HELOISE AND ABELARD

HELOISE

AND

ABELARD

Régine Pernoud

Translated by Peter Wiles

STEIN AND DAY/*Publishers*/New York

First published in English 1973
Copyright © Editions Albin Michel 1970
Copyright © 1973 in the English translation by Wm Collins,
Sons & Co, Ltd, London & Glasgow
Library of Congress Catalog Card No. 72–95915
All rights reserved
Printed in the United States of America
Stein and Day/*Publishers*/7 East 48 Street, New York, N.Y. 10017
ISBN 0–8128–1558–0

CONTENTS

copy

ILLUSTRATIONS

There are only two precious things on earth:
the first is love; the second, a long way behind it,
is intelligence.

THE GIFTED STUDENT

Dum fuisti
manifestus
semper claris
es triumphis
sublimatus

While you lived
You radiated
Brilliance always
And, triumphant,
Soared above us.

Abelard: *Planctus David super Abner*

'PARIS at last!' the young student thought eagerly as the bend
of the river came into view, revealing a small cluster of spires
and towers. For several days he had journeyed along the road
from Orléans, whose all but perfect straightness was a reminder
of the old Roman way. The little church of Notre-Dame-des-
Champs already lay behind him to his left: in those days it
lived up to its name, standing amid well-tilled fields. Away to
his right, he had seen the abbey of Sainte-Geneviève rearing
high above the vineyards which terraced the slopes of the hill.
He had also passed a building which had the look of a large
farmhouse, with its wine press, its rows of vines and its
sturdy walls; this was no farmhouse, however, but the Roman
baths. By now he could see the Petit Pont,* with the church of

* Paris had only two bridges at the time: the Petit Pont, connecting the
Ile de la Cité and the left bank, and the Grand Pont (today the Pont-au-
Change), reaching to the right bank. The districts developing on both banks

Saint-Séverin on the left and the church of Saint-Julien on the right. In the far distance, to the west, he could make out the buildings forming the small market town of Saint-Germain-des-Prés. 'Paris at last!' he thought again, as he began to ride across the bridge, between the two rows of houses and shops perched above the river.

Why was Peter Abelard so keen to see Paris? What made him regard his arrival there as a crucial moment in his life? It would, after all, be difficult to argue with the contemporary poet who wrote: 'Paris at this time was mighty small.'[1] Squeezed, save for a small overspill, into the Ile de la Cité, Paris was as yet far from being a metropolis. The king might occasionally come and stay at the Palace, but he was more often to be found at one of his other residences – Orleans, or Etampes, or Senlis. So Peter was certainly not responding to the lure of the big city, a lure which was then practically non-existent. There were, however, many other reasons why a young man of twenty should take to the road in the year 1100. Six months earlier, Godfrey of Bouillon and his companions had recaptured the Holy City of Jerusalem, previously lost to Christendom for over four centuries. The feudal lords and men-at-arms were drifting home again, one by one, now that they had fulfilled their vows, while others were setting out to lend support to the handful of knights who had remained overseas. The call of the Holy Land had grown strong, and so had the urge to visit the shrines of the saints. The road which Peter Abelard had been following was the main route to Santiago de Compostela, and he must have encountered many bands of pilgrims proceeding slowly southwards, stage by stage – many merchants, too, driving their teams of pack-animals to fairs and markets anywhere between the banks of the Loire and the banks of the Seine.

---

were known as 'Beyond Grand Pont' and 'Beyond Petit Pont'. The Petit Pont, of wooden construction until Maurice de Sully rebuilt it in stone in 1185, had been erected in place of a Roman bridge.

Yet none of this made any deep impression on Peter Abelard. He desired fame but felt no urge to acquire it through knightly feats of valour. Had he wished, he could have followed in his father's footsteps and achieved rapid promotion to an honourable military rank: he was, after all, the eldest son of the lord of Le Pallet, on the borders of Brittany. Instead, he had renounced his privileges in favour of one of his younger brothers, either Ralph or Dagobert. And although he might share in the religious fervour of his time, it was not with the object of reaching any particular abbey – Saint-Denis or Saint-Marcel or Sainte-Geneviève – that he had set out on the road for Paris.

What drew him, as he himself explains in his autobiographical *Letter to a Friend*,[2] was the fact that Paris was already the main bastion of the liberal arts, and that 'dialectic in particular flourishes there'.

In the twelfth century, being a student meant practising dialectic, the interminable pursuit of arguments presented in the form of thesis and antithesis, major premise and minor premise, 'antecedent' and 'consequent'. Every age has its favourite intellectual pursuits. In our own day, pride of place is given to the fields of genetics and nuclear energy; yet only a few years ago the pull of existentialism was so strong that it led everyone under a certain age to argue in terms of being and non-being, of essence and existence. In short, there have always been dominant intellectual themes capable of influencing an entire generation, and this was no less true in the twelfth century than in the twentieth.

At that time the obsession was with dialectic, the art of reasoning, which was then regarded as the highest art of all. Two centuries earlier, a philosophy teacher named Hrabanus Maurus had called it 'the discipline of disciplines', adding: 'It teaches a man to teach, provides instruction in instruction; through [dialectic], reason discovers and reveals what it is, what it intends, what it sees.'

Thus dialectic covers more or less the same ground as logic:

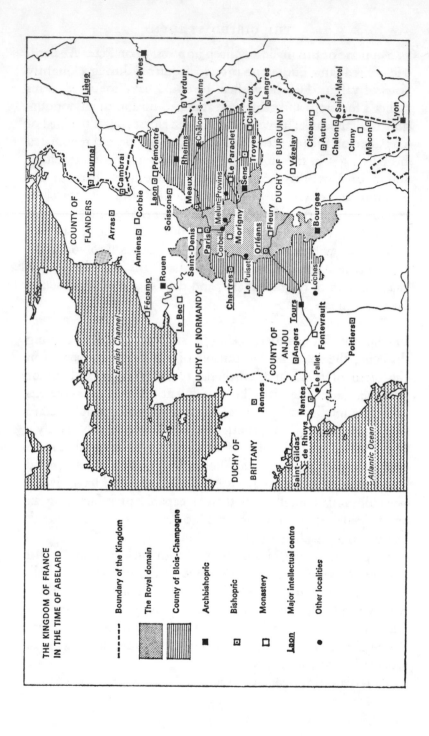

THE KINGDOM OF FRANCE
IN THE TIME OF ABELARD

- - - - - Boundary of the Kingdom

The Royal domain

County of Blois-Champagne

■ Archbishopric

▣ Bishopric

□ Monastery

Laon Major intellectual centre

● Other localities

COUNTY OF
FLANDERS

DUCHY OF NORMANDY

COUNTY OF
ANJOU

DUCHY OF
BRITTANY

DUCHY OF BURGUNDY

English Channel

Atlantic Ocean

Liège

Trèves

Verdun

Tournai

Cambrai

Laon ▣Prémontré

Rheims

Châlons-s-Marne

Le Paraclet

Langres

Clairvaux

Citeaux

Saint-Marcel

Lyon

Autun

Chalon

Cluny

Mâcon

Vézelay

Troyes

Sens

Meaux

Provins

Soissons

Arras ▣

□Corbie

Amiens ▣

Saint-Denis

Paris

Corbeil

Melun

Morigny

Fleury

Orléans

Bourges

Rouen

Fécamp

Le Bec

Chartres

Le Puiset

Loches

Tours

Fontevrault

Poitiers ▣

Angers

Nantes

Le Pallet

Saint-Gildas
de Rhuys

Rennes

it trains man to employ his highest and most distinctive attribute – reason – in the quest for truth. But whereas logic may
be the activity of a lone thinker reasoning his way towards a
private conclusion, dialectic presupposes talk, argument, intellectual give and take. And in the twelfth century the quest for
truth, in every sphere, was invariably conducted in the form of
a debate or 'dispute'. Here, perhaps, lies the real difference
between the worlds of scholarship then and now: in those days
it was not considered possible to arrive at a truth without
preliminary 'disputation'; hence the importance of dialectic,
which trained the mind to set forth the premises of an argument, state the terms of a proposition correctly and assemble
the components of thought and speech, thereby guaranteeing
that the debate would be fruitful.

And this was certainly the view taken by Peter Abelard. He
'prized dialectic and its arsenal above all else that philosophy
can teach'. A fervent seeker after knowledge and ideas, he had
first of all 'scoured the provinces' – to quote his own phrase –
in search of famous dialecticians, from whom he proceeded to
learn all he could. From an early age he had shown unmistakably that the scholar's gown held more attraction for him than
the coat of mail. As he himself observes (the classical references
are typical): he had 'forsaken the court of Mars for the safety
of Minerva's bosom'; he had 'exchanged the weapons of war
for those of logic and sacrificed the triumphs of the battlefield
to the cut and thrust of debate'. It would be a mistake, however,
to see him as a rebellious son and heir defying the wishes of his
family; on the contrary, Abelard's father – Berengar – had
been in complete agreement with the decision to renounce his
privileges. The lord of Le Pallet had offered the young man
every encouragement. He was obviously destined for the
academic life; he had been a brilliant pupil, even as a small
child, and his outstanding gifts were greatly to Berengar's taste.
'Before buckling on his warrior's sword, my father had received
a smattering of scholarship and afterwards became so passionately fond of books that he resolved to give all his sons a

13

literary education prior to training them in the profession of arms. And this he proceeded to do. I was his first-born, and my special dearness to him heightened the zeal with which he taught me.'

Not that literary inclinations were in any way uncommon among the landowners of the day. Fulke the Bad, count of Anjou, composed his own family chronicle. The letters which Stephen, count of Blois, sent home to his wife are among our most valuable sources of information for the First Crusade. There was also William, count of Poitiers and duke of Aquitaine.*

But to continue: after turning his back on the family estate in Brittany, Peter Abelard had moved from school to school ('forever disputing', he recalls), driven by the urge to stock his mind with the whole armoury of definitions and techniques. He had learned how to handle the philosophical vocabulary which was needed for an understanding of Aristotle's *Categories*; he had come to realize what was meant by 'the genus, the differentia, the species, the proper and the accident'. Let us take an individual, Socrates. There is something particular about him which makes him Socrates rather than anyone else. 'But if we disregard the difference (the "socraticness"), we are free to consider simply the man in Socrates, i.e. the rational and mortal animal, and there we have the species (the human species) . . . If, in our minds, we further overlook the fact that he is rational and mortal, we are left with what is implied by the term "animal", and there we have the genus,' and so forth.[3] And Abelard goes on to establish the relationship of species to genus, which is that of the part to the whole; to distinguish

* William IX of Aquitaine (1071–1127) may reasonably be regarded as the first of the troubadours, all poetical works previous to his in the region beyond the Loire, whether in Latin or in langue d'oc, having been anonymous. He was a very great poet. Much of his work is earthy and vigorous, but he was also capable of considerable refinement and subtlety. His poems deal with the principal themes of courtly behaviour – including service to the beloved Lady, a poetic transference of feudal service which was developed in the writings of the later troubadours.

between essence and accident; to set forth the rules of syllogism, premise and predicate (all men are mortal; now, Socrates is a man; therefore Socrates . . .) In the twelfth century the fundamentals of abstract reasoning were habitually summed up in short mnemonic poems:

> *Si sol est, et lux est; at sol est: igitur lux.*
> *si non sol, non lux est; at lux est: igitur sol.*
> *non est sol et non-lux; at sol est: igitur lux.*[4]

If there be sun, there is light; now, there is sun;
   therefore there is light.
No sun, no light; now, there is light; therefore
   there is sun.
Sun and non-light cannot be; now, there is sun;
   therefore there is light.
Etc., etc.

Abelard had probably acquired these first rudiments of dialectic before leaving Brittany, a region famous for producing 'keen minds dedicated to the study of the arts'.[5] He himself declared that he owed his mental agility to the 'properties of my native soil'. And contemporary texts do indeed refer to several schools in Brittany, some of them dating back to the eleventh century: one at Pornic, one at Nantes, where a certain Ralph the Grammarian taught, and others at Vannes, Redon, Quimperlé, and so on. None of these, however, ever achieved the fame of the great schools at Angers and Le Mans; still less could they vie with Chartres, rendered illustrious by two of Abelard's fellow-Bretons, Bernard and Thierry of Chartres. When he spoke of 'scouring the provinces', he was unquestionably alluding to Maine, Anjou and Touraine, and we know for certain that he studied in Loches under a famous dialectician named Roscelin. Long afterwards, Roscelin reminded Peter Abelard of the days when he had sat at his feet 'as the least of his pupils' (in the meantime the two men had become enemies).

This Roscelin was a curious figure who deserves a few lines of comment, for he plays a part in Abelard's story. He led an eventful and unsettled life. For a while he was master of the schools in Compiègne, but it was not long before he began to clash with the ecclesiastical authorities. In 1093 he was condemned by the Council of Soissons and afterwards lived for a while in England, where he occupied himself in protesting against the morals of the English clergy; the English Church was at that time lax over the question of celibacy, and Roscelin was profoundly shocked that the sons of priests should be accepted for ordination. Subsequently he was appointed canon of Saint-Martin-de-Tours. Almost at once he came in conflict with Robert of Arbrissel – another Breton! – the famous wandering preacher whose message brought all who heard him closer to God and who was followed wherever he went by a large and varied flock in which knights mingled with clerks, and harlots with highborn ladies. Roscelin, the kind of man who would nowadays be accused of 'finding evil under every stone', was severe in his condemnation of this weirdly assorted band, whom Robert soon afterwards united for ever as members of the new order of Fontevrault. Eventually Roscelin himself was taken to task by Ivo of Chartres, the renowned expert in canon law, who warned him against 'seeking to appear wiser than was proper'. After this, Roscelin went back to teaching at Loches, and it was probably from him that Abelard first heard mention of the great controversy which was engrossing the entire thinking world at that time – the dispute about universals.

When, employing the terms used in Aristotle's *Categories*, one speaks of 'genus' and 'species', is one referring to realities, or to intellectual concepts, or is one merely playing with words? May one legitimately speak of 'man' in general, of 'animal', and so on? If the answer is yes, does there exist somewhere in nature a reality, an archetype, a sort of model of which every man is, as it were, the more or less successful copy, originating from the same mould? Or is the term 'man' simply a word, an artifice of language, and is there no element of sameness between one man and the next? These questions were keenly discussed and caused considerable disagreement among the leading dialecticians of the time; each put forward his own system and his own solution.

Was Abelard really 'the least' of Roscelin's pupils? One thing is certain: the teaching of his first master made an enduring impression on him. For Roscelin held the view that the universals – genera and species – were mere words. And although Abelard eventually departed from this concept and became Roscelin's rival, his career was permanently coloured by certain aspects of the older man's thought.

His intellectual training was certainly not confined to dialectic. Like all other students of his time, Abelard had been grounded in the 'seven liberal arts'. He had studied grammar, which was considered the basis of all learning; the term, as then applied, covered a much wider area than it does today, extending to what we now call 'letters' or literature. He was well-acquainted with the Latin authors known at the time – Ovid, Lucan, Virgil and many others. He had been drilled in rhetoric, the art of effective speaking, for which he had a natural flair, and also, as we have seen, in dialectic. The other branches of learning – arithmetic, geography, music, astronomy – had clearly not interested him so much: he confesses that he was a complete dunce at mathematics, although he had read the treatise by Boëthius on which the teaching of this science was based. It is perhaps worth adding that although, like most scholars of that era, he had some small knowledge of Greek and Hebrew – just enough to fathom the meaning of certain passages in the Scriptures – his familiarity with the writings of the great Greek thinkers was limited to those works which were available in the West in Latin translations, that is, with the *Timaeus*, the *Phædo* and the *Republic* of Plato, and with the *Organon* of Aristotle. Other works were known chiefly through extracts and through the commentaries of Latin authors – either ancient, like Cicero, or medieval, like Boëthius.

'I arrived in Paris at last.'[6] This 'at last' seems to draw Abelard curiously close to our own time: even in the second half of the twentieth century, a philosophy student turning his back on the provinces would be likely to express the same mixture of relief and elation. Abelard gives no details of his travels. At about the same time, a monk from Fleury (Saint-Benoît-sur-Loire) named Ralph Tortaire bequeathed us a most vivid description of his short journey from Caen to Bayeux, marvelling at the wealth of merchandise displayed in the market-place at Caen and relating how he passed King Henry I of England, clad in a purple tunic, riding in procession with an escort of squires and followed by a veritable menagerie of wild animals, including a camel and an ostrich. Next comes a colourful description of a whale hunt which he witnessed from the shore, and finally he recalls his fear of being poisoned by the raw local wine which he drank on reaching Bayeux.[7] But it is a waste of time looking for concrete details in the *Letter to a Friend*, or indeed in any of Abelard's writings: he was a philosopher, not a story-teller. We may reasonably assume that, as the son of a feudal lord who had urged him to go on with his studies, he was not a member of that large and often penurious band of students who roamed the dusty roads on foot. Doubtless he travelled as any other well-to-do person travelled at the time: on horseback, possibly with a servant, sleeping in inns at night. Moving eastwards, he must have ridden along the road whose course can still be traced on a street-map of Paris, a straight line formed today by the rue de la Tombe-Issoire, the rue Saint-Jacques and the rue Saint-Martin.

He may well have travelled in the company of other students. The Paris schools had not enjoyed their high reputation for long. True, the cloister school of Notre Dame almost certainly dated back to the Carolingian era; but not until the end of the eleventh century – only a very short time before Abelard's own arrival – were there signs of a definite influx of students from other areas. We come across a Lorrainer named Olbert, later abbot of Gembloux, who had studied at the abbey of Saint-Germain-des-Prés, and another named Drogo who seems to have taught in the Cité. Nearer Abelard's own time, a certain Hubald from Liége taught on the Montagne Sainte-Geneviève, while Robert of Arbrissel – like Peter himself – had come to Paris from Brittany to continue his studies in the discipline of letters. But it was the dialectician William of Champeaux, and Abelard himself, who were the true founders of the Cité's renown. Guy of Bazoches, a poet writing in the second half of the twelfth century, later observed that the seven sisters – in other words, the seven arts – had taken up permanent residence in Paris; and not many years afterwards an Englishman, Geoffrey of Vinsauf, drew the following comparison between Paris and Orleans:

> Paris bakes bread which sustains
> The mighty ones, strong in the arts.
> Orleans rears on her milk
> The nursling, the cradle-child.[8]

During Abelard's lifetime Hugh of Saint-Victor, in a treatise written in the form of a dialogue, drew a lively picture of the throng of students in Paris, and of the ardour with which they were animated:

'Turn and look in another direction.'
'I have turned and am looking.'
'What do you see?'
'I see schools, and students in great number. I see people of all ages: children, youths, young men, old men. Their studies are equally varied. Some are learning to adapt their tongues to new sounds and utter unfamiliar words. Others are striving to learn declensions, constructions and derivations, first by listening to them, then by repeating them among themselves, and then by reciting them again so as to fix them in their minds. Others are scoring the wax tablets

with their styles. Others are drawing figures of sundry shapes
and colours, guiding their pens confidently over the parchment. Still others, fired with even greater zeal, appear to
be debating earnest matters among themselves and striving
to defeat one another with an array of subtle arguments and
fine distinctions. I can also see some students engaged in
calculations. Others, plucking at strings stretched tight over
wooden bridges, are producing various types of melody; still
others, with the aid of diagrams, are explaining the methods
of musical notation. Others are describing the courses and
positions of the stars and using various instruments to
explain how the heavenly bodies rotate. Others are dealing
with the nature of plants, the human constitution, and the
properties and actions of all manner of things.'

Such was the world in which Abelard was about to carve a
place for himself, and naturally his place would be among those
who sought to outdo one another with 'subtle arguments and
fine distinctions' – the dialecticians. His prime purpose in
coming to Paris was to listen to the most famous of them all,
William of Champeaux. It is impossible to improve on
Abelard's own summary of his career as a student, a student
who was very soon to become a master in his own right:

I remained at his school for some time. But although I was
well received at first, it was not long before I became a
nuisance to him, for I made a point of refuting some of his
ideas; I would tackle him fearlessly, and now and then I
would win the day. My audacity further excited the anger
of those of my fellow students who were regarded as first
in rank, especially as I was the youngest and newest pupil.
Thus began my series of misfortunes, which have continued
ever since.

In these few words, the scene is set and the actors are brought
of life: the celebrated teacher, the eager bevy of pupils, the
out-of-the-ordinary newcomer who quickly attracted the
wrong sort of attention, interrupting at awkward moments and

initiating clash after clash from which, most galling of all, he often emerged victorious. The result was interminable strife, with the tame, competent pupils siding with the master, and the bolder, more independent spirits with the newcomer. Within a very short time there was chaos where all had once been peace and harmony.

Abelard is certainly justified when he states that his long succession of misfortunes began here. All his life he was to be known as a troublemaker, notorious for his habit of interrupting, disagreeing, baiting, riling. All his life he was to rouse anger as frequently as he roused enthusiasm. Undeniably, such 'troublemakers' have been responsible for some of the most notable contributions to human progress. It must be said, however, that Abelard's magnificent qualities were somewhat marred by his cocksureness. This is not the sort of failing which a teacher will forgive in a young man who seems to threaten his jealously guarded prestige. In consequence, William of Champeaux soon came to regard Abelard as an 'obnoxious' pupil and reacted as all university teachers were to react in future: with that harsh, relentless hatred to which intellectuals are peculiarly prone.

The situation cannot be properly appreciated without reference to the teaching methods employed in Abelard's day. As a matter of common practice, there was what we nowadays call 'dialogue' between a master and his pupils. Moreover, there was no clear boundary between teaching and research. Teaching kept pace with research, and there was interaction between them: any new idea was at once subjected to study, criticism and discussion, whereby it was transformed and made to burgeon anew. At that time, the world of philosophy was animated by the dynamism now to be found in the various spheres of technical advancement.

Basic to this system of education was the reading of a text – *lectio*. The task of the teacher was to 'read'. The use of this term became so deeply embedded in academic life that the office of 'reader' survives in universities to this day. It is in this sense that the term must be understood when, for instance, we ponder the decision of a number of thirteenth-century bishops to prohibit the 'reading' of Aristotle: what they were really prohibiting was the custom of using Aristotle's works as a basis for instruction. The bishops' ruling had nothing to do with placing books on the Index, a procedure which was not adopted by the Church until the sixteenth century.

Thus, to read a text meant to study it and comment on it. After an introductory survey of an author's work and the circumstances in which it was written, the master would proceed to the exposition, or commentary proper. Tradition demanded that this commentary should cover three points: the 'letter', i.e. the task of construing the Latin correctly; the 'sense', i.e. the outward meaning of the text; and finally the 'sentence', the inner meaning of the text, its doctrinal content. Together, these commentaries formed the gloss. The great libraries of the world contain a host of manuscripts which show how this teaching method worked: the text in the centre of the page and, in the margins, the various glosses relating to the *littera*, the *sensus* or the *sententia*. Indeed, we still have the glosses which Abelard himself made in the course of his 'reading' of Porphyry.

But there was more to it than this: the study of the text, especially when its doctrinal content was being examined, raised questions which inevitably provoked dialogue between master and pupils, dialogue culminating in the 'dispute' or debate. This was specifically included in the range of scholastic exercises, particularly in the sphere of dialectic – which, as we have seen, was the art of debating as well as the art of reasoning. Now, dialectic gained ground so rapidly in the twelfth century that the habit of disputation spread to all areas of scholarship, both sacred and profane. The *Summae* of St Thomas Aquinas, composed in the middle years of the thirteenth century, were among the many treatises of that period to bear the title *Questiones disputate*, a clear indication of the circumstances in which they were written: they consist of propositions which have been taught and debated, and are therefore as much the outcome of a series of lessons as the elaboration of a personal line of thought. In addition to disputes between master and pupils, there were disputes between master and master, some of which are still famous. In Abelard's lifetime, for example, a monk named Rupert who taught at the large and influential monastery school in Liége agreed to debate the theological problem of evil with Anselm of Laon and William of Champeaux. Anselm died before the dispute could take place, but the texts report a bitter clash between Rupert and William.

As for the pattern of the students' days, we have the testimony of John of Salisbury, a familiar of Thomas Becket and Henry II, who eventually became bishop of Chartres:

> Each day we all had to do our best to recollect part of what we had been taught the day before; so that, for us, the morrow was the pupil of the eve. The evening exercise, which was known as Declension, consisted of a lesson so stuffed with grammar that, unless he were a half-wit, anyone who kept at it diligently for a year was able to speak and write presentably and understand the lectures which we were normally given.[9]

Thus, the mornings were to some extent devoted to checking the pupils' work, and the evenings to teaching in the more positive sense. John of Salisbury also mentions what he calls the Collation (literally 'bringing together'), presumably a form of recapitulation between master and pupils; this took place at the end of the day, together in all likelihood with some kind of sermon or morally uplifting lecture for the benefit of the students.

A further indication of the way students were expected to spend their time is contained in the words of advice which Robert of Sorbon* addressed to scholars in the thirteenth

* Chaplain and adviser to Louis IX. In 1253 he founded the college which eventually became known as the 'Sorbonne'; the deeds have been preserved

century. In his view, there were six vital rules: (*a*) allocate a set time to each particular type of study or reading; (*b*) give your undivided attention to whatever you are reading; (*c*) copy out some notion or truth from every item of reading and store it carefully in your memory; (*d*) write a summary of everything you read; (*e*) discuss your work with your fellow students (to Robert, this seems even more important than the actual process of reading); finally, (*f*) pray – for prayer, he says, is the true path to understanding.

The general picture to emerge from the writings of the period is of an 'impulsive and riotous' school,[10] and this is certainly the impression given by Abelard himself.

As for his clashes with William of Champeaux, we know the substance of them not only from Abelard but from his master's sole surviving work, *Sententie vel questiones XLVII*. The main point at issue, needless to say, was the question of universals, which at that time obsessed and excited dialecticians throughout Europe. William's view was diametrically opposed to that of Roscelin. William was a realist: in his opinion, the general terms listed in Porphyry's *Introduction* corresponded to independent and unitary realities. He maintained, for instance, that species was something which existed in its own right; that it was to be found whole and identical in every individual; and that the human species was the same in every man.

Abelard forced William to abandon an argument which, if carried to its logical conclusion, would have implied that Socrates and Plato, by partaking of the same species, were the same man. So William of Champeaux revised his initial thesis: Socrates and Plato were not the same man, but the species was the same in both, the humanness of the one was the same as the

---

in the French national archives and can be examined at the Musée de l'Histoire de France. Originally, the colleges were houses providing board and lodging for poor students. As time went by, the students began to receive private lessons on the premises. The lessons grew into lectures, and that was how Robert of Sorbon's college became the seat of the faculty of theology.

humanness of the other. Abelard found this equally unaccept-
able. He forced William to define his terms more clearly. The
humanness of Plato was not identical with the humanness of
Socrates; the two were merely *similar*.

That is a fair summary[11] of the successive phases in a dispute
which lasted several years, and in which the arguments on
either side were backed by dry, voluminous dissertations on the
nature of the socraticness in Socrates, the rationalness in man,
etc. The intricate chains of reasoning in support of every
thesis are set down in a manuscript, probably the work of one
of Abelard's pupils; each of William's statements ('Our master
William says . . .') is immediately followed by a refutation
(We, for our part, declare . . .')[12] Abelard, as we have seen, had
studied under Roscelin before enrolling as William's pupil, and
must therefore have been able to draw on a wide range of
counter-arguments. It seems certain, however, that he was not
content to repeat what he had been taught, for he himself was
about to construct a system which differed both from the
realism of William and the nominalism of Roscelin; indeed, he
was to earn the lasting rancour of the latter. By then, he had
embarked dramatically on his own career. 'Overestimating the
intellectual resources of my years, I ventured to become head
of a school while I was still very young.'

Much later, Abelard began his words of advice to his son
with an injunction which was obviously heartfelt: 'Be more
mindful of learning than of teaching.' And he underlined the
point: 'Learn long, teach late and only what seems certain to
you. And as for writing, do not be in too much of a hurry.'[13]

He was trying to spare someone he loved his own experiences. It therefore seems likely that those experiences
were painful – in the long run, at least; for his initial endeavours
were brilliantly successful, and he describes them with considerable zest:

I had already chosen the arena for my exploits – Melun, at
that time an important town and a royal residence. My

master surmised this aim and surreptitiously made every
effort to put a greater distance between my teaching post
and his; before I left his school, he sought to stop me from
setting up my own and to rob me of the place which I had
chosen. But he had jealous opponents among the mighty of
the land. With their co-operation, I succeeded in my
purposes; indeed, his display of envy earned me a good deal
of sympathy.

So Melun was the scene of Abelard's earliest achievements as
a practising teacher. It was a royal city within easy reach of
Paris, to which it was connected, like Orleans, by an old Roman
road. The schools of Melun – this may indeed have stemmed
from the link with Abelard – came to be highly regarded.
Robert of Melun, an Englishman who subsequently became
master of theology in Paris, owed his name to the time he spent
there as a student. Abelard is believed to have taught in the
schools of the collegiate church, Notre Dame de Melun. Not
for long, however: his ambitions lay elsewhere. He was
patently seeking to establish himself as a rival to his master,
William of Champeaux, and he was encouraged in this purpose
by the successes which he now enjoyed – for, according to his
account, pupils flocked to his classes and his reputation as a
dialectician was no longer in doubt. 'Success was a boost to my
confidence and I lost no time in moving my school to Corbeil,
a town close to Paris, where it would be easier for me to step
up the attack.'
    Thus, even at this early stage in his autobiography, Abelard
reveals the characteristics which predominated throughout his
life: the skill in philosophical debate which ultimately earned
him the reputation of being the best 'disputant' of his time; his
wonderful gifts as a teacher; and, finally, his aggressiveness.
Impossible to picture him without an enthusiastic following of
students who congregated whenever he chose to lecture.
Equally impossible to picture him without an enemy who had
to be routed in battle. The martial spirit instilled in him as a

boy seems merely to have been rechannelled into the ostensibly more pacific realm of abstract discussion, and when he recalls his early days as a teacher he cannot help employing the language of a military strategist.

After the move to Corbeil, however, there was a setback. He now had to pay the cost of the intensive efforts which had launched him so triumphantly on his career. He began to show signs of overstrain and eventually fell victim to a disorder which is all too prevalent in our own day: he had a nervous breakdown. It seems possible that success and failure affected this highly emotional man in the same manner, completely draining him of nervous energy; we shall encounter other instances later in his life.

Whatever the true cause, overwork or over-agitation, Peter Abelard suffered what he calls a 'decline' and spent some time convalescing with his family at Le Pallet. He is at pains to assure us that he was 'sorely missed by all who had an itch for dialectic'.

Abelard hurried back to Paris as soon as he was properly recovered, for life in Brittany had made him feel an exile. By now he was intent on teaching in Paris, an ambition which presupposed final victory in the long-sustained duel with Master William of Champeaux.

During Abelard's absence, William had given up teaching dialectic and had turned to rhetoric. So Abelard became his pupil a second time. Perhaps William was mildly flattered to see him return; if so, his mood must have changed rapidly when he found himself subjected to a further barrage of queries and objections from Abelard. It was at this point that he amended his stand on the vexed question of universals: 'After being compelled first to modify his view and then to renounce it, Champeaux saw his classes fall into such disrepute that he was barely able to go on teaching dialectic.' Although Abelard's account is somewhat unclear at this point, we learn that within a few months he had started teaching again – this time in the schools of Notre Dame, in the very heart of Paris. 'The great doctor's most ardent supporters, my own fiercest opponents, deserted him and flocked to my lessons; even Champeaux's successor came and offered me his chair and joined the crowd which had gathered to hear me within the very precincts where his master and mine had once shone so brilliantly.' From which we gather that William of Champeaux had lost heart and relinquished his post in favour of another pupil, who was quickly supplanted by Abelard.

To arrive at a true estimate of the events and personalities involved, however, we must bear in mind that the rivalry between Abelard and William was not the only point at issue. According to the *Letter to a Friend*, all this happened after 1108, the year when William of Champeaux founded the canons regular of Saint-Victor. At that time, the name referred to nothing more than a small priory on the left bank, downstream from the Montagne Sainte-Geneviève, near a ford in the river Bièvre. It was here that a few clerks gathered round William with the intention of leading a communal life – a decision prompted by the mounting tide of religious reform. Before long, this modest foundation grew into a vast monastery containing schools where some of the greatest thinkers of the twelfth century won renown: Hugh, Richard and Adam of Saint-Victor, and many others besides.

It is probable, however, that in his retreat at Saint-Victor, where he was to teach from now on, William was furious at the manner in which Abelard had taken over from his official successor. 'Having no grounds for engaging in open warfare against me, he secured the dismissal, on a defamatory charge, of the man who had surrendered his chair to me, and substituted another in order to foil me.' Abelard had no choice but to reopen his school at Melun. 'The more blatantly I was pursued by envy, the more I gained in esteem, for as the poet says: "Greatness invites envy; it is against the high peaks that the storms break." ' Once it became clear that William had taken up permanent residence at Saint-Victor, Abelard returned to Paris. His ambition was as keen as ever. 'But, finding that he had installed a rival in my chair, I set up camp outside the city, on the Montagne Sainte-Geneviève, as if laying siege to the man who had usurped my position.'

My chair, *my* position . . . Abelard regarded the Notre Dame school as his private property. It was his reputation which now attracted students from far and wide; they came in ever greater numbers, much to the old master's resentment. 'On learning this news, William cast off all restraint and came back to Paris, bringing such pupils as he could muster and the members of his little community . . . Evidently he planned to rescue the lieutenant whom he had left behind in the city.' Abelard's next words are like a triumphant fanfare: 'But by trying to help him he destroyed him. The luckless [master of Notre Dame school] still had a few pupils: his lessons on Priscian had earned him some regard. No sooner had the master [William] returned than he lost them all; he had to give up his school, and shortly afterwards, despairing of worldly fame, he in turn adopted the monastic life. The arguments which my pupils had with William and his followers after his return to Paris, the successes which fortune conferred on us in these encounters, and the size of my own contribution: these things have long since been common knowledge. This, however, I can say more modestly than Ajax, yet without fear of contradiction: "If you ask me what the outcome of the battle was, I was not beaten by my enemy." ' The quotation is from Ovid. Abelard, as was the custom in his day, strewed his writings with phrases culled from classical authors, sacred and profane; but generally his work was epic in tone and full of cut and thrust. Undoubtedly he had won a comprehensive victory, but his account of these events – the modesty is only assumed – tells us a good deal about his nature. Abelard may have been a superbly accomplished dialectician and a teacher beyond compare, but there are indications that his character was not on a par with his intellect. The envy which he attributes to his old master, William of Champeaux, seems likely enough: it is what any teacher feels when he is outstripped by one of his pupils. On

29

the other hand, Abelard does not hesitate to ascribe certain sentiments to him which are utterly incompatible with the details which have come down to us of William of Champeaux's life. When Abelard tells us that William 'turned coat and joined the order of the clerks regular in the belief, it was said, that this show of zeal would smooth his path to high office', and that 'it soon did so, for he was appointed bishop of Châlons', the charge is invalidated by the fact that William turned down the bishopric of Châlons three times. And it is hard to believe that an institution like Saint-Victor owed its existence to the shallow ambition of a man who, had he really wished to draw attention to himself and 'smooth his path to high office', would have done better to go on teaching in the Paris schools than to retire to an obscure priory on the banks of the Bièvre.

It was enough that Abelard should have vented his native pugnacity on his former master; that he should have demonstrated his superiority in the art of reasoning so conclusively that William was forced to climb down on two important issues; and, finally, that he should have ousted him as the idol of the Paris students. There was surely no need for him to blacken his victim's character. Anyone who reads the *Letter to a Friend* must soon begin to wonder whether Abelard the man measured up to Abelard the philosopher.

His fame was already well-established by the time he started teaching on the Montagne Sainte-Geneviève. And his own words provide the best possible account of the determined, if bloodless, investment of a hill which had previously been subjected to only one kind of invasion: that of the grape-gatherers in autumn.

For it was still a mass of vineyards, tier after tier of them, all the way from Sainte-Geneviève church to the little church of Saint-Julien on the banks of the Seine; they stretched as far as the more distant village of Saint-Marcel, where the relics of the first bishop of Paris were displayed for veneration. This rural landscape was to undergo a complete transformation in the course of the twelfth century, because of the droves of eager students who came to seek enlightenment from the successive masters who taught there. The feud between Peter Abelard and William of Champeaux was to have an unexpected consequence: the swift development of Paris on the left bank of the river, an area which was famed from then on for its distinctive inhabitants – the *scolares*, the students, a youthful, boisterous throng, replenished year after year down the centuries. St Goswin attended the Sainte-Geneviève school as a young man, and his biographer relates how, far from accepting Abelard's statements in a tame, unquestioning manner, Goswin stood up to him, convicted him of error, and afterwards went down and celebrated his victory with some students living near the Petit Pont. Obviously the story cannot be authenticated, but it sounds possible and shows what a memorable feat it was for a student to cross swords with that master of debate, Peter Abelard.

The story also serves as evidence of the influx of students on to the hill. Previously, in the deeds which survive, only arable land is recorded in the vicinity of Notre-Dame-des-Champs, of Saint-Etienne-des-Grez (the little church, no longer in existence, which used to stand approximately midway between the Law School and the Lycée Louis-le-Grand), of the Roman Baths, and of Le Chardonnet. There were just a few houses at the approaches to the Petit Pont and around the church of Sainte-Geneviève itself, with no villages in the strict sense apart from those near Saint-Germain-des-Prés, Saint-Médard and Saint-Marcel. Each abbey had its own school, so that student life already existed in embryo; but it was with the soaring reputation of the Sainte-Geneviève school that the history of the left bank really began. The left bank was the intellectual bank, as opposed to the right bank, which was commercial: merchants had been attracted to it by the ease with which craft could be landed along the shore downstream from the church of Sainte-Geneviève. It was in the twelfth century that the

ultimate shape of Paris* was decided: Les Halles were installed
on the site where they were to remain until our own day, while
on the Montagne Sainte-Geneviève the vines were uprooted
to make room for the houses that were needed for all the
masters and students. And it can fairly be claimed that this
transformation was due in part to Master Peter Abelard and his
success as a teacher.

'At this juncture, my loving mother Lucia pressed me to return
to Brittany. Berengar, my father, had taken vows. She was
preparing to do the same.'[14] So Abelard went home to Le
Pallet. He stayed there long enough to attend the religious
ceremonies and to settle family affairs in his capacity as eldest
son. There was nothing unusual about his parents' decision;
on reaching the age of retirement, men and women frequently
devoted the rest of their lives to prayer within the shade of a
cloister.

But Abelard, as we have seen, could not bear to be away
from Paris for long. Once he had carried out his family duties,
he lost no time in returning to 'France' – the name habitually
applied to what was then the heart of the kingdom, the royal
domain, the Ile-de-France. And now comes another surprise.
One would have expected him to go on teaching dialectic, or
even rhetoric, on the Montagne Sainte-Geneviève. Instead, he
branched out in a new direction: he had decided to study
'divinity', *sacra pagina*, or theology as we usually call it today.
And he made no attempt to conceal his motive: 'William had

---

* In the middle of the twelfth century, Paris still consisted of nothing more
than scattered urban nuclei. The fortified walls, begun on Philip-Augustus's
orders in 1185, did not begin to weld them until the following century.
Already, however, there were signs of those special characteristics which
were to distinguish the three main districts of Paris in the time of St Louis:
the Cité, residence of the king and bishop; the right bank, the commercial
area containing Les Halles, La Grève and La Boucherie; and the left bank,
home of the monks and scholars. Here, as well as the abbeys of Saint-
Germain, Saint-Victor and Saint-Marcel, stood the students' lodging houses
and, before long, the colleges.

been teaching it for some time and had begun to win a reputation for it within his own diocese of Châlons.' We may legitimately wonder to what extent Abelard's continual changes of tack were not dictated by the urge to compete against the man who had once been his master. Admittedly, the study of theology was at that time regarded as the culmination of a scholar's career: it was usual, though not compulsory, for academics to proceed to this science of sciences after completing their studies in the liberal arts. And it was a characteristic feature of the age that a man like Abelard, already a famous teacher in one branch, should have so little difficulty in becoming a pupil in the other.

William of Champeaux 'had received lessons from Anselm of Laon, the most authoritative master of the day'. Accordingly, it was from Anselm that Abelard in turn sought instruction. And so, for the next few months at least, he studied on the venerable hill of Laon, a city which had not entirely lost the prestige it had once enjoyed as capital of a kingdom. Even today, libraries bear witness to the vitality of its schools by the number of manuscripts, especially on theological matters, originating from Notre Dame in Laon.

In the previous year (1112), Laon had been plunged into turmoil by a full-scale urban revolution, vividly described in the eyewitness account of a monk named Gilbert of Nogent. Authority over the city lay partly in the hands of the king of France – for it was owned directly by the Crown – and partly in those of the bishop. In 1106, the see was usurped by a wretched character named Gaudry, who had not even taken holy orders and who very soon earned the hostility of the entire population. The burghers of Laon set up a commune. The bishop attempted to foil them, and violent disturbances broke out. The cathedral and the bishop's palace were set ablaze, and the fire spread to the whole of the surrounding district. Gaudry was trapped in his own cellar and unceremoniously dispatched.

The only man with sufficient influence over the rebels to

persuade them to give their murdered bishop decent burial was
the scholarly Anselm. Paradoxically, he had been alone, six
years earlier, in opposing Gaudry's candidature. He and his
brother Ralph, who also taught in the cathedral schools, had
built up a remarkable reputation. Their fame had attracted
so many students to Laon that lodgings were extremely hard to
come by. Among the documents preserved from that period is
a letter from an Italian clerk warning a compatriot to decide
before winter whether he wished to come and join him, for,
however much he might be willing to pay, finding a room
would be a great problem in a town where there were scholars
from Poitou and Brittany and every province in the kingdom,
as well as Belgians, Englishmen and Germans. Some years later,
recalling the time when Anselm and Ralph had taught in Laon,
John of Salisbury referred to them as *splendissima lumina
Galliarum*, the most brilliant of Gallic luminaries.

Abelard did not share this opinion. He dismisses Anselm in
the most contemptuous terms: 'I went to hear this old man. He
certainly owed his reputation to routine rather than to intelligence and memory . . . He was remarkably glib but the substance of his words was poor and devoid of reason.' He adds
several unflattering comparisons: Anselm was a fire producing
nothing but smoke, an imposing-looking tree which, on close
examination, turned out to be the barren fig-tree mentioned in
the Gospel . . . In the light of this assessment, Abelard applied
himself less and less diligently to his lessons. Some of his fellow
pupils, he claims, were offended by his attitude and made
trouble for him by informing their master of his views. Among
these fellow pupils were a pair who were to play a part in
Abelard's story: Alberic of Rheims and his friend Lotulf, who
came from Novara; we shall encounter them again later, in
Rheims. They were probably among the party of students who
engaged Abelard in friendly conversation one evening. He was
asked what the study of the Scriptures had to offer a man like
himself, who had previously confined himself to the liberal
arts. (Peter Abelard had obviously achieved fame as a teacher

34

of secular subjects, or his views would hardly have attracted interest). Abelard replied that he considered the subject exceptionally beneficial, but that in his opinion it would suffice to have the text of the Bible, and a gloss to clarify linguistic difficulties; he could see no need for the exhaustive commentaries which Anselm was inflicting on his pupils. This was too much for Abelard's companions. They objected loudly and asked whether he was seriously claiming that he could improvise a commentary on the Scriptures. The challenge was direct and obvious, and Abelard was too much of a Breton to decline it. Very well, he said: let them choose a passage and he, with no help except a gloss, would 'read' it in public. Laughter in the audience. Eventually the students suggested a passage from Ezekiel – not the most lucid of prophets – and agreed to judge Abelard's efforts the following day.

Abelard shut himself away with the text and gloss and spent the night in preparation. Next day he conducted his first divinity lecture. The audience was sparse: few people had imagined that he would carry out his promise. 'Those who heard me were so enraptured,' he reports, 'that they lauded me to the skies and urged me to go on with my commentary, employing the same method. The news spread, and those who had missed the first lecture hurried to the second and third, eager to note down my interpretations.' It would seem that once Abelard made up his mind to speak in public, he could not fail. His eloquence and the subtlety of his commentary were irresistible. He had been studying theology for only a short time, yet already he had proved himself a master.

His behaviour had earned him another enemy, however. 'This success excited old Anselm's jealousy. Spiteful innuendoes, as I have said, had already set him against me, and now he began to persecute me because of my theology lessons just as William had persecuted me because of my philosophy.'[15] Anselm, as we have seen, was by no means so negligible a figure as Abelard seeks to suggest. The teaching of Holy Writ owed a great deal to him. He and his assistants had compiled what was known in the Middle Ages as the 'ordinary gloss', a dis-criminating anthology of the most authoritative Bible com-mentaries; this 'ordinary gloss' was to become a standard reference book for students in the twelfth and thirteenth centuries. Abelard had as little regard for the work as for the man. True, Anselm was an old man by then; he died not long afterwards, in 1117. He seems to have been deeply wounded by the ungracious conduct of this supremely gifted pupil. His response was harsh indeed: Abelard was banned from further teaching.

'The news of this ban caused great indignation as it spread through the school: never was an attack so manifestly dictated by envy. Yet this, by its very obviousness, redounded to my credit, and the persecutions merely enhanced my renown.'

Abelard was obliged to leave Laon; but he left as the victor, not as the vanquished. He returned to Paris, and this time his reputation so far outshone that of any other possible candidate that he was immediately offered 'his' chair at the Notre Dame schools. 'Once again I took the chair which had long been intended for me, and from which I had been evicted.'[16] This time he did not have to share his throne. Paris had always been the focal point of his ambitions, and now he was the city's most celebrated master of theology, as well as of dialectic. For he had immediately decided to continue the commentary on Ezekiel which had been so rudely interrupted. He was without peer.

In 1113, William of Champeaux had finally retired to his diocese at Châlons. Abelard enjoyed an unparalleled success. 'These lessons were so favourably received,' he writes, 'that my standing as a theologian soon seemed as great as my previous standing as a philosopher. Because of the enthusiasm, attendances at both my courses rose higher and higher.' An unprecedented number of students flocked to the Paris schools. There is independent testimony of these.

'Distant Brittany sent its clods to you for instruction. The natives of Anjou, mastering their uncouthness, had begun to attend on you. Men from Poitou, Gascony, Iberia, Normandy, Flanders, Germany and Sweden were united in their praises and in the diligence with which they heeded you. The inhabitants of the city of Paris and of the provinces of Gaul, both near and far, were all athirst to hear you, as if no learning were to be found anywhere but in you.' The writer is one of Abelard's contemporaries, Fulke of Deuil. 'Rome,' he continues, 'sent you her pupils so that you might educate them. She who once imparted knowledge of every art showed, by sending you her students, that in her erudition she acknowledged that you were more erudite still. However great the distance, however high the hill, however deep the valley, however arduous the road, nothing could deter them from hastening to you in defiance of robbers and other hazards.'[17]

Many of Abelard's pupils went on to achieve lasting fame. Among them were John of Salisbury and Guido of Castello, who later became Pope Celestine II. Others, less well-known, played an active part in the events of their own day. There was Geoffrey of Auxerre, for instance, who subsequently turned on his former master, and Berengar of Poitiers who remained loyal through thick and thin. When, in 1127, Bishop Stephen ordered the removal of the episcopal school from the grounds of Notre Dame and, with the chapter's approval, refused to allow any more lessons to be given in that part of the precinct which used to be called *Trissantia*, his decision was undoubtedly prompted by the fact that the students who continued to flock to the now famous Paris schools were disturbing the silence proper to the cathedral close. Not many years later, the king chose to send his own son – afterwards Louis VII – to study at Notre Dame. This rapid increase in intellectual activity, which ultimately gave rise to the University of Paris, may have begun in the time of William of Champeaux; but it was Abelard who made the city's schools famous. Henceforth Paris was an acknowledged citadel of learning.

For the students, Paris was a 'paradise containing every

37

delight' – a paradise presided over by the Master, who, according to a satirist of the time, caused a stir whenever he showed his face:

> *Obvius adveniet populo comitante senatus; plebs ruet et dicet:*
> *'Ecce Magister adest.'*
>
> The leading citizens come to meet him, accompanied by the common people; the mob rushes forward, crying: 'Here comes the Master!'[18]

Fulke of Deuil gives the same impression: 'Everyone flocked to you, as to the clearest fount of all philosophy, dazzled by your lucid mind, your smooth eloquence and your skill with words, as well as by your perspicacity as a scholar.'[19] Invincible in the field of logic, Abelard brought the same intellectual clarity to bear on theological matters, and his brilliant style and delivery matched his exceptional powers of insight and reasoning. Having competed successfully against the best brains of his time, he now proceeded to establish himself as the deepest and most penetrating of thinkers. He fired the enthusiasm of all the young students who crowded into the Notre Dame schools. He was the 'Socrates of the Gauls', he was 'our own Aristotle' – as Peter the Venerable referred to him long afterwards. He reigned over his pupils, whose heads swam not only with dialectic but also, at times, with wine from the vineyards on the slopes of the Montagne Sainte-Geneviève. Hymns and psalms were not the only things they sang: they were addicted to those *chansons goliardiques* whose strains lingered in the Latin Quarter until quite recently. A few of Abelard's students un-doubtedly lived up to the portrait which Guy of Bazoches drew of himself:

> *Et ludis datus et studiis, sed rarus in illis, creber in his, doctus atque*
> *docendus eram.*
>
> Given alike to play and to study, the former seldom, the latter often, I learned and was eager to learn.[20]

But others sang a different tune:

38

Obmittamus studia,
dulce est desipere,
et carpamus dulcia
juventutis tenere;
res est apta senectuti
seriis intendere.

Let's away with study,
Sweet it is to play,
And the sweets of springtime
Savour while we may;
Let age to books and learning,
While youth keeps holiday.

The song goes on:

Voto nostro serviamus,
mos est iste juvenum;
ad plateas descendamus
et choreas virginum.[21]

Young men yield to pleasure,
Youth must have its fling,
So we'll go tread a measure
Where maidens dance and sing.

What was the point of spending countless hours reading Ovid if
one did not oneself practise the 'art of love'?

Imperio, eya!
Venerio, eya!
cum gaudio
cogor lascivire,
dum audio
volucres garrire.[22]

Hail, Venus!
Hail, pleasure!

> What sweet wantoning
> Possesses me
> When I
> Hear birds jargoning.

The love song, which soon afterwards began to flourish in the vernacular, and which was carried to every corner of France by the troubadours and trouvères, enjoyed huge success in this high-spirited and sometimes rather unruly company. Its popularity was rivalled only by that of the drinking song and the Goliardic poem, celebrating the adventures of the scholars' hero, Golias (Goliath); in the *Metamorphoses of Golias* he was credited with the most monstrous and absurd exploits, while the *Apocalypse of Golias* even contained parodies of the Scriptures.

There were times when the students became more actively boisterous. They would sally forth from the schools and surge through the streets of the Cité like new wine bursting from the cask. One such occasion was the Octave of Christmas, which contained a number of echoes of the Saturnalia of ancient times. For twenty-four hours, the young scholars became the masters and were permitted to indulge in all kinds of wild and unconventional behaviour; there was a great deal of gorging and carousing and general licentiousness. It was a collective escape from the hard work and strict discipline of student life:

> *Adest dies*
> *optata, socii;*
> *quidquid agant,*
> *et velint alii,*
> *nos choream*
> *ducamus gaudii.*
> *Pro baculo*
> *exsultet hodie*
> *clerus cum populo.*[23]

Friends, the longed-for
Day is dawning;
Whatever others
Will or won't,
We will lead
The dance rejoicing.
In the baton's
Exaltation
Clerk and people join.

For the choirmaster's baton or wand, that traditional symbol of authority, was in their own hands that day, which indeed was known as 'Wand Day'. The festivities were only for those with a broad mind and an open purse; all others were kept at a distance and held in contempt.

Omnes tales ab hoc festo
procul eant; procul esto;
tales odit baculus,
illi vultus huc advertant,
quorum dextrae dando certant,
quorum patet loculus.[24]

Let these from this feast be absent,
Let them go and keep their distance,
Such men the wand abhors.
But hither let the open-handed
Come, our level's for the spender
Whose purse has gaping jaws.

Master Peter Abelard undoubtedly joined in these celebrations. He was not appreciably older than the throng over whom he exercised undisputed authority. And their boisterousness was matched by their craving for knowledge and by their eager quest for the absolute. For all their drinking, wrangling, and occasional debauchery, the students of Paris would accept none but the best in reasoning and the surest demonstrations of given truths. Abelard measured up to their exacting standards: he was not the kind of teacher who sidesteps awkward problems or takes refuge in stock answers. With him, 'disputes' were not mere classroom exercises: 'They [my pupils] insisted that they had no use for empty words, that a man can believe only what he has first understood, and that it is absurd to preach to others when one's understanding of a matter is as small as theirs.'[25] And where was the problem that could withstand the master's reasoning powers? He was Aristotle, but Aristotle born afresh, young in body and in spirit. The conventional image of the author of the *Organon* was that of a frail old man presiding over the brilliant victories of his pupil Alexander: 'Pale, nearly bald, with an austere brow . . . His wan face was proof that he often burned the midnight oil . . . his regular fasting showed in the thinness of his hands, all skin and bone . . .'

No part of this description could ever have been applied to Abelard. His features glowed with youthfulness and vitality. He cannot have been much more than thirty-five, and everything about him was exceptional: his seemingly inborn knowledge of dialectic and even theology, his gifts as a teacher, his quick-wittedness, and finally his physical appeal – for he was handsome, extremely handsome, and this unquestionably contributed to his power over others. 'You had only to show yourself in public, and who did not rush out for a glimpse of you? Who did not stare longingly after you when you chose to depart? What wife or daughter did not burn for you in your absence and blaze up at the sight of you?'[26] One thinks of the countless admirers who must have yearned for the touch of those beautiful hands which he employed to such good effect when making a point. That Abelard should be the focal point of attention whenever he strolled through the streets of the Cité suggests that his fame had long since spread beyond the confines of Notre Dame. 'Was there anywhere a king, a philosopher, whose renown could stand comparison with yours? What country, what city, what village did not long to see you?'[27]

Fame soon brought fortune. 'You must surely know from hearsay,' he writes, 'what gains and what glory I derived from [my pupils].'[28] He charged for his lessons, which was the usual practice; but whereas most masters earned barely enough to live on, Abelard did very well for himself. Some teachers had scruples about dispensing wisdom for gain, but he does not seem to have given the matter a second thought. The remuneration of teachers has always been a problem – a social problem in our own day, a problem of conscience in Abelard's. To what extent, people wondered, was it permissible to sell something as sacred as knowledge, to put a price on the treasures of the intellect? Yet if a priest was entitled to make a living from the performance of his duties, why should a master not do the same? As a makeshift solution to this dilemma, it was decided that the master – the schoolman – should receive a benefice, in other words the income from an endowed church office, sufficient to cover his essential needs. Abelard himself appears to have been paid a stipend as an honorary canon while teaching at the Notre Dame school. This sum was augmented by fees, at least in the case of students who could afford them. A severe view was taken of any master who abused this source of revenue. Baldry of Bourgeuil, among others, roundly condemned 'the venal master selling venal words . . . [and] filling the pupil's ear only if the pupil has first filled his coffers . . .' And Bernard of Clairvaux later denounced those who 'seek to learn so that they may afterwards sell their knowledge, either to make money or to secure advancement.' Abelard profited in both ways, without seeming to worry about it.

His career as a scholar had earned him far more fame and glory than he could have hoped to win as a knight. Had he wished, he could easily have crowned his long list of achievements with triumphs of another kind. Ladies used to spend hours examining the rival claims of clerk and knight, and soon, in the courts of love, there was fierce debate about whether it was preferable to be loved by a man who excelled in the lists or by a man who chose to win his laurels in verbal jousting.

Dulcis amicitia clericis est gloria.
Quidquid dicant alii, apti sunt in opere.
Clericus est habilis, dulcis et affabilis.[29]

Sweet friendship is the glory of all the clerkly rout,
Whatever others murmur, they know what they're about.
The clerk's a skilled performer, gentle and pleasant too.

The term 'clerk', of course, needs to be understood in the sense which was then attached to it. As Rupert of Tuy puts it, 'The title "clerk" is applied to anyone who is suitably educated, whatever his sort and condition.' It did not denote membership of the clergy or hierarchy; it simply meant 'scholar'. Abelard, in his correspondence, employs the words interchangeably. Many poems written at about this time were cast in the form of a debate setting forth the respective merits of clerk and knight:

Meus est in purpura, tuus in lorica;
tuus est in prelio, meus in lectica.
Meus gesta principum relegit antica;
scribit, querit, cogitat totum de amica.[30]

Yours wears the breastplate, mine the scholar's gown;
Yours loves the battle, mine would rather be
Lost in old lays of knights of high renown,
And write, research and dream – for love of me.

That is how the heroine of one such poem sings the praises of her lover, the clerk. And the goliardic songs, of course, likewise champion the scholar's cause. Both his erudition and his manners, they say, make the clerk a better lover.[31] Such is the verdict of the court which the god of Love convened for the purpose of resolving this undecided issue. And if ever there was an attractive clerk, endowed with every appealing quality, physical and intellectual, it was Peter Abelard.

II

HELOISE

Ah Dieu! Qui peut amour tenir
Un an ou deux sans découvrir?
Car amour ne se peut celer.

Ah God! What man has loved a year
Or more, yet let it not appear?
For of its nature love will out.
Déroul. Tristan

'A T that time there was a girl named Heloise living in this same city of Paris.'[1]

It sounds like the opening of a fairy tale: 'Once upon a time . . .' But the story is a true one, and it was enacted with such intensity that after eight and a half centuries its emotional impact is unimpaired.

Like Abelard, the girl Heloise attracted attention whenever she appeared in public. She was much talked of, not only in Paris but throughout the academic world. Her fame had spread rapidly from one religious and educational establishment to another. 'I used to hear reports that a woman, still shackled to a lay existence, was devoting her life to the study of letters and – a rarity indeed! – of wisdom, and that the pleasures of the world, its frivolities and desires, could not distract her from the notion of improving her mind.'[2]

The author of those words was still a young monk at the time, although he was a figure who played an active part in determining the intellectual climate of the period through being in charge of the monastery schools lying in the shadow of

45

the beautiful new abbey at Vézelay. On his hilltop in Burgundy, Peter of Montboissier – who had joined the order of Cluny at the age of seventeen, and had not yet acquired the name 'Peter the Venerable' – sometimes thought of Heloise, a girl whom he had never met but who had aroused so much interest because of her exceptional thirst for knowledge. She was still in her teens, yet it was claimed that she had already embarked on a course of philosophical studies. Paradoxically, she seemed to have no intention of entering a convent. It was quite natural for a nun to develop a taste for scholarship and pursue her studies to an advanced level; nor was there any great cause for surprise if, in the terms later employed by Gertrude of Helfta, an accomplished 'grammarianess' decided to become a 'theologianess'. But there was general astonishment that, at an age when most girls had no thought for anything but their appearance, a young laywoman should be exclusively concerned with furthering her education and should even have begun to master on philosophy, a subject which had proved too much for many men. 'At a time when the whole world . . . shows such deplorable indolence regarding these studies; when wisdom has difficulty in finding a haven – I will not say among the female sex, from which it is utterly banished, but even in the minds of men – your burning zeal has raised you above all women, and there are few men whom you have not surpassed.' Once again the writer is Peter the Venerable, informing Heloise how deeply her reputation had impressed him in his youth.[3]

Heloise had received her early education at the convent of Our Lady in Argenteuil, near Paris; the nuns ran a school there, as was usual at the time. She had shown exceptional gifts, and an eagerness to match. She had been given the usual grounding in the Psalms, the Scriptures and such secular authors as were considered appropriate for the teaching of 'grammar'. She could quote with ease from the Fathers of the Church, and from Ovid and Seneca; on one particularly dramatic occasion in the future, she cited Lucan instinctively and tellingly.

There were no limits to her intellectual curiosity – for, if what Peter the Venerable says is true, she had elected to study not only the complete cycle of the liberal arts, with dialectic in pride of place, but theology as well. Perhaps the nuns at Argenteuil were not sufficiently well-educated to satisfy her thirst for knowledge. At all events her uncle Fulbert, a canon of Notre Dame, offered her the hospitality of his home within the cathedral cloister. He was full of admiration for his ward's intelligence and did everything to smooth her path to greater learning.

Biographers of Heloise have sometimes found it impossible to believe that an uncle would show such deep concern for his niece's education unless her mother and father were dead. In fact, we know nothing whatever about Heloise's antecedents except that her mother – Canon Fulbert's sister – was named Hersent. Reference to the customs of the time produces no support for the assumption that her uncle would have looked after her only if she were an orphan. A broader view was taken of the family in those days, and uncles, aunts and various other relatives frequently helped to rear kinsmen's children. The probable explanation for Heloise's presence under her uncle Fulbert's roof in Paris is that her parents considered it the best place for her to continue the education she had already received at the convent in Argenteuil.

At first sight, it is also surprising to find a girl, or indeed any person, living within the cloister of Notre Dame. This cloister, however, was not monastic but more of a cathedral close, like those of Wells and Salisbury, with a cluster of small houses providing accommodation for the members of the chapter. About forty of these houses stood at the eastern extremity of the Ile de la Cité. They may well have been walled off from the rest of the town, for the area had always enjoyed a considerable measure of autonomy: officers of the Crown were not allowed to set foot in it, and any criminal could claim sanctuary there, however monstrous his offence. Two small chapels, Saint-Aignan in the north and Saint-Denis-du-Pas in the south (the latter owed its name to the fact that the Seine could be forded on horseback at this point), stood within the close. Before the twelfth century was over, they became parish churches, in response to the needs of an ever-increasing population; but in Heloise's day the cathedral-church still seems to have been the place where most people went to worship. It was not the building we know today, for work on that did not begin until 1163, the year before Heloise died. There used to be two churches: Saint-Etienne, standing where the parvis is now, except that the apse protruded slightly beyond the present façade; and the cathedral proper, much smaller than its successor and built on the site of the present chancel. There was also a baptistry, Saint-Jean-le-Rond, which was not demolished until the eighteenth century. Another enclosure lay somewhat farther to the south: this was the *Trissantia*, where the students congregated to hear Abelard, and from which Bishop Stephen expelled them some ten years later. Thus, the tip of the Ile de la Cité was the home of a small, self-sufficient ecclesiastical colony, containing churches and chapels, cloisters and schoolhouses, gardens and private residences – including the house of Canon Fulbert. According to legend, it stood close to the corner of the Rue des Chantres and of the present Quai aux Fleurs.

So Abelard had ample opportunity to encounter Heloise in the course of his comings and goings. He may well have passed the girl while surrounded by a throng of students debating earnestly, for he often taught in the open air, like Aristotle himself; or on his way to class; or on a feast-day, when masters and students mingled in the overcrowded cathedral. Besides, it was no ordinary event for a girl to take up residence in the cloister of Notre Dame with the express aim of furthering her education. This made Heloise all the more noticeable. There were plenty of women scholars in the convents, and occasionally at the courts of feudal lords; but Heloise's presence among the young clerks of Notre Dame was as dramatic, in its way, as the enrolment of the first girl student at university in the late nineteenth century. She must have attracted many stares on

The seal of the university of Paris

Music, one of the Seven Liberal Arts,
as portrayed in a 12th c.
manuscript in the Bibliothèque de Troyes

The ruined chapel of Le Pallet in Brittany, Abelard's birthplace

Tombstones from the chapel of Le Pallet

those occasions when she tore herself away from her books and emerged from the canon's house to go to church or to take a constitutional.

The inclination to stare was redoubled by the fact that Heloise was beautiful. Later, Abelard wrote that she 'was a combination of everything that can rouse a man to love' – a description which, while promising much, is infuriatingly imprecise. Attempts have been made to deduce her physical appearance from the size and shape of her bones, for her remains, like Abelard's, suffered many tribulations before they were finally laid to rest in the Père-Lachaise cemetery. They were exhumed in 1780, and again in 1792, during the Revolution. Those who examined them decided that she must have been 'tall and beautifully proportioned . . . with a curving brow harmonizing with her other features'; her jaw was 'adorned with teeth of an extreme whiteness'.[4] These gruesome deductions are our only guide. It is no use looking for detailed contemporary descriptions: portraiture was an unknown art before the fourteenth or fifteenth century. On the other hand, the literature of the time abounds in similes celebrating the radiance and harmony of womanly beauty: hair shining like silk or glowing like gold, milk-white foreheads, black eyebrows, clear complexions, eyes radiant as two stars . . . Faces and breasts are likened now to roses and lilies, now to snow and ivory; voices are said to be like crystal, legs like marble columns. Innumerable phrases of this kind are to be found in the works of Baldry of Bourgeuil, Matthew of Vendôme, Geoffrey of Vinsauf, and other poets of the early twelfth century, all of whom wrote in Latin; and the same similes occurred, soon afterwards, in the first attempts to produce verse in *langue d'oc* and *langue d'oil*:

> *Plus ot que n'est la flors de lis*
> *cler et blanc le front et le vis;*
> *sor la color, par grant mervoille,*
> *d'une fresche color vermoille*

que Nature li ot donée,
estoit sa face enluminée.
Si oel si grant clarté radoient
que deus estoiles ressambloient.

The lily-flower is not more fair
And white than was her brow, and there,
Marvellous to tell, the rosy hue
Of her complexion mingled to
Create the radiance of her face,
A miracle of natural grace;
And her bright eyes gave forth such light
As made them seem two stars by night.

That is how Chrétien de Troyes describes his heroine in *Erec et Enide*, and it seems reasonable to suppose that Heloise's appearance tallied with what was then considered the ideal of feminine beauty. Abelard assures us in his heavy rhetorical style: 'If in physical appearance she was not the least of women, in wealth of scholarship she was supreme.'[5] It is worth noting, incidentally, that although he favoured the use of litotes when discussing other people, his praise is more direct if relating to himself: 'I enjoyed such high renown, and was so graciously endowed with youth and good looks, that I felt I need never fear rejection from any woman whom I favoured with my love.' For suddenly the detached, self-contained philosopher, hitherto driven by no demon other than dialectic, found himself in the grip of sensual appetites to which he had previously paid little heed. There is an extremely apt student song dating from about that time:

Ignoras forsitan ludos Cupidinis?
sed valde dedecet si talis juvenis
non ludit sepius in aula Veneris.[6]

Can it be you're ignorant of Cupid's pranks?
For a young man like you to shun the ranks
Of those who play in Venus's courts were shame.

Abelard himself is perfectly blunt about the kind of fever which now beset him: 'I had always led a life of extreme continence, but now I began to give free rein to my passions. And the farther I progressed along the path of philosophy and theology, the farther the impurity of my way of living led me from the philosophers and the saints . . . I was consumed with the fever of arrogance and lust.'[7]

In other words, natural instincts were beginning to assert themselves as vigorously as ambition had asserted itself in the past. By now he was convinced that he was 'the only philosopher on earth', and so his urge to engage in public disputation was receding. But the urge to enjoy the pleasures of the senses, which he had never yet tasted, had become a raging obsession.

Abelard had every intention of gratifying this new urge. But with whom? 'The lewd dealings of debauchery repelled me; the hard work of preparing lessons left me little time for associating with women of noble birth, and I was almost entirely unacquainted with those of the burgher class.'[8] He longed for a woman, but not just any woman. There were plenty of prostitutes in twelfth-century Paris; true, they lived herded together at the far end of the town, but that was no great distance. Abelard had no wish to consort with harlots, however. And at the same time he was far too busy to establish the social links which would have brought him into contact with the wives and daughters of the bourgeoisie or the nobility. Yet here, within easy reach, was a girl who matched his requirements exactly. He found her physically attractive ('she was endowed with charms of every kind'), and she had the additional advantage of being highly literate. 'Even when we were apart, we could keep in touch by means of letters.'

Once again Abelard showed his gifts as a strategist. He began to manœuvre as he had once manœuvred against William of Champeaux, digging in on the Montagne Sainte-Geneviève and then proceeding to invest the citadel and take command of it. He would have been a poor logician had he not, in these present circumstances, drawn on the reserves of logic which had served him so magnificently in the past. 'I thought of getting in touch with her, and I assured myself that nothing could be simpler.' Plainly there was no trace of feeling in all this – just the intellect and the senses, two poles which may seem far apart but are often closely related. Abelard, as we have already seen, was an archetypal academic.

It only remained for him to decide his tactics and implement them. He had to find some way of 'establishing a close, every-day relationship which would accustom this girl to his presence and thus induce her to succumb more readily.' In the event, circumstances made his task unexpectedly easy. 'I got in touch with her uncle through the intermediary of some friends. They urged him to take me into his house, which was very close to my school, on his own terms. I alleged that the bother of running a home of my own interfered with my studies and was too great a burden to me. Fulbert loved money. In addition, he was anxious to do everything in his power to advance his niece's career as a scholar. By catering to both obsessions, I won agreement from him without difficulty and so succeeded in my aims.'

The canon was dazzled by the thought of entertaining so eminent a boarder, who might well be prevailed upon to give private lessons to his niece. The combination of such a master and such a pupil would surely produce remarkable results. On his own initiative, therefore, he put forward a proposal which to Abelard must have seemed almost too good to be true: 'He entrusted Heloise to my entire control, asked me to devote all my free time to her education, night and day, and said I should not hesitate to chastise her when she was at fault.' For all his conceit, Abelard admits in the *Letter to a Friend* that this success was beyond his wildest dreams, and that he 'could not get over his astonishment'. He had been prepared for a long, hard struggle – yet suddenly, without any real effort on his part, he was given full control of the girl whom he had decided to appropriate in the manner, as he puts it, of a hungry wolf stealing a tender lamb. Fortune was certainly kind to him: fame, honours, and now love – or at least gratification, which was the prize he had been seeking.

And so Master Peter moved into the house in the cathedral close, together with all his books and belongings. Did he, as he crossed the threshold, experience some small sense of disquiet, a fleeting presentiment of the tragedy in which he was about to involve himself? Apparently not. Indeed, once his astonishment had abated, he was not even afflicted by that form of vertigo which sometimes follows too easy a success. He was Peter Abelard, the most gifted, intelligent and shrewd man of his time. He had laid his plans, and those plans were succeeding. Could anything be more natural?

'We were united first by [the experience of living under] the same roof, and then by our hearts.' Abelard's very brevity is expressive. Heloise obviously made no attempt to resist him. She was his from the moment their eyes first met. And how could it have been otherwise? Heloise was seventeen or eighteen, a time of life when any girl is living in anticipation of the man who will awaken her – for, by her very nature, a woman receives in the moment of giving. Heloise was especially responsive to the charms of intelligence and erudition. She herself was committed to a life of scholarship. Like Abelard at the same age, she had turned her back on frivolous pleasures, and shunned the amusements available to a girl of her station, so that she might devote all her time to literature, dialectic and philosophy. If Fulbert, her uncle, had welcomed Abelard with alacrity, it is easy to imagine how thrilled Heloise must have been when she learned that she was to become his pupil. For her, there was no weighing the merits of clerk and knight: the former commanded all her enthusiasm and admiration. And her uncle's lodger was a superb representative of clerkly qualities: he was the most influential teacher of his time, the most eminent of contemporary thinkers, the master who held unchallenged sway over the young. What is more, he was endowed with a handsome face, a stylish appearance, a persuasive tongue – all the attributes to beguile a young girl. She could not help being captivated. In the very moment of meeting him, she decided that here was the man she was going to love for the remainder of her days. She loved him fiercely, with a love which nothing could cool or weaken, for Heloise was wholehearted in everything she did. She was too young, too artless and too emotionally involved to realize that Abelard's arrival in her uncle's house, and in her own room, was the result of some rather shabby scheming, and that his feelings were not of the same quality as hers. She loved him. She would love him until the day she died. Abelard was to pass through various phases and undergo a gradual change in his manner of loving. But not Heloise. In this lay her greatness – and at times, as we shall see, her weakness. Her love was unfluctuating and free of any flaw: it was love pure and simple.

This was a memorable coming-together. If ever two people were made for each other, it was Heloise and Abelard. They claim to have enjoyed perfect physical accord, and there is no reason to disbelieve them. But their minds were on the same plane, too: the whole of their correspondence testifies to this fact. Abelard was the greatest philosopher of his day, and Heloise was hardly less gifted than the master whom she was soon to jolt from his chosen path. And the harmony between them was intensified by the fact that both were new to passion and without previous experience. Their love was pristine as the love of Adam and Eve in the garden of Eden. 'The newness of these joys served only to make us prolong them ecstatically; we could not weary of them.' And in a few sentences Abelard draws an adequately evocative picture of this blissful time: 'On the pretext that we were studying, we gave ourselves un-reservedly to love; lessons provided us with the opportunity for the mysterious converse which love demands; the books lay open, but the lessons were interspersed with more words of love than words of philosophy, more kisses than construed sentences; my hands returned more often to her breast than to our books; our eyes shone with love more often than they pored over texts. Sometimes, to allay suspicion, I went so far as to strike her – not in anger but in love, not from hate but from affection; the blows were sweeter than any balm. What more can I say? In our eagerness, we went through all the phases of love; we exhausted every refinement that passion can devise.' And Heloise, embroidering on the same theme, asks: 'What queen, what princess did not envy both my joys and my bed?'[9]

Before long, this unrivalled passion began to find expression in literature. Apart from the white-hot correspondence which has survived the passage of the centuries, it inspired many poems – or perhaps one should rather call them songs, for at that time all verse was still performed to music. 'You, more than any other man, had two talents which are instantly successful in capturing a woman's heart: talent as a poet and talent as a singer.' We today can only endorse Heloise's comment. It is surprising to find that the poet or singer was as glamorous a figure in the twelfth century as he is now; for the songs which Abelard composed in Heloise's honour were not written for their ears alone: '[Your] poems and love-songs . . . were performed far and wide because of the matchless grace of their words and music, and your name was on everyone's lips. Their mellifluousness was sufficient in itself to keep the greatest dunce from forgetting them. It was this above all else which set women's hearts yearning for you, and those verses, mostly celebrating our love, soon spread my name through many lands and sharpened the jealousy of countless women.'[10] What wouldn't one give for a knowledge of Abelard's love lyrics! Generations of scholars have pored over the poems of that time, especially the goliardic songs, in the hope of recognizing his hand, his style, his inspiration, but no unchallengeable discoveries have ever been made. Perhaps a few will one day be culled from the endless mass of inadequately perused and often unidentified writings, just as a large number of his hymns were eventually found in the library at Chaumont long after the publication of the *Patrologia Latina*, previously regarded as complete. It would be a wonderful enrichment of our poetic heritage, and it would certainly throw new light on this matchless pair of real-life lovers who have long held a place beside the legendary Pyramus and Thisbe, Romeo and Juliet, and Tristan and Iseult. At present, our familiarity with Abelard's poetry is confined to the liturgical hymns and a few lamentations.

At this point in their relationship, Abelard's obsession with these lost poems took the place of his previous concern with dialectic and theology. For the Philosopher had undergone a change which surprised him even more than it surprised others. He no longer found any interest in the issues which he had debated so hotly only a few months earlier. Writing love poems was now his only concern. Never for a moment had he suspected that by following the dictates of his senses he would lay himself open to a feeling strong enough and deep enough to transform him. Some lines which he wrote years later, as an old man, show how shaken he was by the realization of what was taking place within him:

> Quecumque est avium species consueta rapinis
> quo plus possit in his, femina fortior est
> nec rapit humanas animas ut femina quisquam.[11]

> Whatever bird of prey's most ravenous,
> Woman outrivals him. No beast more apt
> To prey on human hearts and minds than she.

The completeness with which he surrendered to love affected every aspect of his behaviour: 'As the craving for pleasure took possession of me, I gave less and less thought to studying and to my school. I found it intensely boring to go there or, having gone, to remain there. It was tiring, too, for my nights were given over to love and my days to work.' What had become of the brilliant teacher of only a few short weeks ago? 'I conducted my classes in a mood of lukewarm indifference. I no longer spoke from inspiration, but from memory. I did little more than repeat my earlier lessons, and if I felt free enough in my mind to compose a few scraps of verse it was love and not philosophy which dictated them to me.'

He clearly considered the fame which his poems brought him of less value than the renown which he had won as a logician and a theologian. With his customary self-satisfaction, he adds: 'As you know, most of these verses have achieved popularity in many lands and are still sung by people who find themselves in the grip of the same feeling.' But his sense of gratification, however pleasurable, could not match the excitement which he had once derived from his pupils' enthusiasm.

In the event – and here is yet another indication that Abelard's career was primarily that of a teacher, a pedagogue, inextricably bound up with the effect on his listeners, and their response – it was his pupils who were the first to notice the change in their beloved master. Comparisons have sometimes been drawn between Abelard in this new role, and the figure of the 'recreant' knight who appeared in many of the romances written at a slightly later date – *Erec et Enide*, by Chrétien de Troyes, for example. Marriage to Enide makes Erec the happiest of men, but it also renders him indifferent to the knightly ideal: he no longer rides off in search of situations in which he can prove his valour; he keeps away from tourna- ments; he never thinks of anything but love, comfort, the easy life.

Another image seems even more appropriate and was, indeed, to become the subject of many medieval pictures and stories: that of the harassed and derided Aristotle, about whom the thirteenth-century Norman poet, Henri d'Andeli, wrote a highly mischievous lay depicting the great philosopher as a man enslaved by a woman, even to the point of crawling on all fours and assuming a variety of other humiliating postures.

Meeting Heloise taught Abelard that there was one thing against which logic was of no avail. He had fondly supposed that he had nothing to fear; yet the enterprise on which he had

embarked for the express purpose of satisfying what he un-
hesitatingly dismissed as the baser side of man's nature was
already injuring the reputation which he prized above all else.
And it was his pupils who made him realize this fact: 'You
cannot imagine how sad and pained and regretful my pupils
were when they became aware of my preoccupation, or rather,
my obsession.'

'My nights were given over to love and my days to work . . .'
But it was the nights that really mattered. How he longed for
curfew, for the dying away of noise within the unlit house, for
the moment when he could safely steal along the corridor
and up the stairs to the door which led to paradise.

> *Plagues a Dieu ja la nueitz non falhis,*
> *Nil mieus amics lonh de mi nos partis,*
> *Ni la gaita jorn ni alba ne vis:*
> *Oi Deus, oi Deus, de l'alba! Tant tost ve!*[12]

> God grant the night may never end
> Nor my love leave my side,
> The watchman never see the dawn.
> Ah God, how soon dawn breaks!

A good many poems written about this time were concerned
with the callousness of dawn; it was a subject to which the
troubadours and trouvères returned again and again. Another
favourite theme was the jealousy of the *losengier*, the scandal-
monger roused to enmity by the sight of lovers' happiness.

> *Mesdisans sont en agait,*
> *amis, pour nous agaitier.*

> The evil-tongued, my sweet,
> Spy on us through their spy-holes.[13]

Not that scandalmongers played any active role in the story
of Heloise and Abelard. There were plenty of them hovering
round Canon Fulbert, but for a long time he refused to see the

truth of a situation which was obvious to everyone else. He was affectionately devoted to his niece and had complete trust in the philosopher, a trust amply justified by everything he had ever heard about Abelard. He was as wholehearted and single-minded as Heloise: like her, he loved or hated unreservedly, unwaveringly and for ever. Heloise's name was on everybody's lips, thanks to the songs her lover wrote about her; Abelard made his own state of mind all too obvious every time he gave a lesson; and round about Notre Dame there can have been talk of little else but this almost openly paraded passion. Yet Fulbert persisted in turning a deaf ear. His behaviour prompted Abelard, in the *Letter to a Friend*, to quote a remark made by St Jerome: 'We are always the last to know of the ills afflicting our own homes, and remain unaware of our wives' and children's vices even after they are the object of public mirth.' It was too good to last, however. 'A man may learn of something later than other people, but he still learns of it in the end, and a truth which is known to everyone else cannot remain hidden from him alone. That was what happened to us after a few months.'[14]

A little later in his account, Abelard confesses that he and Heloise were caught together in the same circumstances as Mars and Venus. The contents of Ovid's *Art of Love* were familiar to every educated man and woman of the time. Abelard's statement, therefore, is open to only one interpretation: they were surprised in the act of love.

It seems almost certain that they were surprised by Fulbert himself, for Abelard expressly states: 'What a lacerating discovery for her uncle!' And it is easy to imagine the poor canon's grief and anger at this sudden collapse of all the hopes which he had so trustfully pinned on his beloved ward, his profound shock at this brutal revelation of the truth, his consternation at the thought that he himself had set the trap into which Heloise had fallen, and finally his fury with Peter Abelard, as great as the esteem in which he had previously held him.

The immediate consequences can be visualized without much

difficulty. For a start, Abelard was ordered out of the house. And at this point in his narrative he sounds, for the very first time, like a man in love. The passionate songs, the 'intense boredom' which he had felt while teaching dialectic, could have stemmed from a wholly physical, sensual joy. But enforced separation made him aware of an overwhelming emotion. He had entered Fulbert's home as a cynic, a seeker after pleasure; he left it emotionally committed to his partner: 'Oh, the agony of lovers faced with separation . . . ! Each of us bewailed the other's lot rather than his own; each of us sorrowed, not over his own misfortune but over the other's.' Gradually, step by step, Abelard had progressed towards the state of love which Heloise had experienced spontaneously, at first sight; his continual lucid self-analysis brings out the steady progress from *eros* to *agape*, from physical excitement to a feeling which possessed him entirely: 'Parting merely tightened the grip on our hearts; deprived of all gratification, our love became even more impassioned.'

Abelard moved to another address in the Ile de la Cité and went on with his teaching. Employing the ingenuity which love always seems to impart, he and Heloise devised innumerable ways of keeping in touch, if not of meeting.

This *voidise*, or lovers' guile, was another theme often treated by contemporary poets, who were alert to all the subtleties and intricacies of passion. It is perfectly possible that, by bribing a servant or exchanging prearranged signals, they were able to exchange a few words on the sly. And in fact, although they both had good cause to fear Fulbert's anger and evade his vigilance, they were wholly unmindful of the opinions of others, whether pupils or associates. 'The thought of the scandal which we had already had to bear made us impervious to scandal.' Now that everyone was saying aloud what had previously been spoken in whispers, they felt liberated from all sense of shame. At this point, however, Heloise realized that she was with child. She lost no time in writing to Abelard and communicating the news 'with transports of joy'. She felt no trace of alarm or consternation, only a certain perplexity. 'She consulted me as to what she should do.' The days went by, and then at last their opportunity came: Canon Fulbert was called away. Abelard stole into the house after dark and carried his mistress off. To prevent her being recognized and to facilitate her journey, he clothed her in a nun's habit – a strange omen, though he was unaware of it. He then 'got her to Brittany'. Abelard's phraseology does not make clear whether he escorted her there himself or left the task to devoted friends. His sister made her welcome at the family home in Le Pallet. It was here that she gave birth to a son whom she named Peter Astrolabe.

These developments call for a few words of comment. Many historians, falling into the usual trap of judging Heloise's reactions in the light of modern attitudes, have claimed that she was a woman 'considerably ahead of her time', meaning that she was remarkably free of all forms of 'bourgeois prejudice'. They forget that she lived *before* the advent of bourgeois civilization and the resulting outlook on life. It would take volumes to clear up the misunderstandings stemming from the fact that mental attitudes are attributed to the Middle Ages which properly belong to later times. A short anecdote – highly significant and possessing the additional merit of being a 'true story', written not for literary effect but simply because it relates to an episode in the life of William Marshal* – may serve to throw some light on this. One day, William was ambling along in the company of a squire, Eustace of Bertrimont, when they were overtaken by a couple on horseback – a

---

* The story is taken from the *Histoire de Guillaume le Maréchal*, a historical poem – probably the work of a herald of arms – dealing with the life and exploits of a figure who was the devoted friend and adviser of Henry II of England. He was partly responsible for the upbringing of the king's sons, Henry the Young and Richard the Lionheart. After the latter's death, he espoused the cause of John Lackland out of loyalty to the Plantagenets and subsequently safeguarded the line of succession by acting as regent during the minority of John's son, Henry III.

man and a woman. The man looked worried, the woman was sighing and weeping. William glanced questioningly at his companion. They set spurs to their horses and overtook the suspect pair, and a brief interrogation revealed that the couple did indeed have something to hide: the man, a monk, had absconded from a monastery and had eloped with the woman. William and Eustace expressed sympathy with them for suffering the pangs of love, which were responsible for so many human errors, and did their best to console the woman in her obvious distress. Just as the two pairs of riders were about to go their separate ways, William asked: 'Do you at least have enough to live on?' The unfrocked monk was quick to reassure him: he had a well-filled purse containing no less than forty-eight pounds; he proposed to lend the money, and they would live on the interest. William exploded with wrath. 'So you plan to live by usury, do you? By God, that shall not be! Take the shekels, Eustace!' And without more ado they flung themselves furiously upon the man, took all he owned, consigned him and his lady to perdition, and returned to the castle. That same evening they related their adventure and divided the money among their friends.

In other words, whereas usury was adjudged an inexpiable crime because it entailed living on others, a highly indulgent view was taken of those led astray by passion – even when, as in this case, love impelled them to renounce holy orders.

'Progress' has not always brought greater enlightenment. Consider, for instance, the changes in the laws relating to bastardy. The deterioration in the legal standing of illegitimate children began during an era which is quaintly regarded as free of all forms of prejudice – the eighteenth century. As late as the sixteen hundreds, few people thought of concealing illegitimate births. The tendency began at about the time of the regency of Philippe of Orleans and was later reinforced by the Code Napoléon. Under the Code, it was the woman who incurred the gravest censure; actions for affiliation were either prohibited or seriously impeded, and the illegitimate child was effectively shorn of rights. Throughout the medieval period, however, bastards were brought up as members of the father's family; they were publicly accorded his surname and, in noble families, entitled to bear his coat of arms, charged with a brisure – the famous 'bar sinister'. In theory, they were deemed unsuitable for certain offices and debarred from holy orders; but many exceptions were made, and the son of Heloise and Abelard was to be one of them.

Vindictiveness, on the other hand, is a quality which has steadfastly resisted changes in legislation and moral outlook. Fulbert's temperament made his rancour as resolute as the trustfulness which had preceded it. When he found that Heloise had escaped, he became 'like a man demented; his wild grief and helpless confusion are inconceivable to anyone who did not see them.' Abelard even feared for his own life. 'I was on my guard, for I was convinced that he was a man who would attempt anything he could – or *thought* he could – accomplish.' And Fulbert was indeed to prove that he was capable of anything.

It was not until after the birth of Astrolabe – in other words, at least five or six months after Heloise's flight from Paris – that Abelard finally decided to make the gesture which one would have expected of him: he sought out the canon, presented his apologies and offered to make reparation. The step did not come easily to him: not only was he afraid of coming face to face with Fulbert, but the feelings which his actions implied had been slow to stir in him.

'At last,' he writes, 'moved to compassion by his inordinate sorrow, and telling myself accusingly that the theft which love had caused me to inflict on him was an abominable act of treachery, I went in search of him.' For all his intellectual dash and brilliance, Abelard was clumsy and incompetent at coping with human feelings. Only gradually was he learning to sympathize with other people's sufferings. Compassion was outside his province, and he might not have discovered it even now but for the sight of the intense distress which he himself had occasioned. Unfortunately, this kind of imbalance is all too common among intellectuals. It is a disillusioning but observable fact that character development does not necessarily keep pace with cerebral growth: think of the middle-aged academics who will never be anything but overgrown schoolboys. Abelard might be a master in the art of reasoning, but he was still only a child in his knowledge of human beings. Intellectually, he was mature; emotionally, he was not yet a true adult.

The account which he has bequeathed of his own tragic story enables us to follow the slow change in him and observe how this worshipper of logic was gradually brought to the realization that there were more things in heaven and earth than were dreamed of in his philosophy. Already his first dealings with a woman had made a new man of him; he had been sidetracked by a passion which he had expected to steer and control like a rational argument; he was painfully coming to terms with a transformation which made him a lover first and a scholar second. And the future held other revelations in store for him.

This meeting between the two men must have been charged with emotion: on the one hand the old canon, blinded by fury and despair; on the other the young master, finally prepared to admit that he had done wrong. Abelard gives an extremely partial account of their tête-à-tête, for never once does he tell us what Fulbert said. But one thing emerges clearly from the *Letter to a Friend*: the dialectician within him was active and proficient even on this occasion: 'I implored him, I promised to make any reparations he wished. I protested that what I had done would come as no surprise to anyone who had ever experienced the violent intensity of love, and who knew to what depths women had brought even the greatest men since the world was first created.' If the wealth of classical quotations and allusions in his letters to Heloise are any guide, he must have furnished the old man with instance after instance, including Samson and Delilah, Socrates and Xanthippe, Hercules and

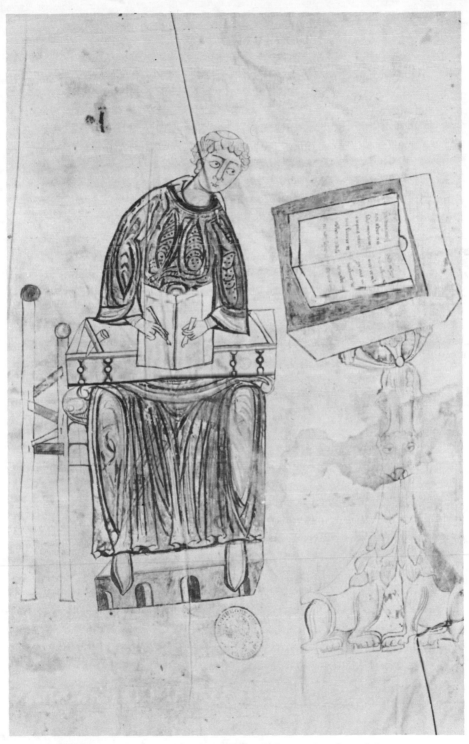

Clerk copying a manuscript. Note desk, parchment, reed pen,
inkhorn, eraser

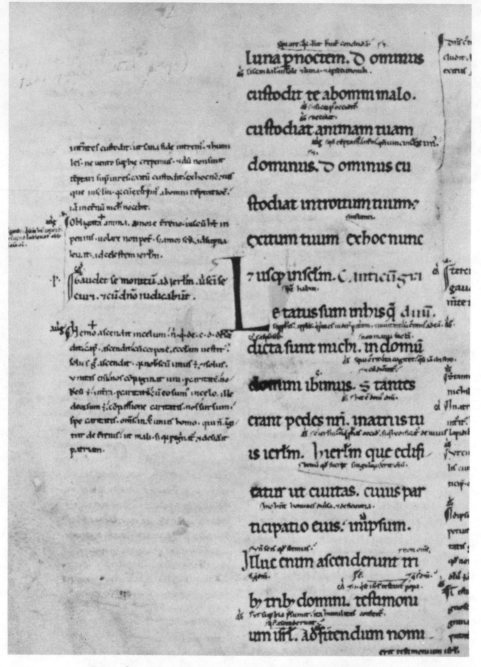

Part of a 12th c. Psalter, in which the text has almost
disappeared beneath the marginal and interlinear commentary

Omphale, Caesar and Cleopatra, and Adam and Eve. This
flood of eloquence produced the desired result: the two men
came to an understanding. 'To placate him even more fully,
I suggested a form of atonement which must surely have surpassed all his hopes: I offered to marry the girl I had seduced,
on one condition – that the marriage should be kept secret, so
as not to damage my reputation.'

It is impossible not to be taken aback, first by the smug
manner in which Abelard makes a favour of what seems to us
the most obvious solution, and second by his peculiar reason for
insisting on secrecy – to avoid damaging his reputation!

Be that as it may, Abelard felt that his talk with Fulbert had
settled the problem. He had found an intellectually satisfying
solution: Heloise would become his wife, and he would still be
the leading philosopher of his time. He immediately set out for
Brittany, 'to collect my mistress and make her my wife'.[15]
He does not actually say so, but there is no reason to doubt that
Heloise was staying with his sister at the family home at Le
Pallet. Today nothing remains of it except a few ruined
sections of wall and a chapel which probably stands on the same
site as the one in Abelard's day. A few gravestones bearing
ansate crosses have been dug up, and a crucifix has been erected
on top of the hillock. It is not hard to imagine the feelings
which this homecoming awakened within him, or the in-
expressible happiness of the reunited lovers, or – though he does
not refer to it – his joy at seeing his son, Peter Astrolabe. He
must have been buoyed up throughout the journey by a mood
of eager and confident anticipation.

What he had *not* anticipated was Heloise's attitude, and the
way she would react to the plan he was about to lay before her.
It is at this point in the story that her personality begins to
reveal itself. Up to now – though each of them had her interests at heart – her uncle and her lover had taken it upon
themselves to determine her future without reference to her
own views. Both men had been confident of her approval,

especially Abelard. Did he not know her better than anyone? Had she not always given in to his every wish, yielding to him, leaving Fulbert's house, exiling herself to Brittany?

But he had not allowed for the fact that Heloise was a live human being, not a mere cipher in a logical proposition. She was no longer the innocent young girl, the lamb offered up to the ravenous wolf and marvelling that her master should condescend to notice her. Her personality had strengthened in direct proportion to the love he had shown her. She was a woman now, and this time it was she, not Abelard, who had the last word. Never before had she said no to his plans, but she would not hear of their marrying, either in secret or in public.

Abelard's bewilderment is obvious even today. For the first time he gives pride of place to her comments, her motives, her line of argument. He even quotes some of her remarks verbatim – a rare occurrence with him.

Her decision is bewildering to the reader, too; indeed, it is incomprehensible unless we take the whole of her long argument into account.

She makes only passing reference to what would seem to us the most likely objections: 'Surely you, a clerk and a canon, will not prefer the shameful pleasures of the senses to the holy ministry?' In the absence of other documents and information about the period, we might well conclude that the Church did not permit Abelard to marry. But the terms 'clerk' and 'canon' must be considered in the light of their twelfth-century meanings. To be a clerk, as we have seen, did not necessarily entail being a priest. The merest student was a clerk in those days – and so was his manservant, if he was lucky enough to have one. Canon law stipulated that 'clerk' was not a grade within the Christian ministry: one could be termed a clerk, enjoy clerical privileges all one's life, yet lead what we would regard today as a thoroughly lay existence. The clerk was tonsured, but free to marry. He was prohibited from doing certain other things – from setting up as a merchant, for instance, or worse still a banker. But there was only one restriction concerning marriage: he must not marry more than once and his bride must be a maiden. Any clerk marrying a widow was deemed guilty of bigamy. This may seem strange to us, but the feeling at the time was that the marriage of a clerk should represent Christian marriage in its purest form: he and his bride must be 'the first man and the first woman'.

And the title of canon was not, as in the Roman Catholic Church today, conferred on ecclesiastical dignitaries. At about this time it had begun to be generally applied to members of the chapter who assisted the bishop in the administration of the diocese, advising him in matters spiritual and temporal. But the word may also have retained its original meaning. One was a canon, *canonicus*, when one's name appeared on the church register, *in canone*. The cathedral, in fact, was not just a large stone edifice, but a complex living organism embracing all manner of clergy and institutions. Among the latter were the schools, sometimes run by lay canons who had a stall but no 'voice in the chapter'. In other words, they had no say in the election of the bishop or in the management of the material or spiritual possessions administered by the chapter proper. They belonged to the large and varied group of persons occupying a position midway between the hierarchy and the laity. Not until much later did the great divide appear between the clergy and their flock, a divide which eventually led to the habit of using the phrase 'the Church' in the restricted sense of 'the ecclesiastical hierarchy'.

So Abelard could have married Heloise without losing any of his clerical privileges, and probably without forfeiting his stall.[16] She did not dwell on this aspect of the situation; instead, she reviewed the drawbacks which matrimony would entail for him. The picture she drew of married life was enough to alarm and repel any intellectual: 'Think of the situation wedlock would inflict on you. What connection can there be between scholarship and running a home, between a desk and a cradle, a book or tablet and a distaff, a pen or stylus and a spindle? Is there anywhere a man who, with his mind on

Scripture or philosophy, can endure the wailings of a new-born child, the songs of the nurse lulling it to sleep, the comings and goings of the household staff, the dirtiness of early infancy?'

What a prospect for a man of intellect! How could anyone who had dedicated himself to philosophy bear to contemplate a secular life, the life of an ordinary man beset by material worries? 'You will point out that the rich manage very well. Yes, because in their palaces or domains there are apartments set aside, because money is no problem to them and they are not burdened with everyday cares. But philosophers do not enjoy such conditions, while those who seek to make a fortune, whose life is bound up with this world's goods, have little time for the study of the Scriptures or of philosophy.' Heloise seems to be enunciating a general rule, recognized in her day and still valid in ours: there is a choice to be made between money on the one hand and the joys of the intellect on the other. Her greatest wish was that Abelard should be of that select band who rise above the common herd. That was how she had seen him at the time of their first meeting, and that was how she wanted him to remain; it was her responsibility, she felt, to ensure that he stayed true to himself. She could not bear to think of this exceptional man reduced to the level of a domesticated husband and father. Is that in itself so strange, so remote from us? Exactly the same stand was taken by a modern woman very typical of her era, who indeed has exercised a profound influence over it: Simone de Beauvoir. Of the occasion when she might have married Sartre, she recalls: '... Not for a moment was I tempted to fall in with his suggestion. Marriage brings a twofold increase in family responsibilities and irksome social duties. By altering our situation vis-à-vis the rest of the world, it would inevitably have marred our relationship with each other. I was not unduly concerned to preserve my own independence . . . , but I saw what it was costing Sartre to say goodbye to travel and freedom and youth in order to become a provincial schoolmaster and, finally and conclusively, an adult. Joining the

68

ranks of the married would have been a further renunciation.'[17] Both women advance similar reasons for saying no, though the mood and emphasis of their remarks mirror the differences between the two centuries.

And Heloise went further still. It was not merely the prospect of children, family responsibilities and social obligations that she feared for Abelard: she dreaded the thought that she herself might become a burden to him. Like Simone de Beauvoir, she had no wish to see her idol become an ordinary married man. Abelard was a treasure to which the world laid claim, and it would be wrong for her to seek to appropriate him. The sage must never marry, for marriage imposed and legalized too many harassing demands. A husband and wife had duties towards each other, and Heloise was not prepared to contemplate any curtailment of her lover's freedom. It is fascinating to observe the precedents which she invokes, and the order in which she invokes them. She begins by quoting St Paul: 'Art thou loosed from a wife? seek not a wife. But and if thou marry, thou hast not sinned; and if a virgin marry, she hath not sinned. Nevertheless such shall have troubles in the flesh: but I spare you.' There could be no stronger and simpler statement of the choice between retaining one's independence and entering into the partnership of marriage. A couple forfeited their individual autonomy when they married, for each had rights over the other. Of course, the point at issue was not sin but mutual obligations, and such obligations should not be borne by anyone who had decided to devote his life to a cause transcending the self. That was why priests were subject to the rule of celibacy, a rule energetically promulgated as a result of the reformist movement which had begun half a century or so earlier. It is somewhat ironical to find the passionate Heloise emphasizing that priests – those dedicated men set apart by the task of serving God and worshipping Him – had a duty to keep their personal liberty intact. But the following passage affords a closer understanding of how her own and her lover's minds worked: 'If I was not won over by the apostle's advice or the saints' exhortations concerning the shackles of marriage, then I must at least, she said, listen to the philosophers and heed what has been written on the subject, either by them or about them.' Like the master who had moulded her, she was so full of admiration for classical antiquity that the example of the Sage meant more to her than that of the Saint.

She was determined that it should never be said that the new Aristotle had let himself be enslaved by a woman. She cited authority after authority, quoting chapter and verse: Cicero, Theophrastus, Seneca in his *Letters to Lucilius*. She reminded him of the ancient Jewish sects: the Nazarites, the Pharisees, the Sadducees, the Essenes. She bade him think of the Pythagoreans. And finally she spoke of Socrates, a name which would surely reverberate alarmingly in the mind of any man in Abelard's position. At this point it becomes a little easier to understand why Abelard – who, as we have seen, was extremely mindful of his own pre-eminence as a philosopher – should have felt that by offering to marry the canon's niece he was making fuller atonement than anyone would have expected.

But Heloise had yet another reason for saying no, a reason which Abelard was quite unable to grasp. It lay in the intrinsic quality of her love, wholehearted and perfect, in so far as anything human can ever be perfect. In this lay her secret, the underlying motive for her refusal. Hers was a love which insisted on being free and unconditional. Only if one appreciates the full force of this feeling can one hope to understand the age in which she lived. It was the impulse which soon afterwards found expression in courtly love – a love so total, so exacting, that it spurned anything in the nature of a reward and might fairly be said to feed on its own bestowal. Thus, in poem after poem, we find the troubadour abasing himself before the Lady and deriving joy from the very suffering he experiences at knowing she will remain inaccessible to him for ever. And just as the poet will not betray the identity of his Lady (his most treasured secret), just as he shrinks from anything that might sully the reputation of the woman he loves, so Heloise refused to tarnish Abelard's distinction by chaining him to a marriage which, as she well knew, stood no chance of being kept secret.

Abelard may have been aware of this fundamental motive, but it seemed as obscure to him as it seems to us. He gives a full report of her logical reasonings and classical parallels: these he could cope with, for they were part of his intellectual stock in trade. Not until the end of his account, however, does he make passing reference to an attitude which obviously mystified him: 'She bade me realize . . . how much more honourable for me, and therefore dearer to her, the rank of mistress would be than that of wife; for she wished to hold me enthralled by love, not bound by marriage.'

Later she upbraided him fiercely for failing to realize that it was the very strength of her love which made her reject the easy way out. The contents of the *Letter to a Friend* brought her to the painful realization that, although his love may have been as passionate as hers, it had not been of the same quality: 'You have condescended to recall a few of the reasons whereby I strove to dissuade you from a fatal marriage, yet you say nothing of those which led me to prefer love to matrimony, freedom to a chain.' It came as a great shock and disappointment to her that he had failed to comprehend what in her view was the very essence of her argument: 'Never, as God is my witness, did I seek anything from you but yourself: it was you alone I loved, not your possessions. I had no thought for the circumstances of married life, or for the smallest dower, or for my own enjoyment, or for my personal wishes. It was your wishes, as you well know, that I was concerned to satisfy. The term 'wife' may seem at once holier and more substantial, but another was always dearer to my heart, that of your mistress, or even – allow me to say it – of your concubine, your whore. It seemed to me that the humbler I made myself in your eyes, the more I should be entitled to your love, and the less I should impede your glorious destiny.'

However intense his feelings may have been, Abelard had

not dreamed of a love so great that it would far outreach the gratifications to which it aspired. Yet it is this which gives Heloise her distinctive personality; she herself regarded it as fundamental, indeed sacred. Twice she solemnly calls upon God to witness the truth of assertions which seem to us almost blasphemous, or at least paradoxical: 'As God is my witness, had Augustus, the master of the world, adjudged me worthy of marriage, and had his sovereignty of the universe been assured for ever, being known as your courtesan would have seemed sweeter and nobler to me than being known as his empress.' That is what love meant to Heloise: self-giving carried to sublime extremes. And Abelard had not understood. Love may have flared within him, but not a love transcending the self; which is why, although he made an honest and determined attempt to set down what she had said, he failed to grasp the kernel of her observations. Nothing was beyond the scope of his vast intelligence: his extraordinarily keen mind gave him access to the highest truths and enabled him to unravel the most intricate problems. Yet he had remained blind to a truth which for Heloise was clear as day.

This in itself shows how much farther than Abelard she had travelled along the road of human love, to which she brought a generosity of which he was incapable. The difference had already been perceptible when Abelard had artlessly recalled their mutual despair at being forced to part after Fulbert surprised them together: 'How brokenheartedly I bewailed the poor child's affliction! And to what outpourings of despair she was moved by the thought of my own dishonour!'[18] No doubt they shared in each other's feelings, but one senses that even at this juncture Abelard was not prepared, like Heloise, to 'forget' his own dishonour and think exclusively of hers – for which he was, after all, to blame. Similarly we shall find that at a later point in their story he was incapable of putting complete trust in her, even though she had given ample proof of her undivided love. Heloise's skill in argument, and her somewhat wearisome evocations of the classical past, put her on the same level as Abelard: we are dealing with two intellectuals. But Heloise reached greater heights of love because she was a woman, and as a woman she showed genius in the art of giving.

And it was again because she was a woman, endowed with feminine intuition, that she was quick to grasp the reality of the situation confronting them. She saw what Abelard was incapable of seeing, another truth beyond the reach of logic: even if a marriage did take place, it would be no more than a blind, a pretence. Fulbert had not forgiven them. He would never forgive them, she knew he wouldn't. Uncle and niece were cast in the same mould: both were inflexible. He would not keep his promise, the marriage would not be hushed up, and heaven alone knew what perils she and Abelard would have to face afterwards. 'Then finally, seeing that her efforts to dissuade me were of no avail against my folly, yet not daring to clash with me, she began to weep and sob, saying: "This is the one action which will destroy both of us for sure and open the way to a sorrow as great as our love." And in this, as the whole world has acknowledged, she was illumined by the spirit of prophecy.'

For the time being, logic and reason prevailed. Heloise and Abelard set out for Paris. They left their son with Abelard's sister, who was to attend to his upbringing. If the marriage was to remain secret, there could be no question of keeping him with them.

'We therefore commended our young child to my sister and returned surreptitiously to Paris. A few days later, after an all-night vigil in a church, we were married at dawn in the presence of Heloise's uncle and several of his friends and ours; then we went our separate ways and never afterwards saw each other except at long intervals and by stealth, so that our union should remain hidden as far as possible.'

Obviously it was wishful thinking to imagine that a marriage could be kept secret when the wedding was an act of reparation performed in the presence of witnesses – the kind of witnesses who, at another time and in another place, might have been summoned to a duel.

Fulbert and his friends were itching to broadcast the news. The affront had been public, the reparation must be public too: such, no doubt, was the canon's excuse for failing to keep his word. 'Heloise denied it loudly and swore that nothing could be further from the truth. Fulbert lost all patience and subjected her to considerable ill-treatment.'

At this point, Abelard devised a subterfuge which hardly commends itself. It was perfectly right and proper that he should wish to shield Heloise from her uncle's brutality, but the step which he now took appears to have been prompted chiefly by concern for his own reputation, by the desire to give the lie to gossip: 'On hearing of this situation, I sent her to a convent near Paris, at a place called Argenteuil, where she had been brought up and taught in early youth. To accord with the monastic background, I made her don the habit, all except the veil.' It is hard, at this point, not to share the indignation felt by Fulbert and his friends. Abelard's sudden decision could surely have no other purpose than to hush up the marriage. Heloise had been publicly observed to enter the convent, not as a boarder but as a novice; she was attired in the habit of a nun; only the veil was missing, until such time as she took her vows. It was an act of sublime self-sacrifice on her part, but of no benefit to anyone except Abelard. 'Her uncle and relations thought I had tricked them,' he writes, 'and assumed that I had installed Heloise in the convent in order to be rid of her.'[19]

Everyone who knew them must have thought the same, and there is no proof that this was not Abelard's intention. No doubt he still loved her, and it is abundantly clear from one of his letters that he did not hesitate to give full expression to his feelings: 'After our marriage, as you know, and during your retreat at the convent of Argenteuil, I paid you a secret visit. You will remember the excesses to which passion drove me in a corner of the refectory, for there was nowhere else we could retire to. We were unrestrained in our lewdness, despite the respect due to a place dedicated to the Blessed Virgin.'[20] So his decision to attire her as a nun did not imply that he was willing to deprive himself of her love – merely that he was willing to deprive her of her freedom.

That Heloise should have consented to all this was only to be expected; that Abelard should have chosen such a dubious way out of his difficulties, leaving her to suffer all the disadvantages, casts an unflattering light on this philosopher infatuated with his own reputation.

And then came the terrible act of violence which Abelard describes in grim and simple terms. The Fulbert clan – the canon and his friends and relations – were 'beside themselves with indignation'. 'They conspired together; and one night, while I was resting in a secluded room at home, a bribed manservant let them in and they took their revenge on me in the most barbarous and shameful fashion, a deed of which the whole world learned with stupefaction: they cut off the parts of my body with which I had committed the offence of which they complained, and then they fled.'

No one could have been more obsessed with his own fame than Abelard, and now suddenly that fame was hideously transmogrified. 'By morning, the whole town had gathered round my house.'[21] And one can well imagine the scene. The attack had occurred at dawn. The various noises – shouts, stealthy footsteps, scurryings, howls of agony – had roused the neighbourhood. People rushed to the scene from all directions. And the news spread like wildfire. Within a short time the cathedral close was packed with Abelard's pupils, indeed with everyone who had ever heard of him. The rumour of the mutilation was on everyone's lips. 'It would be a difficult, an impossible task to convey the astonishment, the general stupor, the wailing and crying and moaning to which I was exhaustingly subjected.'

Abelard cannot be accused of exaggeration. A letter from his friend Fulke, prior of Deuil, is couched in the same terms. Fulke's purpose was to calm him and allay his desire for revenge, yet his letter presents a picture even more striking than Abelard's: 'Almost the whole of the Cité has shared deeply in your suffering ... The canons and noble clerics weep, and so do your fellow citizens. It is a dishonour for their city; they are grieved to see their town profaned by the shedding or your blood. What can I say of the lamentations of the count-less women who – for such is the nature of women – have shed as many tears over losing you, their knight, as if their husbands or lovers had perished in battle.'[22] Whatever his personal failings may have been, whatever scandals he may have pro-voked (and perhaps partly on account of those scandals), Abelard had been a kind of hero to the general populace. His fame, first bruited by his adoring students, had spread beyond the academic world; it could fairly be likened to the rather curious renown which certain great painters enjoy in our own day. No one, therefore, could remain indifferent to the attack. The women who had secretly yearned for him, the girls who had envied Heloise's happiness, the lovers who had sung his songs with such relish – all felt personally involved in what had happened. It caused as much distress as a public catastrophe. In doorways and workshops, in churchyards and market-places, his fate was the sole topic of conversation. Reports of the occurrence were conveyed along the roads by the pilgrims and merchants and wandering scholars. News circulated with surprising swiftness in those days, spreading from fair to fair, from monastery to monastery, and soon the story was known throughout the West, or at least in all its main centres of teach-ing and learning.

'The scholars especially, and above all my own pupils, tormented me with their unbearable wailings; I suffered worse from their compassion than from my wound; I felt my shame more deeply than my mutilation; I was more overwhelmed by confusion than by pain.' He had sought to achieve fame through the loftiest exercise of human reason, and now his fame derived from the most humiliating of physical injuries. He was more talked about than ever before, but for a reason which he would dearly have loved to hide. He had courted admiration; he was obliged to endure pity. 'What fame I had still enjoyed only a short while earlier! With what ease it had been abased, destroyed, in a single moment!' To think that the brief hacking motion of a blade could reduce the best, the *only*, philosopher of his time to a eunuch, a gelding! Each time he evokes this appalling memory, he insists that the physical pain was easier to bear than the blow to his pride, that his suffering was not so much physical as mental. Fulbert and his friends could not have exacted harsher vengeance: in addition to the mutilation and its physiological consequences, Abelard had sustained a serious injury to the intellectual pride which was the one chink in his armour. He felt he had become a figure of fun, a teased and derided Aristotle.

His thoughts at this moment of disarray are highly revealing. 'What contributed even further to my sense of prostration was the thought that, according to the deadly letter of the Law, eunuchs are such an abomination in the sight of God that men reduced to this state by the amputation or crushing of the male parts are driven from the threshold of the Church as foul and unclean.' And he goes on to quote two passages from Leviticus and Deuteronomy which insist that castrated animals must not be offered for sacrifice, and that the eunuch must not enter into the congregation of the Lord. Here, Abelard unexpectedly adopts the stand of a strict upholder of Mosaic Law. His reaction is that of the Hebrew whose behaviour is determined by the Old Testament rather than the New. Just as his philosophy remains remarkably close to Aristotle, so his religion tends to be that of a man still bound by the Covenant. True, there was to be a gradual change within him; but his temperament inclined him towards the Law rather than towards Grace. It did not occur to him to open the Gospels. Not until later did he derive some comfort from St Matthew's reference to 'eunuchs which have made themselves eunuchs for the kingdom of heaven's sake', and from the example of Origen, who is said to have castrated himself because he took Matthew too literally and wished to cast off the temptations of the flesh. For the time being, he was mindful only of the abhorrence expressed in the Old Testament.

Nothing could temper the shame that overwhelmed him, the sense of having suffered an irreversible defeat. 'What a triumph for my enemies to see the punishment fit the crime! What inconsolable distress the blow which I had been dealt would cause in the minds of my friends and relations! How quickly the tale of this unparalleled dishonour would spread across the world! Where was I to go? How was I to show myself in public? Fingers would point at me, tongues would defame me, I should become a kind of monster in everyone's eyes.'

On one point, however, logic came to his rescue: 'How just was the sentence of God which struck me in the part of my body which had sinned! How right and proper was the reprisal chosen by Fulbert, who had repaid treachery with treachery!'

The whole of Abelard's claim to moral greatness lies in these two observations. And it must be emphasized that they were spontaneous, among the 'thousand thoughts' which, he says, came into his head in the moments following the infliction of the wound. His acceptance was total, both towards God and towards the man he most hated: a thinker so enamoured of strict logic could not fail to acknowledge that the punishment had been appropriate.

> *Novi, meo sceleri*
> *talis datur ultio.*
>
> *Cujus est flagitii*
> *tantum dampnum passio.*
> *Quo peccato merui*
> *hoc feriri gladio.*[23]
>
> I undergo just punishment
> For mine iniquity.

I suffer grievous chastisement
For wreaking injury.
I merit, to my detriment,
That sword should transpierce me.

And he never afterwards deviated from this feeling. Much later, addressing Heloise, the human being to whom he lied least, he repeated emphatically: 'In accordance with justice, the organ which had sinned was the one which was assailed and which atoned through pain for the crime of its pleasures.' If there was a seed of salvation within him, the trace of an attitude which might eventually enable him to triumph over despair, it surely lay in this immediate and total acceptance.

Yet although his inner acceptance may have been immediate, he was still anxious to secure justice. The prior of Deuil's letter, which cannot have been written more than a few months after the crime was committed, reveals that the assailants had fled, but that at least two of them had been caught and punished: 'Some of your assailants have had their eyes put out and their genitals cut off. The one who denies that the crime was his handiwork has now been punished by the complete spoliation of all his possessions. Do not lay the blame for your loss and for the shedding of your blood at the door of the canons and the bishop, who have done everything in their power to obtain justice for you and for themselves. Listen instead to the sound advice and consolation of a true friend.' Which suggests that Abelard considered the sentences inadequate. One of the victims of this terrible punishment was Abelard's servant, the man who had made the crime possible by betraying his master's trust.

The story of Heloise and Abelard might well have ended at this point. A relatively brief relationship – two years, three at most. Not long in the lives of an ordinary man and woman. The commonplace solution would have been for Abelard to hide his shame in some distant monastery and eventually start teaching dialectic again; Heloise, for her part, might have been expected to forget this youthful first affair, obtain an annulment, and marry another man. They would then have been forgotten in their own century, and quite unknown in ours.

But their story did not end there, for Heloise and Abelard were no ordinary human beings. Moreover, they were mentally and spiritually attuned to a time when sexual appetite was not the be all and end all of love. Their behaviour cannot be properly understood until we recall that they lived in the age of courtly love:

> *Ailas! Tan cujava saber*
> *D'amor, e tan petit en sai!*
> *Quar eu d'amar no. m puesc tener*
> *Celieys don ja pro non aurai;*
> *Tout m'a mon cor e tout m'a se*
> *E me mezeis e tot lo mon;*
> *E quan si. m tolc no. m laisset re*
> *Mas dezirier e cor volon.*[24]

> Of love I thought to know so much
> And find my knowledge small indeed,
> For never by love can I hope to touch
> My lady, who pays me little heed.
> She has raught my senses all away,
> My heart, myself, my every part,
> And, stealing all, lets nothing stay
> Except desire and a jealous heart.

And the Provençal songs of the troubadours were preceded by similar love poems in Latin:

> *Inspiciunt sine re, sed juvat inspicere.*
> *Praemia magna putant dum spe pascuntur inani,*
> *irritantque suos hanc inhiando oculos.*[25]

> They can but gaze, yet gazing find delight,
> And deem it rich reward on hope to feast,
> Vexing their eyes by keeping her in sight.

The relationship between Heloise and Abelard belongs unmistakably to a time when the distinguishing quality of love was held to be the capacity to reach beyond the self, to transcend the very pleasures on which love feeds; and that is why their story has come down to us. It is sheer paradox that they have been looked upon ever since as the incarnation of the Couple, the Lover and his Mistress, when really they were united in happiness for so short a time.

And indeed they were not united at a deep level until the time of their first parting. We have seen the base and shallow schemings to which Abelard resorted in his efforts to get his hands on the girl: initially he saw her as no more than a means of satisfying his sexual hunger. Love, in the true sense of the word, does not seem to have stirred within him until he was turned out of the house in the cathedral close. So they were not animated by the same intensity of emotion until their physical union was thwarted; and by that time its final savage termination was already in sight.

'We both took the habit at the same time, I in the abbey of Saint-Denis, she in the convent at Argenteuil which I mentioned above.' These words, with which Abelard writes finis to their passion, gloss over another rather squalid truth. Two lines earlier, with embarrassed sincerity, he records: 'Heloise, carrying out my orders with complete self-sacrifice, had already taken the veil and entered a convent.' From this we must conclude that he had bidden her become a nun at Argenteuil, where – again on his instructions – she was already staying; previously she had been wearing the habit, but not the veil which symbolized final withdrawal from the world. In short, he saw to it that she took her vows before he took his.

So it was Abelard who devised and imposed this solution. Perhaps it was really self-imposed: Heloise was his wife in the sight of God and of men, but he could no longer be her husband in a physical sense. A mutual and simultaneous decision to take vows was the only way of dissolving the link which still existed between them.

Entering a convent or monastery may not have had quite the same implications then as it has now. Today we tend to associate the word 'convent' with high walls, total seclusion and the surrender of all freedom and pleasure; it is a place set apart where a small number of elect souls answer a personal, carefully examined call; even in the eyes of a believer, the act of becoming a monk or nun presupposes a high and exacting vocation. Much of this was equally true in the twelfth century, but the context was rather different. The monastery was a human hive made up, like any other institution, of persons holding various ranks and exercising various duties. They lived side by side, ordained and unordained, choir monks and lay brothers, conversi and oblates . . . Some people were linked to the monastery in a purely material manner, because they had been born on the estate and now grew vines or wheat there; for others, the link was spiritual – they were bound to the place by prayer or works of mercy; still others had official connections with the abbey, stemming from their work as lawyers, bursars or ministerials – the term applied to stewards and bailiffs employed by feudal estates, abbeys, dioceses, etc.

So the basic conception of religious life has been considerably refined over the centuries. There has, however, been a corresponding loss in contact with the masses, a contact which made a monastery a sanctuary for the criminal and a haven for the tramp. The situation which then existed is well summed up in a proverb which has been handed down to us: 'The cowl maketh not the monk,' meaning that a great many people wore the cowl without being bound by strict vows. Within the context of the prevailing pattern of life, therefore, entering a convent or monastery did not arouse quite the same feelings as in our own day, although the regulations, when rigorously observed, were no less exacting.

The fact remains that for Heloise the personal sacrifice was considerable. She was only twenty years old, and she was irrevocably signing away her freedom. The decision to take vows was Abelard's. Not for a moment did he doubt her readiness to comply with it, although he knew the step would call for extreme self-denial on her part. Afterwards she spoke of it as 'a decision which was yours alone'. Gilson[26] argues, not without reason, that the most reprehensible thing Abelard ever did was to insist that Heloise should take her vows before he took his. She loved him so much that she would have followed his lead without hesitation; but his failure to trust her, when he had every cause to do so, wounded her deeply and caused an enduring sense of bitterness. Later, much later, she reproached him with a ferocity which greatly startled Abelard.

At the time, however, she complied without a word. Abelard had commanded her to take the veil: she would take it of her own free will. The two halves of this statement may sound contradictory, but much light is thrown on them by his account of what occurred at the covent in Argenteuil.

Her friends and relations condoled with her. They entreated her not to take the veil. They bade her remember how young she was, and how stringent were the demands of convent life. Could she seriously intend committing herself to such a future?

'She made no reply except to give voice, through her tears and sobs, to Cornelia's words of lamentation: "O noble husband, so ill suited to such a marriage, can it have been my destiny to exercise that right over so lofty a head? Criminal that I am, did I have to marry you and so bring you to disaster? Accept in atonement this punishment, which I meet willingly."[27] She was uttering these words as she walked towards the altar, received the blessed veil from the bishop's hands, and publicly recited her vows.'

Many have found it strange that a woman on the point of becoming a nun should approach the altar quoting a passage from Lucan. Heloise was a worthy pupil of Abelard. Just as he had felt crushed with shame when he recalled the Hebrews' attitude to eunuchs, so she was weighed down with despair at the idea of having brought tragedy upon her husband, like the heroine of the *Pharsala*. There was nothing to choose between them in their passionate addiction to works of antiquity.

But although these various quotations may give a slightly artificial flavour to the narrative, the events themselves remain deeply affecting despite the passage of time, whether one thinks of Abelard, deprived for ever of the fame to which he aspired, or of Heloise, pitched at twenty into this harsh, secluded way of life which was not of her own choosing. And over and above their individual destinies, this was the tragic ending of a matchless love-affair, the final, irremediable rift between two human beings who could never belong to each other after this, not even in thought. Two exceptional creatures had come together and for a brief while tasted the joys of Paradise; and now they were driven out, even more cruelly than Adam and Eve, for they were separated from each other as well as from Eden.

III

THE WANDERING PHILOSOPHER

'IT was, I must confess, a feeling of shame rather than a sense of vocation which led me to seek the shade of a cloister.'[1] Abelard longed for oblivion as fervently as he had longed for fame. The relish with which he had once enjoyed being talked about and publicly applauded and stared at in the street was more than equalled by his present desire to pass unnoticed. He was desperately anxious to hide himself, to vanish from human sight, at least until such time as the humiliating event had been forgotten and he could be sure that the interest people showed in him was not inspired by compassion, pity or even irony.

Hence his decision to enter a monastery. But not just any monastery. There were innumerable cloisters throughout the West which could have afforded him the salutary shade he was seeking. In the Paris area alone, he was free to choose between Saint-Germain-des-Prés, Saint-Magloire, Saint-Martin-des-Champs, and a great many others.

In the event, it was at Saint-Denis that he sought and obtained admission, and the choice is a revealing one.

No religious institution was at that time more revered and more illustrious than the royal abbey of Saint-Denis. It was here that Pope Stephen II had anointed King Pepin, his wife Berthe, and his two sons, Carloman and Charles – the Charlemagne of history and of the *chansons de geste*; and it was in the presence of Charlemagne himself that the completed church had been consecrated in the year 775. Ever since, the abbey had been treated with special solicitude, first by the emperors and then by the kings of France.

Consciously or not, Abelard must have been looking for a setting in which his intellect would be appreciated. There were very few abbeys which would not have been honoured to open their gates to him, but he was obviously anxious to select a retreat worthy of his powers. Retirement from the world was one thing, solitary confinement another.

Coronations took place in Rheims Cathedral, but it soon became the tradition for kings to be crowned a second time at Saint-Denis, and the sword and regalia were kept there. King after king expressed a wish to be buried at Saint-Denis: Pepin the Short, Charles the Bald, and several of their descendants; and later Hugh Capet and his son Robert the Pious. Naturally its status as a royal abbey had attracted grants of land from each new monarch, so that in time it had become the centre of a considerable estate. Evidence of this succession of royal gifts – vineyards, areas of arable land and even whole forests, such as the forest of Les Yvelines – is contained in the precious cartularies housed in the Archives Nationales. Side by side with its material wealth, Saint-Denis enjoyed the prestige of a religious past going back to the days when Christianity first came to Gaul; and this counted for a great deal in an age when every institution took a pride in its origins similar to the pride which every individual took in his lineage. Had not the earliest church of Saint-Denis been erected over the remains of the saint himself, reputedly the first man to preach the Gospel in Paris? The traditional story of how he and his companions were martyred – and such accounts were already circulating in Merovingian times – has in recent years been challenged by students of the texts, yet confirmed by archaeologists. In particular, the excavations carried out by S. McK. Crosby have established that the series of sanctuaries built at Saint-Denis (a chapel possibly dating from the fourth century; a late fifth-century church rebuilt on King Dagobert's instructions round about the year 630, together with a hospital and some monastery buildings; and finally the church which stood there in Abelard's time, and which had been consecrated in the presence of Charlemagne) were all erected upon the axis of a single tomb containing the 'holy bodies' – those of St Denis and his companions, who were put to death on the heights of Montmartre, and whose remains were then delivered to the Christian cemetery at Catolacus, the ancient name of Saint-Denis.[2] Catolacus may well have been the name of a Gallo-Roman villa which in time became the focal point of a small market town; it was here that St Denis and his companions were said to have been buried after their execution. Abelard lived long enough to see work begin on a new church, for the existing one had become too small to cope with the large numbers attending the special ceremony held annually on 9 October, the feast of St Denis; the crush was so great that the monks responsible for the safekeeping of the relics sometimes had to clamber out by way of the window. He died two years before the building was consecrated on 11 June 1144, but he had been a companion of the man responsible for the undertaking – Abbot Suger.

The *Letter to a Friend* does not contain a single reference to Suger. This is all the more extraordinary in that he was a most remarkable figure. He did not become abbot until 1122, two years after Abelard's arrival at Saint-Denis; he was elected on the death of Abbot Adam, who *is* mentioned in the Letter. It seems strange that two men like Suger and Abelard could live within the walls of the same monastery, yet fail – apparently – to establish any real contact with each other. Suger was of lowly origins, coming from a family of serfs; but his intelligence and his brilliant talents had soon won recognition. King Louis VI of France, a fellow pupil at the abbey school of Saint-Denis, had been sufficiently impressed to make him his adviser. Suger, like Abelard, was what we should nowadays call a humanist. His works show that he was a man of wide culture. He was a fine poet, an artist, and the possessor of a bold, innovatory spirit. When he rebuilt his abbey, he became the first man of his time to employ the ribbed vault and the audacity of this step can fairly be likened to the decision to engage an architect like Le Corbusier to redesign the chapel at Ronchamp. There is no need to dwell on its repercussions: the introduction of the ribbed vault determined the whole future development of Gothic art. Admittedly, Suger's interests lay in history,

87

architecture and tangible achievement rather than in philosophical debate. However, there was one point over which he
and Abelard might have seen eye to eye: the reforming of
Saint-Denis, which was to be his great achievement.

For the abbey which Abelard had chosen was unquestionably
in need of reform. 'It was addicted to all the licentiousness of
worldly living. The abbot's sole claim to pre-eminence was the
dissoluteness and foulness of his morals.'³ This was true of a
great many abbeys at the time, and the material wealth of
Saint-Denis was a further inducement to laxity. The history
of the entire feudal period, right up to the fourteenth century,
was marked by reformist movements which reminded
monasteries of their prime purpose and restored them to their
true wealth; once these reforms ceased, monastic life went into
a decline which became almost total during the classical
period of the seventeenth and eighteenth centuries. At Saint-
Denis, reform was overdue. Abelard recognized the fact and
proclaimed it openly: 'More than once I had inveighed against
these scandalous excesses, both in private and in public.'⁴ But
his reforming zeal met with no response: it must have seemed
out of place, even offensive, to his new companions. Who was
he to talk of virtue, after such a scandal? And it was easy for
him to condemn other men's weaknesses – he was no longer
subject to temptation. Was he going to preach to monks who
were so much his seniors in the monastic life?

In fact, as the remainder of his life was to prove, this reformist zeal sprang from a genuine impulse, a sincere inner
conversion. The terrible ordeal which he had been through
might well have prompted a negative reaction, making him
prickly and withdrawn. Instead he had bowed to it, in a mood
of immediate and total acceptance. He may have entered the
monastery without a true vocation, but in his case the cowl *had*
made the monk.

> *Quidquid agis quamvis etiam si jussus obedis,*
> *quod facis hoc quia vis, id tua lucra putes.*⁵

Whatsoever you do, even if you are obeying an order,
If you do it because you desire to, you must account it
    your gain.

This precept was among those which Abelard addressed to
his son. He had begun to apply it to his own conduct, and
therein lies his greatness. In later times he was to be thought of
as a champion of intellectual freedom; and it is right that he
should be so regarded, for the first use he made of that freedom
was to accept the tragic circumstances in which he found himself. The transformation is reminiscent of the change which
occurred in the mind and heart of an illustrious contemporary,
Thomas Becket, the once vainglorious chancellor of Henry II
of England; on being appointed archbishop of Canterbury
through the gracious intercession of his master, Becket immediately became as pious, poor and dedicated to the service
of God as he had hitherto been ruthless, wealthy and con-
scientious in the service of the king. Such metamorphoses were
true to the spirit of an age deeply in love with the absolute.

At the time, however, his conversion seemed highly suspect
to the monks of Saint-Denis and his efforts met with total
failure. Oddly enough, reforms were introduced shortly afterwards; they were implemented by Suger, at the behest of
Bernard of Clairvaux. Bernard succeeded where Abelard had
failed. Although neither then knew it, the two men were to
be dramatically in conflict with each other for the rest of their
lives. Abelard records this present setback briefly and starkly:
'I had made myself odious and intolerable in everyone's eyes'.[6]

Life was made easier to bear by his return to teaching.
'Almost before I had recovered from my wound, the clerks
came flocking [to the monastery] and began to weary me and
our abbot with their entreaties. They insisted that what I had
previously done from love of money or fame I should now do
from love of God. They argued that the Lord would demand
repayment with interest of the talent which he had bestowed
on me; that hitherto I had concerned myself almost entirely

with the wealthy, but that I must now dedicate myself to the education of the poor. Surely, they said, I could not fail to realize that, if the hand of God had touched me, it was so that, freed from the enticements of the flesh and from the tumult of secular life, I could give all my time to scholarship, becoming God's true philosopher instead of the world's.'[7] God's true philosopher . . . The expression was not coined by Abelard: it occurs frequently in contemporary texts. God's philosopher was the monk, monastic life being regarded as *vera philosophia*, true philosophy. The quest for wisdom was deemed synonymous with the quest for God, which was the exclusive aim of all who entered a monastery. The term implicitly contrasts this new wisdom, based on love, with the purely intellectual wisdom of the ancients. But in Abelard's hands the phrase was to acquire a new meaning: was it not his ambition to reconcile the two wisdoms, Aristotle's and Paul's? A philosopher by inclination, and a monk by compulsion, he realized that his ordeal had set him on a new path and made him conscious of his true vocation.

> *Si qua neges ex arbitrio contingere nostro*
> *arbitrio fuerit liberiore Dei.*
> *Nil igitur temere fieri temere reputabis*
> *cum prestet cuncta summa Dei ratio.*
> *Quidquid contingerit justo non provocat iram:*
> *disponente Deo scit bene cuncta geri.*[8]

If you deny that an action has been brought about by our
    free will
You must accept its causation as the freer will of God;
Therefore you must not conclude that any wrong comes
    about wrongly
Since all wrongdoing is subject to God's sovereign righteous-
    ness.
The just man is never provoked to anger, whatever befall
    him,

For he knows that, since God is its author, every disaster is
well wrought.

The monks and abbot of Saint-Denis were only looking for
an excuse to rid themselves of this unendurable critic. 'And so,
delighted by my pupils' daily renewed requests, they took
advantage of this opportunity to get me out of the way. Beset
by the students' continual pleadings, and yielding to the intercession of the abbot and the brothers, I retired to a priory and
there resumed my teaching practice.'[9] And at once the throng
of enthusiasts gathered round him again. The priory in question was at Maisoncelles-en-Brie. It is hard to imagine a world-
famous teacher of our own day setting up school at Maisoncelles-en-Brie and watching the students pour in; but here, not
for the first time in Abelard's story, we must allow for the fact
that our modern habits of centralization simply did not exist in
those days. Moreover, Maisoncelles-en-Brie was near Provins –
a prosperous city which, twice yearly, on the occasion of its
famous May and September fairs, became one of the chief
economic centres of the West. The atmosphere may have been
different from Paris, but still the students came. 'There was such
an influx of students that the place was not big enough to
accommodate them, nor the soil rich enough to feed them.'[10]
Now began the most prolific period in Abelard's life, the
period during which he perfected his method and wrote his
principal works. He supplies his own explanation of how he
proposed to fulfil his new programme and live up to his vocation as 'God's philosopher': 'I devoted myself especially to the
teaching of [theology]. At the same time, I did not quite turn
my back on the study of the secular arts in which I was more
versed and which pupils tended to expect of me . . . And as the
Lord appeared to have favoured me with a comprehension of
Holy Writ at least as great as that of profane writings, the size
of my audience, attracted by both courses, soon swelled, while
those of the other [masters] dwindled.'[11] Plainly his misfortunes
had not shaken his arrogant self-assurance, which seems to have

been justified by the equally lavish confidence of those who came to his classes. A significant detail reveals the influence which he was to have on teaching – an influence which, according to one of his maxims, would survive him and carry his renown beyond the grave:

*Per famam vivit defuncto corpore doctus
et plus natura philosophia potest.*[12]

The scholar's repute lives on after his body is dead,
And philosophy shows herself a mightier contender than
   nature.

Previously the term 'theology', by which we now habitually refer to the teaching of dogma and religious knowledge in general, had been applied only to pagan religions, as in the writings of the ancients. Knowledge of God had always been alluded to as Holy Writ, *sacra pagina*, or else, with more emphasis on the actual process of teaching, *lectio divina*. Abelard's personal example would seem to have accounted for the adoption of a term which was to acquire such great importance in the vocabulary of religion, and it is not without interest that this term looked simultaneously back to the past and forward to what would in the following century embrace the entire field of scholasticism. Thus the use of the term 'theology' marks an extremely important stage in the evolution of religious life and thought. The task of Christian writers – and this was as true in the twelfth century as in the days of the Church Fathers – was to pore over Holy Writ, either to extract its doctrinal riches or to cull arguments which would serve to defend their faith; nearly all the sermons and other writings of the spiritual leaders of the age were devoted to exegesis.[13] The spiritual life of the believer was entirely sustained by Holy Writ. This was true of everyone, from the most illustrious doctors of the church to the humblest peasants, whose familiarity with biblical texts derived from hearing the words read and sung during services, or explained in sermons and homilies. A close acquaintance with the Bible was rooted so deep in the customs of the time that learning to read was inextricably bound up with learning the Psalter; the most recent researches into the subject suggest that the young scholar was required to identify letters and spell out words from the Psalms, which he had already learned orally, having sung them so often, since biblical Latin was then widely enough known for the most popular Psalms, at least, to be sung in their Latin versions. In this domain, as in secular poetry, the vernacular was beginning to establish itself in Abelard's time, and before long the Bible was translated and annotated in everyday speech; the manuscripts in our libraries bear witness to the large number of Bibles in French, a few of them couched in mnemonic verses.

Abelard was among those who helped to reshape the teaching of religion so that it became a systematic exposition of doctrines, with definitions and proofs, in the manner of the theological Summae of the following century: what would henceforth be known as 'theology'. Slowly but surely, more importance was attached to theology than to Holy Writ. To summarize a long, intricate process of transformation which went on for several centuries: where pupils had begun by studying the Psalms, they eventually studied a catechism, a set of questions and answers. And this must surely have produced enormous changes in outlook and in the nature of human piety, for there is a world of difference between learning to repeat 'God is an omnipotent Being' and learning to address oneself straight to God and say: 'Thou art my rock.'

Abelard's efforts, as revealed by his successive writings, establish his claim to be considered the father of scholasticism. The purpose of his teaching was to set forth a series of clear and comprehensible definitions. 'I composed the *Tractatus de Unitate et Trinitate divina* for the benefit of my pupils, who were demanding human and philosophical arguments on the subject – not words, but proofs.'[14]

The treatise in question unleashed the first of the storms

which were to break over Abelard's head. It prompted disquiet, suspicion and misunderstandings of every kind. These misunderstandings were not fully cleared up until recent years, for only now is it possible to see Abelard's thinking in perspective and subject it to clear analysis. His manner of presentation, together with his afterthought: 'A man can believe only what he has first understood,' was regarded in the intervening centuries as a plea for pure rationalism, or even free-thinking, which as we shall see was far from his intention. This work contains the seeds of Abelard's entire philosophy, of everything which was to scandalize his contemporaries and constitute his originality in the eyes of later generations. We must therefore pause and consider it for a moment, even though the subject matter may seem rather dry.

In the first place, why was it devoted to the Trinity? To the nineteenth-century historians who sought to show Abelard as a rationalist, a free-thinker born into the wrong era, this was clearly something of a problem: for the *Tractatus de Unitate et Trinitate divina* contains no hint of disbelief, or even scepticism, concerning the dogma of the Trinity.[15] On the contrary, its whole purpose was to establish as clearly as possible that God was One in Three Persons. Abelard's approach was that of a sincere believer exhibiting and explaining the object of his faith; he had not the slightest intention of shedding doubts on that object, still less of destroying it.

Moreover, the fact that his very first work should deal with the subject of the Trinity shows the extent to which Abelard's preoccupations were in line with those of his time, for this central dogma of Christianity was then being studied and pondered with extraordinary fervour. The problem which had obsessed Augustine on the shores of Ostia, which earlier still had been the prime motive for assembling the first ecumenical council in history (at Nicaea), and which had drawn pronouncements from Athanasius, Hilary of Poitiers, and other early doctors of the church, was at the very centre of the studies

94

and meditations of the mystics and philosophers of Abelard's day. It would be impossible to list all the treatises and sermons devoted to the Trinity in the twelfth century; following in the wake of masters like Fulbert of Chartres and Peter Damian came Hugh and Richard of Saint-Victor, Anselm of Canterbury, Anselm of Laon, William of Saint-Thierry, Rupert of Deutz, Honorius of Autun, Gilbert of La Porrée, and many others; indeed, there were very few writings on spiritual subjects which did not broach the question in one way or another.

Signs of preoccupation with this mystery were to be found in the everyday life of the age. For instance, it was general practice for royal charters, and indeed the simplest legal documents, to begin with the words: 'In the name of the Blessed and Indivisible Trinity.' In schools, it was expounded and debated more conscientiously than any other subject. Even the terminology employed in respect of the Trinity was marked by a certain imprecision: scholars spoke now of person, now of substance; or, employing the Greek terms, now of hypostasis, now of ousie. In the following century, the mystery was to be formulated in terms which one had to accept unless one wished to be regarded as a heretic, but the twelfth century was characterized by an extremely active, and indeed competitive, spirit of inquiry. Bishops and abbots exchanged letters and met in synods at the first sign of a suspect doctrine, which, after a great deal of discussion, was either approved or condemned. Any quest for truth inevitably opens the door to error.

Today this may seem much ado about nothing, but at that time concern with the problem was ubiquitous and of far-reaching importance. Consider, for instance, the writings originating from the profoundly influential monastery of Saint-Victor: the question of how the three Divine Persons are interrelated is examined in such a light that any believer – and in those days almost everybody was a believer – is bound to feel involved. When Richard of Saint-Victor speaks of the

95

Trinity, he raises the whole question of what is meant by 'person', in the human sense of the term, and of what is meant by 'love'. For him, as for most contemporary thinkers, God was One. Richard did not take a Monarchian's view of this Oneness, however. God was Three, made One by the fact that he was Love. A Love which is never-ending gives and takes on the basis of perfect equality, total communion; so that when the believer thinks of God, he has not the static notion of a superior Being, but the dynamic vision of a loving impulse.

Richard's belief in the Trinity was founded upon a requirement inherent in the fundamental nature of love: 'The essential ingredient of true charity is not merely to love the other as one loves oneself and to be beloved in return, but to want the other to be loved as one is loved.' Thus real love was incomplete without the desire to see that love shared; and it was perfect love which demanded the existence of the Third Person, 'whose equal participation in the love and joy of the other Two is a requirement of the same love carried to its perfection'. Nothing could be more indicative of the mood of the age than the readiness of most thinkers to regard the very beauty of this conception – absolute love demands a plurality of persons – as more or less conclusive proof of the doctrine. To Richard, such a vision of God was 'too beautiful not to be true'.[16]

For God, therefore, being was synonymous with loving. And man was personally involved in this exchange of love. No credence was given to the idea that God's love of man might manifest itself either in an authoritarian manner, compelling him to 'love', or in a paternalistic manner, subjecting him to an uninterrupted torrent of love. Instead, it was felt that His love invited man to participate in the trinitarian cycle and thereby rediscover 'God's image' within him. This was the general conception of God's relationship with man, and inevitably it was mirrored in secular attitudes. A few decades ago, Charles Seignebos talked of 'love, that twelfth-century invention'. It is hardly surprising that in an age so richly imbued with liturgy the subject which preoccupied the leading religious thinkers should also find expression in art and poetry. To anyone familiar with this background and conscious of the fervour with which mystics and theologians, poring over the Song of Songs, dwelt on the quest for the Bride (the soul) by the divine Groom (Christ), it seems in no way astonishing that courtly love should flourish in literature. *Fin Amors* was directed towards a remote, inaccessible, highborn lady, and there was never any question of sexual fulfilment. The poet derived his *joy* from this self-imposed transcendence of physical desire, and from the rapture to which it roused him. Every era is dyed through and through with its own philosophical hues – a point which does not need proving in an age like ours, when nearly every piece of writing, including prose and poetry which comes under the heading 'pure literature', shows the influence of Marxism or existentialism or some other ism. There is certainly no difficulty in equating the ecstatic love of Richard of Saint-Victor with the *joy*[17] of the troubadours or the various conceptions of profane love explained in Andreas Capellanus's *De amore* and illustrated in the deeds narrated in the romances.

To be properly understood, Abelard's story must be set against this background. Its full paradoxical intensity becomes apparent only if we bear in mind that he was a contemporary of the most illustrious exponents of this theology of ecstatic love. His ideas were developed in an intellectual climate dominated by the attitudes of Hugh, Richard and the other great masters of Saint-Victor. And the paradox is that we tend to regard him as the hero of a love-story, whereas in his own time he was known primarily as a philosopher.

In the eyes of his contemporaries, however, Abelard's position was not paradoxical but extremely critical. He was grappling with the most burning issue of the day, not only as a 'theologian', to use his own term, but as a dialectician, a master in the art of reasoning. He himself had already drawn attention to

97

his dual role: this, he believed, imparted real value and interest to his teaching. Not that he was the first to attempt such a role. Others had already tried, with varying degrees of success. And if the question of universals was exciting renewed interest among scholars, it was because this purely dialectic issue was reflected in the problem of the Trinity. Abelard's clash with William of Champeaux, which had compelled the latter to make the revisions in the doctrine which he was teaching, had been no mere philosophical quibble: pupil and master alike had realized the full importance of their respective stands because of the implications they would have in the religious sphere. If the universals did not exist, if they were mere words, if there was no element of sameness among individuals, if one could speak only of 'men', without discerning any form of relationship between them which was not a mere word ('humanity'), was it possible to perceive anything more than a word in the Oneness of God? Acceptance of this line of argument would turn the dogma of the Trinity, in the eyes of the thinking believer, into a form of tritheism: three gods, three distinct persons devoid of that Oneness of nature which was at the core of biblical revelation.

By writing this treatise, Abelard was joining in an old quarrel which had already brought condemnation on the heads of his former master, Roscelin, and Berengar of Tours. Anselm of Canterbury had spoken out strongly against Roscelin: 'Those dialecticians are heretical who think the universals are mere words . . . whose reason is so clouded by its corporeal fancies that it cannot break free of them and is incapable of discerning what it alone can contemplate clearly. How can anyone who has not understood how several individual men are a single man in terms of species understand that there are several Persons in this very mysterious nature, that each is fully God, that they are a single God ?'[18] And he carries his argument further, citing various examples: if one cannot understand that the colour of a horse may be something distinct from the horse itself, that the wall may be something other than the house, etc., etc.

Abelard was about to take up a similar position against Roscelin. At a date not easy to determine, but certainly prior to the Council of Soissons [1121], he sent a letter to Gilbert, bishop of Paris, stating that he was the victim of attacks and underhand schemings by a man whom he did not name, but who, he said, was easily recognizable, having attracted sufficient attention by his faithlessness and disreputable way of living. 'Some of our pupils,' the letter went on, 'have come and reported to us that this old enemy of the Catholic faith, whose loathsome heresy implying the existence of three gods was demonstrated by the fathers attending the Council of Soissons [in 1093] . . . is spewing out insults and threats against me because of a short treatise which we wrote out of loyalty to the Blessed Trinity, a treatise composed chiefly to contradict the heresy of which he was guilty. Moreover, one of our pupils has stated . . . that he [Roscelin] was awaiting your return so that he might denounce certain heresies to you which I am alleged to have set forth in that treatise, his purpose being to set you against me, just as he tries to set everyone else against me. If this is so . . . we ask all of you champions of the Lord and defenders of the Faith to determine a suitable time and place and summon him and me before estimable Catholic persons of your choice, so that what he reproaches me with in secret and behind my back may be heard and submitted to their enlightened judgement [and a ruling given] whether he is wrong to bring such a charge against me or whether I am guilty of daring to write such things.'[19]

The odd thing is that Abelard makes no mention of this clash with Roscelin in the *Letter to a Friend*. He merely declares that the other masters found their audiences dwindling, which 'roused them to jealousy and envy against me'. 'All of them,' he continues, 'were toiling to defame me, but two in particular took advantage of my absence to assert at my expense that nothing was more contrary to the aims of the monastic profession than to go on studying profane books, and that it was presumptuous of me to teach theology without the aid of a theologian. Their purpose was to ensure that I was banned from all teaching, and to this end they persistently urged the bishops, the archbishops, the abbots and everyone else of note in the ecclesiastical hierarchy.'[20] A little later on in the letter he names the two persons determined to destroy him as his old rivals, Alberic of Rheims and Lotulf of Lombardy. Roscelin is never mentioned.

It is plain, however, that this particular quarrel was precipitated by Abelard, and his letter becomes easier to understand once we realize that his treatise was in essence an attack on Roscelin's nominalism. A fair estimate of their dispute can be formed from the celebrated argument about the walls and the house which Abelard was to take up and develop in his later works. In Roscelin's view, the parts of a whole were, like species, mere words. Thus, wall was only a word, since the house itself was nothing other than the wall, the roof and the foundations. Abelard refuted this, arguing that 'although one may say that the house is wall, roof and foundations, this does not imply that it is each of these parts taken separately, but all three united and taken together . . . So each part exists before forming the whole in which it will be included.' And he went on to develop his own original system which was afterwards called conceptualism and which insists that species and genus are a collective notion at which reason is capable of arriving by process of comparison and abstraction; mankind, for instance, the human species, is a collection of individuals who resemble one another: 'The whole of this collection, although essentially multiple, is alluded to by the authorities as a species, a universal, a nature, just as a people, although made up of several persons, is treated as singular . . . Mankind, garnered from the natures of different individuals, is summarized in one and the same conception, in one and the same nature.'[21] In other words, by its ability to abstract, the intellect can distil the general from the particular. Abelard arrived at this doctrine in the course of his arguments with William of Champeaux and expounded it in a whole series of works, first in the treatise on the Trinity, and later in writings which carried the same ideas further – notably the *Introduction to Theology* and *Christian Theology*, and also his *Dialectic* which he wrote and revised several times for the benefit of his brother Dagobert's sons.[22]

The facts of the situation in this year 1121 would appear to have been that Abelard realized he was under attack from several quarters, as much because he was a successful teacher as because of the propositions advanced in his treatise. These propositions, by virtue of advocating an original solution to the problem of universals, aroused the mistrust of the ecclesiastical authorities, already highly sensitive to a problem which had been the cause of frequent quarrels in the past, and infuriated the supporters of both the opposing schools of thought – the realists, William of Champeaux's disciples, and the nominalists, headed by Roscelin, to whom Abelard's independent view may well have seemed a personal betrayal, and who was probably the most bitter of all these opponents. Abelard realized the need to defend himself and felt it best to strike the first blow by arraigning Roscelin before the bishop of Paris.

This is very much in keeping with the behaviour of the young strategist who had set up camp on the heights of Sainte-Geneviève like a military commander keeping the enemy's movements under observation. Moreover, there was a kind of latent aggressiveness in Abelard, as the *Letter to a Friend* reveals clearly, and also a calculating streak. Whether his purpose was to open a school or to establish a personal relationship with Fulbert, he proceeded in the manner of a chess-player offering a gambit which would eventually lead to his adversary's defeat. His letter to the bishop of Paris was in all likelihood a manœuvre of this kind. Sensing that he was on dubious ground in the eyes of the ecclesiastical authorities, he took the initiative and was shrewd enough to attack Roscelin, who was himself a suspect figure: his personal reputation was tarnished, while his philosophy had been publicly condemned as heretical. And indeed Abelard did not hesitate to put his finger on the weaknesses of the rival who had once been his master: 'This man has

dared to write a defamatory letter against the eminent herald
of Christ, Robert of Arbrissel, and he made himself so detested
by that illustrious doctor of the Church, Anselm, archbishop of
Canterbury, that when he sought refuge at the court of the
king of England the insolent wretch was ignominiously
deported; he barely escaped with his life. His desire is to
have a companion in infamy, so that his own infamy may be
alleviated by the pleasure of seeing reputable persons incurring
disgrace.'

The reply, when it came, was crushing. Not only did he fail to
obtain the confrontation which he had sought, but his letter
provoked a long epistle from Roscelin, written in a tone which
emerges clearly enough from the following extracts: 'You
have sent letters bristling with attacks on me and reeking of the
filth of their contents, in which you describe my person as
covered with many and varied taints of infamy, like sores on a
leper's skin . . . It is not surprising that you should pour out dis-
graceful words against the Church, for your way of living has
conspicuously revealed you as her enemy. And it is true, we
have decided to forgive your presumptuousness, for you are
acting not as a rational human being but under the enormous
weight of your sorrow; just as the damage done to your body,
which causes you so much suffering, is irreparable, so the
sorrow that prompts you to oppose me is inconsolable.' There
follows an unquotable passage made up of hideous puns and
obscene comparisons with the bee's sting and the serpent's
tongue. Roscelin then proceeds to answer each of the points
raised in Abelard's letter. He defends himself – not without
a certain obvious embarrassment – against the accusation that
he had earlier attacked Robert of Arbrissel and Anselm of
Canterbury, and hotly denies the charge of heresy, of which he
claims he had been cleared long ago: 'Never have I defended
my own or anyone else's error; on the contrary, there is no
question of my ever having been a heretic. Since your foul
mind has spewed forth the suggestion that I was held in public

opprobrium and condemned in council, I shall disprove it by the testimony of those churches [within whose shade] I was born and raised and educated; and in view of the fact that you seem to be a monk of Saint-Denis, although you have left the place, I shall come and try conclusions with you there; and have no fear, you shall be informed of my arrival . . . through your abbot . . . and I shall await you as long as you wish. And should you disobey your abbot, as you unquestionably will, I shall seek you out and find you wherever you may hide on the face of the earth. And how can you possibly claim that the whole wide world has closed its doors to me when Rome, its capital, receives me gladly, listens to me even more gladly and, having listened, follows my advice very gladly indeed? And what about the church at Tours, and the church at Loches where you sat at my feet as the least of my pupils, and the church at Besançon of which I am a canon? They all revere me and welcome me and, in their desire to learn, joyfully accept what I say. Are they beyond the compass of the globe . . . ?' After this comes a long passage proving that his doctrine concerning the Trinity was in no way heretical, and that the suspicion of heresy stemmed solely from confusion over the use of certain terms. After which, the old man returns stubbornly and with even greater fury to the story of Abelard's downfall. Although he insists that this story was known 'from Dan to Beersheba', he eagerly recalls the less savoury details in his efforts to shed doubt on the validity of Abelard's conversion and the sincerity of his monastic vows. 'I aver, having heard as much from your fellow monks, that when you return to the monastery of an evening with the fees which you have exacted for teaching falsehoods you throw all decency to the winds and deliver the money speedily to your whore as a brazen reward for past debauchery.' The letter ends on a suitably offensive note: 'Since you have suffered the removal of that which makes a man a man, you should no longer be known as Peter but as Incomplete Peter. And ample proof of the ignominy of the incomplete man is contained in the seal which you have affixed to your foul letters, depicting two heads, a man's and a woman's. How can anyone doubt that a person who shamelessly adorns his letters with these two heads shown side by side is still obsessed with love? I might,' he adds, 'have shamed you further by dictating many other manifest truths, but since the opponent whom I am taking to task is an incomplete man I shall leave the performance of my labours equally incomplete.'[23]

On reflection, it is not surprising that Abelard should have preferred to make no mention of such a letter. No other writings by Roscelin have come down to us in their entirety – only extracts quoted and refuted by Anselm of Canterbury. Perhaps it is unfair to judge him on the basis of a document from which he emerges as little more than a foul-mouthed old man. There is a strong likelihood that he died soon afterwards. What other explanation can there be for his absence from the Council of Soissons? And this may have been another reason for Abelard's total silence about the ugly missive which he had rashly provoked.

> *Oui scribunt libros caveant a judice multo*
> *cum multus judex talibus immineat.*[24]

Let those who write books be mindful that a many-headed
  judge
Pronounces their doom, for their judgement is that of the
  multitude.

Roscelin's letter seems to have been a signal for the various calamities which befell Abelard in the year 1121.

We have no source for the details of his condemnation at the Council of Soissons that year other than the account which he himself gives in the *Letter to a Friend*. That account may be biased, but it is sufficiently dramatic to enable us to follow the proceedings stage by stage without bogging down in the rather abstruse discussions, which today seem to be mere hairsplitting.

Abelard insists that the decision to try him in council was entirely due to the jealousy of Alberic and Lotulf, who had been students in Laon at the same time as he: 'Ever since the death of our mutual masters, William and Anselm, it had been their ambition to reign supreme and establish themselves as their sole heirs. Both of them were teaching in Rheims. Their continual promptings persuaded their archbishop, Ralph, to call upon Conon, bishop of Praeneste and at that time legate to France, to convene a [. . .] council in the town of Soissons and invite me to lay before them the celebrated work which I had composed on the subject of the Trinity.'

So Abelard journeyed to Soissons with his controversial treatise. He was given a hostile reception. Stones and abuse were hurled at him as he rode through the streets: the people of Soissons had been primed against his person and his doctrine; the general assumption was that he was a dangerous heretic who maintained in speech and writing that there were three gods. Such violent treatment of a man suspected of heresy may seem excessive by our standards – we live in an age of religious freedom and tolerance – but the mob reactions of Abelard's time become a little less startling if we forget religion for a moment and consider what can nowadays happen in other spheres. For the people of that period, believing in the Trinity was as fundamental to existence as, say, subscribing to Marxist doctrines in countries behind the Iron Curtain. And sometimes these doctrines have been imposed so vigorously on an entire nation that even scientific data have been disregarded. For instance, the political masters of the Soviet Union insisted on the adoption of Lysenko's theories, as opposed to Mendel's, in the field of genetics; and this in the twentieth century, at a time of extraordinary scientific progress, when science has in large measure taken the place once filled by religion, ethics, philosophical inquiry, and so on. We have only to imagine a Mendelist, or a deviationist of any kind, arriving in a Soviet town or collective farm thirty-odd years ago, and it becomes a good deal easier to understand why Abelard should have had stones thrown at him because of his alleged belief in the existence of three gods.

As soon as he arrived, Abelard delivered his work to the Papal Legate. He stated that he was ready 'either to amend his doctrine or to make reparation' if it was found to contain any heretical proposition. The legate, probably with some embarrassment, asked him to submit other copies of the treatise to the archbishop of Rheims, Ralph le Vert, and to his two accusers. Abelard records this fact with a certain bitterness. 'Our enemies are our judges,' he sighs, quoting the Scriptures.

In the event, however, the council began its proceedings without reference to the treatise. '[Alberic and Lotulf] studied the book page by page, examining it in every possible light, but found nothing they would dare to lay before the assembly; the condemnation for which they were longing was therefore deferred until the end of the council.'[25] In the meantime Abelard braved the storm and spoke in public, certainly in the local churches and perhaps also in the streets and squares – a regular practice at the time. His efforts, he says, were directed towards 'establishing the bases of the Catholic faith in the import of his writings'. He obviously defended his beliefs with all his renowned skill as a master of debate, and slowly but surely opinion swung in his favour. The feeling grew that, far from being a heretic, he was advancing new evidence concerning the mystery of the Trinity. Both the ordinary people – who at that time were actively involved in religious events – and the scholars began to wonder how anyone preaching such an irreproachable doctrine could possibly be charged with heresy, and why the council should continue its proceedings without examining his case. Could it be that the judges had realized that it was they, and not he, who were in error? Alberic made every attempt to catch him out in private conversations, but met with no success.

'On the last day of the council, before the session began, the legate and the archbishop had a long talk with my rivals and a number of other persons as to what decision should be taken concerning myself and my books, which had been the principal reason for convening the assembly.'[26] Whereupon one of the prelates spoke out in defence of Abelard. This was Geoffrey of Lèves, bishop of Chartres and one of the most eminent figures of his day. At that time he had been in charge of his diocese for five years, and he was to remain bishop of Chartres until he died in 1148, leaving behind a great reputation for godliness and wisdom. He was always a loyal friend to Abelard, standing by him in moments of crisis and continually trying to preserve him from the difficulties to which his rash behaviour exposed him. Abelard may well have had Geoffrey in mind when he evoked the figure of the 'Friend'. Certainly, he extolled friendship in the strongest and warmest terms:

> *Omnia dona Dei transcendit verus amicus*
> *divitiis cunctis, anteferendus hic est.*
> *Nullus pauper erit thesauro preditus isto,*
> *qui quo rarior est hoc pretiosior est.*[27]

A tried and true friend surpasses every good gift of God's
    giving
And ought to be valued above all riches and this world's
    goods.
No man is poor who possesses a treasure of value past telling,
One all the more precious for being a golden rarity.

And so on for line after line celebrating friendship in much the same manner. Apart from the hypothetical friend to whom the long, autobiographical *Letter* is addressed, it is hard to see whom he had in mind. A scholar has expressed the view that one of Abelard's very beautiful *plancti*,[28] written shortly before his death and extolling the Friend in the person of David, was inspired by the unfaltering friendship and protection which the bishop of Chartres had afforded him.

Abelard gives a verbatim report of the bishop's speech to the council, a speech which was at once fairminded and full of sympathy for the accused: 'Every one of you lords here present knows that this man's universal knowledge, and his superiority in all the fields of scholarship to which he has applied his brain, have won him many loyal supporters; he has put his masters and our own into the shade, and his vine, if I may so express myself, has spread its branches from sea to sea. If – as I do not think you will – you burden him with condemnation without first hearing him, then his condemnation, even in the event of its being just, will offend many people and more than one of them will wish to defend him, especially since the work against which accusations have been levelled plainly contains nothing resembling an open attack. It will be said that, as St Jerome observed, any display of strength attracts the jealous, and that, in the words of the poet, it is the lofty peaks which are assailed by lightning . . . But if you wish to proceed according to rule, let this man's teaching or his book be produced before the whole assembly, let him be questioned, let him be directed to answer, and let him, thus confounded, be led to confess his guilt or else be reduced to silence . . .'

But Abelard's opponents would not hear of this: to debate with him was to court disaster. 'His arguments and sophistries would defeat the whole wide world.' Alberic must still have been riled by his failure to trap Abelard in their private talks together. So then Geoffrey put forward another sober and reasonable solution. He pointed out that the present council – consisting, as it did, of not more than twenty clerics – was too small to pronounce condemnation in so grave a matter. Would it not, he asked, be better to take Abelard to Saint-Denis? A full-size council could be convened there, and doctors of the church who were thoroughly versed in the topic could make a comprehensive examination of his treatise. The legate, who showed signs of being somewhat embarrassed by the pattern of events thus far, quickly assented to Geoffrey's plan, and they all went off to Mass.

The rival faction had different ideas, however. 'Reflecting that all was lost if the case were removed from their diocese to a place where they had no jurisdiction, and showing scant faith in justice, [they] persuaded the archbishop that it would be greatly to his discredit if the case were referred to another court.' They then sought out the legate and insisted that an immediate condemnation be issued. Conon of Urach was no theologian and failed to grasp the full implications of the dispute.

Inwardly, he began to feel – as a German – that the French clergy was a disquieting mixture of controversialists and bigots. He would have preferred to leave the matter to the man who was endowed with absolute religious authority over the area: the archbishop of Rheims; but the archbishop was a puppet in the hands of Alberic and Lotulf. Geoffrey of Lèves realized that the cause was lost. 'Sensing what the outcome of these intrigues would be, he gave me warning and strongly advised me to redouble my meekness and show no other reaction in the face of an obvious outrage. This conspicuous overstraining of the law, he said, could only injure them and prove to my ultimate advantage . . . And thus, mingling his tears with mine, he did his best to console me.'

As soon as the session opened, Abelard was summoned before the council. 'There, without discussion, without examination, I was forced to throw the book on to the fire with my own hand.' A long silence followed. It was broken by one of Abelard's opponents who, no doubt impelled by the need to justify his behaviour, cited a heretical proposition which he claimed he had found in the condemned work. This was enough to precipitate a general discussion. A member of the council, referred to by Abelard as 'a certain Thierry', spoke out warmly in his defence and quoted the words with which young Daniel championed the chaste Susannah: 'Are you so stupid, sons of Israel, as to condemn a daughter of Israel unheard, and without troubling to find out the truth?'

At this point, the archbishop intervened and attempted to allow Abelard to have his say at last: 'It would be good if our brother were to state his beliefs publicly so that they may, as appropriate, be either approved or censured or rectified.' The philosopher was on the point of being granted the opportunity which his enemies dreaded. 'As I rose to make my confession of faith, with the intention of enlarging on it in my own way, my adversaries said that all I need do was recite the Athanasian Creed.' This, of course, was a statement of faith setting forth the Church's teaching in respect of the Trinity and was traditionally regarded as the work of the great bishop of Alexandria. Its wording is still perfectly familiar to the average Christian. 'The merest child could have recited it as well as I,' complains Abelard, and to add insult to injury his opponents set the written text before him as though the contents were unknown to him. 'I read as best I could through my sobs and sighs and tears.'

The council broke up at once. It had been decided that, as a penance, Abelard should be confined within the near-by monastery of Saint-Médard, whose abbot had taken part in the proceedings. Clearly he was not among those who were animated by feelings of hostility towards Abelard, for the latter himself declares: 'The abbot and monks of that monastery, convinced that I was going to remain with them, welcomed me with transports of joy and lavished all kinds of attentions on me, in a vain attempt to console me.' He was beyond consolation. He describes his suffering in poignant terms:

'Today I should be at a loss to convey the frantic grief, the muddled shame and the desperate agitation which I felt at the time. I considered the two together, the punishment inflicted on my body and the torments endured by my soul, and I accounted myself the most wretched man alive. Compared to the present outrage, the earlier treachery seemed of little consequence, and I grieved less over the mutilation of my body than over the slur on my name.'

It would be a mistake to dismiss these words as the momentary outburst of a man whose pride had been injured. Abelard was cut to the quick because, although he had deployed the full force of his intellect in defence of his beliefs, he had failed to win understanding, failed to clear up a misapprehension stemming from the manifest ill-will of his opponents, and been

unjustly treated in the matter closest to his heart. 'The persecution which laid me low today sprang from no other cause than
the upright purpose and attachment to faith which had impelled me to write.' He had accepted the barbarous punishment
which had been meted out to him earlier precisely because it
was a punishment, a penalty for a transgression. But now he
was being punished for no reason – and in direct connection
with the work to which his whole life was devoted. Abelard
could be cynical at times; but this did not alter the fact that he
was a man of feeling, and his outraged sensibility found expression in a moving outcry: 'O God, who judgest fairly, with
what gall of soul and bitterness of mind did I rashly rebel and
accuse Thee in my delirium, often repeating that complaint
of the blessed Anthony: "*Jesu bone, ubi eras?* Good Jesus, where
wert Thou?" '[29]

Not until much later did the full significance of this loving
complaint emerge, for at the time of writing Abelard was
unaware that what had occurred was no more than a prelude
to the sustained tragedy of his last years.

Someone, however, appears to have glimpsed what the future
held. A few weeks earlier, Peter of Montboissier had been head
of the relatively obscure priory of Domène in Dauphiné. On
learning of the death of the abbot of Cluny, Hugh II, he had
set out for the mother house in Burgundy in common with all
the other priors of the order. If we are to believe a contemporary chronicle, he had scarcely set foot inside the chapter-
house when 'all the monks rose, hurried over to him, took him
from his place and, as the Rule requires, led him to the abbot's
chair and did obeisance to him.'[30] Peter, who was soon known
as 'the Venerable', was now established as abbot of Cluny. He
was not yet thirty, but his authority extended to more than
fifteen hundred monasteries, convents, churches and priories;
for as he himself wrote: 'The vast multitude of monks . . .
covered most of the French countryside.' And the increase in
numbers was in large measure ascribable to the influence of

Cluny: the abbey had fostered the religious revival which had begun in the eleventh century and was spreading steadily in the twelfth. The man who was to preside over the order for more than thirty years was a frail, retiring figure with no obvious claim to attention except his extraordinary capacity for fellow-feeling. 'Everyone found him lovable,' wrote his lifelong companion, Ralph of Cluny. 'His peculiar goodness made him public property.'

Peter the Venerable had heard of the decision to hold a council in Soissons, and of the sentence subsequently passed on Abelard. It would not have been surprising if the onerous responsibilities of his new position had left him with too little time and energy to intervene in the matter, but it was to Abelard that he addressed one of his first letters as abbot. He was as familiar with the philosopher's career as anyone else – indeed he had followed it more closely than most, for in early youth he had been excited by reports of Heloise and had acquired an interest in her, and he had without question been profoundly affected by the tragic course of their relationship. He sensed the lack of understanding which the philosopher had encountered and the isolation in which he risked finding himself.

'Why wander from school to school as you do, dear friend? Why alternate between being a pupil and being a teacher? Why seek, so wordily and laboriously, something which you can find without difficulty, in a single word, if you so wish?' And since he was dealing with a thinker who set such great store by the classical past, Peter went on to list the achievements of ancient times and to point out that all those achievements had suddenly been transcended by the advent of Wisdom: 'The sages of Antiquity wore themselves out looking for happiness; they made arduous attempts to extract the elusive secret from the bowels of the earth. Hence the invention of the arts, hence the cryptic arguments, hence all those sects, infinite in number and perpetually in conflict with one another: some asserting that happiness lay in sensual enjoyment, others in intellectual

Dialectic (above left) and
Aristotle (below left); Grammar
(right). Figures from the 12th c.
west doorway of Chartres
cathedral

(left) The 12th c. crypt of St Denis, where Abelard first entered as a monk (right) Seal of the cathedral of Soissons

The crypt of St Médard, Soissons

powers, others seeking it somewhere above and beyond man, still others refuting these theories and inventing new ones. While they blundered about in this manner, asking the human intellect for a light which only God could grant, Truth gazed down on them from heaven; it took pity on their destitution; it appeared on earth. So that it should be visible to all, it assumed flesh and blood like sinful man; it shared their sufferings and said to them: "Come unto me, all ye that labour and are heavy laden, and I will give you rest . . ." And so, without the aid of platonic meditations, of academic disputes, of Aristotle's cavillings and the philosophers' views, we were suddenly shown where bliss lay and how to reach it . . .' At this point, Peter's note of exhortation grew more urgent: 'Why waste your time performing like an actor, declaiming like a tragedian, flaunting yourself as courtesans do . . . ? Make haste, my son, to go where the Divine Master calls you . . . Take the path of spiritual poverty . . . Then you will be a true philosopher of Christ . . . I shall welcome you as a son . . . We shall not want for help from on high, we shall defeat the enemy; having defeated him, we shall be crowned and, true philosophers, attain the goal of philosophy, which is eternal bliss.'

Peter the Venerable was opening the doors of Cluny to Peter Abelard.

But his affectionate invitation met with no response. Peter wrote a second letter, shorter and more insistent. In vain. The wound Abelard had suffered was still too painful. And in all likelihood he was not yet ready to voice the 'yes' which meant self-renunciation, forfeiting the right to choose for himself and follow his own ambitions. What he needed was a victory, regardless of cost. Certainly he wished to be a philosopher of Christ, but on his own terms; and those terms did not – so far, at least – include renunciation.

Geoffrey of Lèves had been right to counsel meek acceptance. Abelard's period of residence at the monastery of Saint-Médard was a rare haven of peace and grace in his troubled life.

The persons responsible for condemning him started pinning the blame on one another. As for the legate, Conon of Urach, he gradually came to realize that he had been talked into perpetrating an injustice, and he bitterly criticized the French clergy, so quick to engage in self-destructive feuds over obscure issues. After a while he publicly lifted the condemnation and allowed Abelard to return to the abbey of Saint-Denis. The philosopher insisted that this shabby episode had been wholly inspired by the ambitions and resentments of Alberic and Lotulf. Experience teaches us daily that there is nothing more enduring or virulent than the jealousies existing between former students. Yet if we look more closely and bear in mind that this was no isolated occurrence in Abelard's career, the episode points to something more fundamental than personal rivalry; it brings into the open the lack of understanding which continually beset him. And today, with the benefit of hindsight, we realize that Abelard was no isolated victim of this failure in comprehension. He epitomizes the long, slow process of historical evolution. He was not only the hero of an unforgettable love story, but – in the realm of thought – the carrier of a seed which took more than a century to ripen to maturity. The true importance of that seed could not be calmly evaluated much before our own era.

Abelard gave a commendably clear statement of his position when he declared that at the Council of Soissons he rose to 'make [his] confession of faith with the intention of enlarging on it *in* [*his*] *own way*'. His faith, as he was to demonstrate time and again, was not in doubt. He may occasionally have put forward propositions which smelt of heresy; these are of no interest except to specialists in the history of religious doctrines,[31] and a discussion of them would be out of place here. In fact, Abelard never hesitated to offer his works for official scrutiny or to accept the Church's judgement. He was no self-willed heretic. And a thorough examination carried out in our own time by various scholars concerned with the history of philosophy[32] has rectified many of the hasty conclusions advanced by authors sympathetic or hostile to Abelard. However, one of his contemporaries – Otto of Freising – seems to have captured the truth when he remarks that Abelard mixed theology and dialectic *non caute* – incautiously.[33]

The 'own way' to which Abelard refers in the phrase quoted above was to treat logical reasoning as a tool which could be employed in approaching the truths of faith. For the believer, then as now, logic and faith were incommensurable: there was literally no common measure between the two. This was not, of course, to say that man must deny himself the use of reason and logic in elucidating the truths of faith: doctors of the church had been doing that since the days of the apostles. In Abelard's time, religious opinion – practically synonymous with general opinion – was particularly sensitive over the question of how reason and faith were related. Some thirty years earlier, the influential Anselm of Canterbury had ruled that they were equally valid sources of knowledge at man's disposal. His celebrated formula was developed from St Augustine: 'I do not seek to understand so that I may believe, rather do I believe so that I may understand.' Although, in his view, faith came first and was supported by revealed truth, he felt that men should still make every effort to arrive at a rational understanding of their beliefs. 'He who has not believed,' wrote Anselm, 'will not experience, and he who has not experienced will not understand; for just as experiencing a thing is better than hearing about it, so knowledge which stems from experience outweighs knowledge derived through hearsay.' In other words, faith was essential in his view because faith was inner experience and there was no substitute for that method of acquiring knowledge; but at the same time he goes on to state that 'through dialectic [i.e. logical reasoning] the mind is uplifted to the point of gaining some inkling of the joy of the Lord'.[34]

And it was precisely because Abelard was a born dialectician that he initiated a new advance in the rational study of the truths of faith. All his writings were dedicated to the task of making logical reasoning serve the interests of doctrine. For naturally the Council of Soissons had not quelled his activities as a thinker and teacher. His treatise on the Trinity may have been publicly burnt, but he lost no time in returning to the same ideas and expanding them in his next work, the *Introduction to Christian Theology*.[35] He was as pugnacious as ever and proceeded to attack, one by one, all the most prominent masters teaching the 'sacred sciences'. He did not go so far as to name them but, by stating their whereabouts, made their identities obvious to every reader. He referred, for instance, to a master living in Bourges: this was the future bishop of Poitiers, Gilbert of La Porrée, who – at the opposite extreme from Roscelin – professed complete realism. He referred also to a master living in Anjou: a man named Ulger, who enjoyed a considerable reputation at the time. A third, in Burgundy, must surely have been Gilbert the Universal. And with marked vehemence Abelard went on to declare: 'And there is another in France . . .' meaning Alberic of Rheims: 'He claims to be sole master of the divine science and fiercely contests whatever he finds in the writings of other men . . . He has even gone so far as to declare – and I for one have heard him say it – that God begat Himself, since the Son was begotten by the Father. And this creature, more puffed up with arrogance than any man alive, imputes heresy to all who do not profess the same belief . . .'[36]

In another work, entitled *Christian Theology*, Abelard emphasizes what he states to be his underlying intention: that of employing dialectic – in other words rational argument; for dialectic, he says, is the 'mistress of all reasoning' – to establish religious truth in the eyes of the unbeliever. 'And because the arguments which they bring against us are mainly philosophical, we in turn have made use of those which nobody, I believe, can understand fully unless he has spent years studying philosophy and, more especially, dialectic. Indeed it is imperative to combat our opponents with arguments which they too accept, for a man can only be convinced or refuted by [arguments] which he is prepared to admit.'[37] His chief targets of attack in this latest work were Bernard and Thierry of Chartres, both ardent Platonists. Abelard, on his side, represented Aristotelian thought, and this revived duel between two ancient philosophical systems is exciting when we consider the historical setting. Here was the dramatic confrontation of two distinct trends, two attempts at a synthesis reconciling Christian revelation with the great masters of classical thought, the school of Chartres finding support in Plato ('divinity is the essential form of all things . . . the Holy Ghost corresponds to what Plato used to call the *anima mundi* . . .') while Abelard allied himself with the logic of Aristotle. He was laying bare the foundations of that logic at a time when the West was still in possession of only a small proportion of Aristotle's writings. His efforts anticipated the masterly work which was carried out in the following century by Albertus Magnus, Thomas Aquinas and others; in the intervening period, however, an event of vital importance in the history of western ideas had occurred: the re-emergence of Aristotle through the medium of Arab thought. Averroës, otherwise Ibn Rushd, was not born until 1126, and by then Abelard had written, or was in process of writing, his principal compositions. Only the *Organon*, and a number of extracts quoted by Porphyry and Boëthius, were familiar to western readers of Aristotle. It was many years before the other writings of this prince of philosophers gradually filtered through in translation. Abelard may therefore be regarded as a precursor. His works looked forward to the great Summae in which the scholastic philosophers were to define their thinking. Indeed, the *Introduction to Theology* was a summa in its own right – not just another commentary on Holy Writ but a treatise divided into three parts, as was to become general practice: Faith, the Sacraments, Charity. The method was elaborated further in another of his writings, the one which probably had most importance in his lifetime. He entitled it *Sic et non*, 'Yes and No'.

Sic et non seems to have given rise to more disquiet among Abelard's contemporaries than any of his other works, and it forms the basis of his subsequent reputation as a sceptic. It is, moreover, a perfect example of the methods of reasoning employed by its author. The title gives a clear indication of the nature of this treatise: yes and no, pro and con . . . In respect of a certain number of questions – a hundred and fifty-eight, to be precise – concerning faith or dogma, Abelard draws up a methodical catalogue of the contradictions to be found in the Bible and in the writings of its principal commentators, the fathers and doctors of the church – the men who were referred to as 'authorities' because they did indeed exercise authority in all matters of faith. *Sic et non* is remarkable for the boldness with which reason was brought to bear on those authorities. It is not surprising that Abelard should have aroused so much enthusiasm in his pupils: he was the exact opposite of the run-of-the-mill commentators whose chief skill lay in glossing over difficulties; whenever a question required elucidation he examined it clearly from every angle, with no attempt to disguise contradictions. Some of the questions raised were trivial, but most were burning issues; either because they remain valid for believers in any age, or because they bear on major preoccupations of twelfth-century theology. It will suffice to quote the first and most significant hypothesis: 'That faith should be founded on human reason – and the reverse.' Then comes a list of quotations, some maintaining that the basis of faith eludes rational proof, others that the faithful can and must exercise reason in demonstrating revealed truths.

A composition of this kind might indeed be the work of a sceptic assembling all the pros and cons for the glib satisfaction of proving that they cancel each other out. Abelard's intention was very different. *Sic et non*, he insisted in the prologue, was the product of an inquiring mind employing dialectic to arrive at a positive truth; he aimed to show that on any given question the various texts were inconsistent but not contradictory: rather than cancelling each other out, they revealed different aspects, and the logician's task was to analyse the differences in order to overcome the apparent conflict between them. 'Since, in such a multiplicity of texts, some of the saints' words seem not only divergent but opposed to one another ... we must believe, taking our weakness into consideration, that it is we who lack the grace to understand [those words] rather than they who lacked the grace to write them.' And he went on to outline a method which largely anticipated what we now label textual criticism. The differences might, he said, be superficial, stemming from the various meanings covered by a single term or from the careless or ignorant alterations made by a copyist. On the other hand, the cause might go deeper. Sometimes for instance – St Augustine was a case in point – an author had clarified and developed his thinking to such a degree that variant texts represented stages in his progress towards truth. Or again, the divergences might arise from the fact that on a particular question text A referred to the rule and text B to the exception. When the differences seemed insoluble, the texts must be arranged in order of rank and preference must be given to the one with the highest claim to authority. In conclusion, Abelard asserted that only one text was completely free of error – the Bible. 'Should anything therein seem nonsensical, you have no right to say: "The author of this book was not conversant with the truth." ... Either the manuscript is faulty, or the translator has blundered, or it is you yourself who do not understand.'

The work represented a major step forward in the history of critical thought. It was uncompromising in its intellectual honesty, rigorously analytical, a manifestation of total commitment. 'The first key to wisdom,' he wrote, 'is assiduous and frequent questioning ... It is through doubting that we begin to seek, and through seeking that we eventually perceive the truth.'[38] All this was very much to the taste of young scholars eager for enlightenment and impatient of that brand of overcautiousness which, for fear of jeopardizing an acknowledged truth, took refuge in false comparisons and evasive generalizations.

Sic et non laid the foundations of a method which was later adopted by all the scholastic philosophers. Abelard did not create that method, but he provided a rational basis for it: he 'established the technical rules for all medieval speculation in philosophy and theology.'[39] Thomas Aquinas followed much the same course in his various treatises, symmetrically aligning dissimilar views on a given subject as a preliminary to drawing a positive conclusion from apparent contradictions. The machinery of scholasticism was now complete: *lectio*, reading; *sententia*, the form of study which brought out the inner meaning of a text; and *disputatio*, the method of debate which analysed, and compared and challenged in order to lay that meaning completely bare. The profound and lasting influence exercised by Abelard becomes apparent when we realize that some of the questions which he put forward were repeated almost word for word in books which afterwards became required reading for the medieval student; among these was the *Book of Sentences* by his pupil Peter Lombard. Abelard's second question was on an issue of vital importance to any believer, for it was concerned with nothing less than the definition of faith: 'That faith applies only to non-apparent things – and the reverse.'[40] Abelard proceeded to assemble the texts which established the proper domain of faith: *fides est de non visis*, faith applies to invisible things. His presentation of this statement, subsequently adopted by schoolmen everywhere, led to a general acknowledgement that, in the case of phenomena apparent to the senses or of truths capable of being arrived at by reason alone, the question of faith did not arise; it was simply a matter of rational knowledge. Faith was specifically concerned with that which the senses could not discern, and that which reason would be incapable of perceiving without assistance. 'Understanding or believing is one thing, knowing or perceiving distinctly is another; it is faith to accept non-apparent things, it is knowledge to experience things in their own right, by dint of their presence.'[41]

Sic et non did not draw conclusions, however. It presented contrasting propositions without establishing a synthesis. Abelard's efforts did not bear fruit until long afterwards, and the work was viewed with suspicion during his lifetime. But for modern readers it is the composition which evokes most fully his restlessly questioning cast of mind. He was a teacher, yet he never ceased to enquire and explore with all the eagerness of a student. How he must have fascinated the youthful audiences whom he schooled in this method, which he called 'permanent inquisition'. The word inquisition is nowadays full of dark overtones, but the notorious tribunal which it conjures up in our minds was not brought into being until 1233, and in Abelard's time – indeed, throughout the feudal period – it implied no more than the process of enquiry, investigation, research.

Considered from this viewpoint, and in the light of the developments to which they gave rise in later centuries, the attitudes embodied in Abelard's various writings take on their full significance: he was truly one of the fathers of scholasticism, and consequently a precursor of those methods of rational knowledge which were to play so powerful a role in the evolution of Western thought that they effectively excluded any other form of knowledge. It was in keeping with the same Aristotelian line of thought that Descartes gave fresh impetus to this evolution by taking doubt – more extreme than enquiry or questioning – as his point of departure and by refusing to accept anything as true unless it was manifest, visible from without. Not until the twentieth century were the flaws and limitations of this extraordinarily prolific way of thinking revealed, partly through the exploration of the inner recesses of the mind, leading to discoveries which upset all the trust previously invested in man's reasoning faculties, and partly through the very nature of scientific development, which has led us to acknowledge that the use of the imagination, for instance, can be helpful even to the scientist – for the instruments at his disposal, enabling him to probe far beyond the earlier confines of human knowledge, have afforded a glimpse of realms as yet beyond his capacity for analysis and observation.

As soon as the condemnation was lifted, Abelard left Soissons and returned to Saint-Denis. This change of surroundings brought him no pleasure: 'Nearly all the brothers were old enemies.'[42] Most of them violated the rules of monastic life, and Abelard would have found communal existence trying enough in the best of circumstances. There was bound to be an explosion sooner or later, and in the event it came after only a few months. The immediate cause seems astonishingly slight: 'Whilst reading one day, I came across a passage from Bede's commentary on the Acts of the Apostles in which the author claimed that Dionysius the Areopagite had been bishop of Corinth, not Athens. This opinion greatly vexed the monks of Saint-Denis, who fondly believed that the founder of their order, Denis, was this same Areopagite.' With his unfailing instinct for making enemies, Abelard had put his finger on a lingering sore dating back to Carolingian times. Three centuries earlier Abbot Hilduin, chaplain to Louis the Pious and head of the abbey for more than forty years (814–55), had gone to great lengths to establish the common identity of Dionysius, the member of the Areopagus who according to the Acts of the Apostles had been converted by St Paul; St Denis, who had brought Christianity to Paris and whose remains were buried beneath the high altar of the abbey; and finally the author of *Celestial Hierarchies*, a shadowy figure who even today, for want of further information, is known as Pseudo-Dionysius. The earliest manuscript of the latter's work to reach the West had been deposited at the abbey, and it was the same Abbot Hilduin who had produced a Latin translation of the Greek text. His gifts as a historian, however, were clearly not on a par with his skill as a linguist. The attempt to show that the three Denises were really the same person had been contested in his lifetime. The monks of Saint-Denis defended it all the more vigorously. It was an age when men took immense pride in their origins – as indeed they always do, our own era being no

exception: the public record offices are kept busy with genea-
logical queries from persons driven by a perfectly valid desire
to trace their ancestry. In Abelard's time this urge was not confined to individuals and expressed itself in all kinds of ways: in
the care with which the abbeys maintained their annals, or in the
insistence with which the goldsmiths and shoemakers claimed
that their statutes had been conferred on them by SS. Eloy and
Crispin in person. Some monasteries went so far as to forge
charters showing that they owed their privileges to Charlemagne or even to Clovis.

To voice doubts about Dionysius the Areopagite in the
abbey of Saint-Denis was to invite a storm, and it broke without delay:

'I communicated the passage from Bede . . . to a few brothers
who happened to be close at hand. At once, beside themselves
with indignation, they protested that Bede was an impostor
and that they attached greater credence to the testimony of
Hilduin, their abbot, who had travelled the length and breadth
of Greece checking the authenticity of the story and who had
afterwards banished doubt once and for all in his history of
Dionysius the Areopagite.' When asked whose word carried
more weight in the matter, Bede's or Hilduin's, Abelard further
aggravated the general feeling against him by siding with
Bede. The monks could scarcely contain themselves: 'Seething
with anger, they bellowed that I had just given clear proof that
I had always been a bane to the monastery and that I was a
traitor to the whole country, for by denying that the Areopagite was their patron saint I sought to rob it of a glory which
it held especially dear.' They informed the abbot at once, and
he took an extremely grave view of Abelard's offence: 'In the
presence of all the assembled brothers, he issued severe threats
against me and stated his intention of sending me straight to the
king so that he might punish me for undermining the reputation of the kingdom and doing injury to the crown. He then
recommended that I be kept under surveillance until he handed
me over to the king.'

Literally an affair of state: Abelard had dared to cast doubts on what we should nowadays call one of the glories of France's national heritage. And if it seems surprising that the monarch should intervene personally in such a trivial matter, we must recall the limited powers which a king of France enjoyed at the time. Louis VI did not exercise much real authority except within the confines of his own meagre domain, which stretched – just – from Senlis in the north to Orleans in the south. In Paris he had only one possession, the royal palace; and throughout the rest of the kingdom he could claim little more than moral sovereignty over feudal lords whose rights and revenues were often greatly superior to his. To make up for this, the king took a personal interest in all matters pertaining to his fief – and Saint-Denis was part of that fief. Indeed, of all the abbeys within the royal domain it was the one on which he chose to lavish particular care. He had spent most of his childhood there, and never wearied of declaring that it was the place where he wished to die. So the abbot would probably have little difficulty in persuading him to deal harshly with Abelard, a man whose scandalous life was already the talk of the kingdom, a man who had been condemned for heresy, a man who had now cast a slur on the royal abbey, a crime almost tantamount to high treason.

Abelard thought it wiser not to wait for the royal verdict. A few of the brothers were moved to pity by his plight, and with their assistance he escaped the following night and sought sanctuary on the lands of Count Theobald of Champagne. He had taught there earlier, at Maisoncelles-en-Brie, and might still have been at the same priory had he not been condemned by the Council of Soissons. He was warmly welcomed on his return: 'I was slightly acquainted with the count himself. He was not unaware of my misfortunes, and was sympathetic towards me.' At first Abelard stayed in Provins castle, the traditional seat of the counts of Champagne; a few remains are still to be found near Saint-Quiriace church – a hall, now below ground level, and part of the romanesque chapel; already the castle was dominated by the keep which in neo-classical times, when so many medieval walls were mistaken for Roman, acquired the fanciful name of 'Caesar's Tower'.

Even if Louis VI had chosen to harbour a grudge against the philosopher for undermining the prestige of the royal abbey, Theobald of Champagne ran no great risk in sheltering Abelard, for he was among those vassals who had far more wealth and power than the king, their overlord. The puny royal domain was completely hemmed in by the territories which he had gradually garnered through the complicated interplay of inheritances and alliances. In addition to Champagne – in other words the counties of Troyes and Meaux, extending from the banks of the Aisne to the Armançon – he ruled the counties of Blois and Chartres, which his mother had just relinquished on taking the veil at the abbey of Marcigny; she was the famous Countess Adela of Blois, daughter of William the Conqueror, one of those strong-willed, mettlesome women who abounded at the time. Fêted by most of the poets of her day Baedry of Bourgeuil, Geoffrey of Rheims, Hildebert of Lavardin – she had administered her domain almost single-handed during the long absences of her husband, Stephen, who had gone on crusade with Godfrey of Bouillon and died while on a second mission to the Holy Land. When he inherited her estate, Theobald was still afflicted by an event which had brought great grief to all his family, both in England and in France. In 1120 he and his uncle, Henry Beauclerk, had watched, powerless to help, as the *White Ship* sank after striking a reef. The flower of the young Anglo-Norman nobility perished because of a steering error. Among them were Theobald's sister Matilda – wife of Richard, earl of Chester – and his cousins William and Richard, heirs presumptive to the English throne. The tragedy disturbed him so deeply that for a while he thought of following his mother's example and withdrawing from the world. But he was dissuaded by Canon Norbert, founder of Prémontré. The canon convinced him that he ought rather to remain in public life and show what could be achieved by a great feudal lord truly enamoured of justice and piety. And sure enough, throughout his thirty years as ruler of a vast domain, he set a fine example as a pious, charitable prince, so attentive to the needs of the poor and the suffering that he even, it was said, visited them in person. Rumour had it that whenever he was in residence at the castle he went out every day and washed the feet of a leper. There came a time when, returning after a long absence, he called on the poor wretch and performed the customary service for him. When the neighbours saw him emerge from the hovel they were astonished, for the leper had died while the count was away. Thus Theobald learnt that the feet he had washed were those of Our Lord. Many such stories circulated after his death.

At the time of Abelard's request for asylum, therefore, Theobald was undergoing a religious crisis of his own. Yet he complied without hesitation. Only a few weeks later he had to speak and act in his protégé's defence. By then Abelard had entered Saint-Ayoul priory, a daughter-house of the Carthusian monastery at Moutiers-la-Celle, near Troyes. The prior knew him of old and treated him with great personal kindness, but Abelard sensed that it was time to seek a permanent place of retirement. He was reasonably confident that, with the support of the count of Champagne, he would obtain permission to settle wherever he wished. In the event, however, count and prior were equally unsuccessful in their attempts to sway Abbot Adam of Saint-Denis. 'They [Adam and his advisers] thought I was planning to enter some other abbey, and that would have been a tremendous affront to them. For they gloried in the fact that I had chosen their monastery in preference to all rivals and it would, they said, be exceedingly ignominious for them if I now cast them aside.' The monks of Saint-Denis were plainly in a quandary. On the one hand Abelard was a source of great pride to them, a jewel which they had no intention of relinquishing; on the other he was an unendurable thorn in the flesh. The abbot remained obdurate, dismissing all arguments and entreaties. He threatened to excommunicate Abelard unless he returned to the fold, and he warned the prior of Saint-Ayoul to expect the same treatment if he continued to harbour him.

There appeared to be no way out. But within days of these abortive negotiations Abbot Adam was dead; his passing seemed almost providential. Two months later, on 12 March 1122, Suger was elected to succeed him. Abelard saw the wisdom of deciding the issue without further delay. He won the support of the bishop of Meaux and of the royal favourite, Stephen of Garlande. Through Stephen he secured the patronage of the king, reinforcing that of the count of Champagne. And so at long last an agreement was arrived at, in the presence of Louis VI and his council. 'I was given leave to withdraw to a place of my own choosing, with the proviso that I should not attach myself to any abbey.' Abelard was still a monk and officially he was still subject to the authority of Saint-Denis; but he had won his freedom.

He had no thought of venturing beyond the estates of the count of Champagne, for the count's protection was of the utmost value to him. 'I therefore removed myself to a lonely tract in the region of Troyes, an area with which I was already familiar. Certain persons had presented me with a piece of land and with the consent of the local bishop I built a kind of oratory with reeds and thatch, invoking the blessing and protection of the Blessed Trinity.'[43]

Master Peter's retirement from the world came barely four years after he unwittingly brought on the 'history of his calamities' by taking Heloise as his mistress. In that brief span he had tumbled from fame and success to the lowest degradation. He had had to renounce his manhood and to burn in person his scholarly writings.

The land which he had now acquired lay a few miles to the south of Nogent-sur-Seine in a rather marshy plain beside the gently winding Ardusson. The scenery was flat and uneventful, like so much of the Champagne countryside, yet it was not without charm: there were always the poplars, and the meandering river with its clumps of reeds.

A new era began in his life. Suddenly he found himself surrounded by the peace and solitude which must often have seemed the supreme blessing in the stormy years when he had striven so desperately for worldly success. 'There, hidden away with one of my friends, I could truthfully echo Our Lord's own cry: "Lo, then did I wander far off and remain in the wilderness." '

Peace and solitude . . . Petrarch, who kept up a kind of spiritual friendship across the centuries, wrote the word *solitudo* in large letters in the margin of his treasured copy of the manuscript of the *Letter to a Friend*. Like him, we may picture Abelard slowly coming to terms with silence as he strolled by the riverside or roamed the empty woods and fields.

Yet it could not last. Solitude was wholly alien to his temperament. He was a born teacher, a born schoolman, and he needed the lively bustle of pupils about him. How could such a person harbour a permanent desire for solitude? The bitter wranglings at the Council of Soissons may well have overtaxed his patience with his fellow men, and the prospect of returning to a religious community doubtless appalled him after his unpleasant experiences at Saint-Denis; but solitude in itself held no meaning for him. It is with obvious relish that he immediately goes on to describe, in the *Letter to a Friend*, how the students invaded the quiet countryside and put an end to his privacy. 'As soon as they knew where I had retired to, [they] poured in from all directions, turning their backs on cities and castles so that they might come and live in a wilderness, forsaking large homes in favour of small huts which they built with their own hands, dainty dishes in favour of wild herbs and coarse bread, soft beds in favour of thatch and moss, tables in favour of grassy banks.' This string of antitheses may sound self-congratulatory, but it contains an undeniable element of

Seal of the abbey of Cluny, showing St Peter, its patron saint

House in Cluny, said to be the former abbey mint

'Caesar's Tower' in the castle of the Counts of Champagne at
Provins, where Abelard took refuge

The banks of the Ardusson, where he became a hermit

truth: before long a substantial colony had gathered by the banks of the Ardusson. And here one is conscious of an interesting link between Abelard's time and our own. We too have grown used to seeing young people congregate in the open air – to enjoy a pop festival, perhaps, or stage a demo, or share in the work of a kibbutz. So we should have little difficulty in imagining the scene as the simple, thatched-roofed huts went up one by one to accommodate the students who had gathered to hear Master Peter. He could no longer deny himself the pleasure of teaching – and if any special inducement had been needed, it would have lain in his lack of material resources. Quoting St Luke's Gospel, he writes: 'I could not dig; to beg I was ashamed.' And so he became a schoolman again. His pupils paid for their lessons by labouring long and hard, so that in time the colony became self-sufficient. Through careful husbandry they ensured a plentiful supply of food and drink. And soon these self-taught builders felt qualified for a more ambitious undertaking than the construction of rudimentary living quarters. The oratory which Abelard had erected before their arrival proved altogether too small for their needs, so they set to work on a full-size chapel. They built it to last, using stone and wood, and when they had finished Abelard dedicated it to the Paraclete, a name derived from a word meaning Intercessor or Comforter and designating the Holy Spirit. He must surely have been conscious of repaying a debt, for here in this place he had found the comfort and serenity which are the quintessential gifts of the Third Person of the Trinity, to which his original oratory had been dedicated.

Unfortunately Abelard's own description of the Paraclete school is the only one which has come down to us, but the general atmosphere of the place is hinted at in a charming little poem written by a student from England. Its author, Hilary, humorously bewails Abelard's decision to suspend classes because a manservant had complained of disorderly conduct by a handful of pupils:

Detestandus est ille rusticus
per quem cessit a scola clericus . . .
Heu! quam crudelis est iste nuntius
dicens: Fratres, exite citius
habitetur vobis Quinciacus
alioquin non leget monachus.

A curse upon that lout and fool
Whose tale-bearing has closed the school.
No lessons will our master give
Until in town we go and live.

Each stanza ends with the same refrain, written in the vernacular: 'The master has done us wrong – to us he has done wrong.' Hilary wonders what he should do:

Banishment cruel, yet why do you dither?
'To Quingey!' he says, so hie thee thither.
But Quingey's far, the days are short,
And you've grown fatter than you ought.[44]

He then paints a truly desolate picture: the fount of logic has ceased to flow, the students are tormented by their unslaked thirst for knowledge, the oratory has become a house of tears – a 'ploratory'.

The incident may have been a storm in a teacup; on the other hand, it may have been a major cause of Abelard's decision to leave the Paraclete. Students could be at least as 'difficult' then as they are today, and it was impossible to keep proper discipline in the conditions prevailing at the Paraclete. Once the initial excitement of having so brilliant a master had worn off, there must have been a good deal of drinking and debauchery in the makeshift living quarters – and no doubt there were easy conquests to be had among the local peasant girls. It was only natural that Abelard should wish to minimize his responsibility in these matters by insisting that his pupils find proper accommodation in the village. He himself makes no reference to the episode.

Not long afterwards we find Hilary – author of the lines quoted above – completing his studies in Angers. For Abelard's spell of teaching at the Paraclete was short-lived. Why, exactly ? The *Letter to a Friend* is rather vague on the subject. It alleges that his success had once again aroused the jealousy of his 'rivals', by which he most likely means Alberic and Lotulf. 'Increasingly, as [the students] continued to pour in and accept ever greater privations in accordance with my precepts, my rivals felt that I was adding to my prestige and humiliating them. They had done all they could to harm me, and it pained them to see the situation working out to my advantage . . . "Everyone has gone chasing after him . . . our acts of persecution have achieved nothing; we have merely added to his fame. We meant to extinguish his reputation, but we have made it more lustrous than ever." '

An echo of the enduring rivalry between Abelard and Alberic of Rheims is to be found in a poem by Hugues Primat, a contemporary of theirs and a well-known scholar and goliard. It sings the praises of the school at Rheims, where theology was taught in an atmosphere of calm and reverence, without the noisy bickerings which were all too often heard elsewhere.

On the other hand, he goes out of his way to attack Abelard. He does not actually name him, but the identity of his victim is plain to anyone who knows that Gnatho – the sobriquet which he inflicts on Peter – is the parasite in Terence's play, *The Eunuch:*

> *Vos, doctrinam qui sititis,*
> *ad hunc fontem qui venitis*
> *audituri Iesum Christum,*
> *audietis furem istum?*
> *In conventu tam sacrato,*
> *audietur iste Gnato?*
> *Dignus risu vel contemptu,*
> *cur hoc sedes in congentu . . .*

revertatu ad cucullam
et resumat vestem pullam.[45]

O you who doctrine's depths would plump,
Who to the fountainhead are come
To hear rehearsed the true belief,
Will you listen to this thief?
Will you, in this sacred gathering
Listen to a Gnatho's blathering?
Fit only for a gibe or sneer,
How do you dare to lecture here?
Get you back behind your desk,
A monkish habit suits you best.

These lines may be taken as a fair sample of the attacks
to which Abelard was subjected from all sides. He accuses
Alberic and Lotulf of deliberately fostering the mistrust –
which soon turned to animosity – of persons who, though he
does not name them, are easily recognizable as two of the most
influential men of the time. 'One of them bragged that he had
revitalized the laws governing the behaviour of canons regular,
and the other that he had done the same for monks.'[46] It is
beyond all doubt that he is here referring to Norbert, the
founder of Prémontré, and to Bernard of Clairvaux.

And at this point it becomes more and more difficult to
accept Abelard's account at face value, or to share his point of
view. We may at a pinch grant him his opinions of Anselm of
Laon, say, or William of Champeaux, if only because his
allegations cannot be fully checked. But we really cannot
underwrite his contemptuous dismissals of men like Norbert
and Bernard. Both had incontestably done far more than 'brag':
they had carried out major and necessary reforms. Norbert
had reawakened secular priests to the spiritual benefits of living
together as a community, and Bernard had breathed new life
into the Benedictine order, making it far stricter than ever
before. Their influence and their holiness speak for themselves.

Abelard does his own cause a considerable disservice when he seeks to present them as 'braggarts' and goes on to say: 'For a while these men who travelled the length and breadth of Christendom, shamelessly picking me to pieces in their sermons, managed to discredit me in the eyes of certain ecclesiastical and secular authorities, and the outrageous things they said about my beliefs and way of life turned some of my best friends against me. Even those who still had some affection for me were afraid to show it.'

In other words, his present troubles had been occasioned by a calculated effort to blacken his character. What grounds are there for such a claim? It is totally unsupported by any of Norbert's or Bernard's surviving letters or sermons. The most one can say is that Bernard's treatise *De baptismo*, addressed to Hugh of Saint-Victor, may in part have been written to counter certain errors attributed to Abelard – though even here there is no direct reference to him. True, their work has not come down to us in its entirety, and their biographers have omitted, voluntarily or otherwise, various episodes in their lives.

But the question arises: to what extent was Abelard his own worst enemy? There can be no denying that he was somewhat unstable, and as he grew older he viewed his fellow creatures with mounting distrust. Misfortune had made him a pessimist. Despite his religious conversion, he remained self-centred and was quick to regard other people as his enemies. And indeed we can observe these dark attitudes taking hold of him more and more as the *Letter to a Friend* progresses – for although one may jib at his judgements of others, one cannot but admire the clearheadedness which invariably informs his moments of self-analysis. His sense of despair at the time of escaping from Saint-Denis had made him feel that 'the whole world was conspiring against me'.[47] And it was the same story at the Paraclete: 'As God is my witness, I could never hear that a meeting of churchmen had been called without thinking that their sole purpose was to censure me.' Admittedly the memory of the Council of Soissons was enough to justify such suspicions, but it may also be that his particular cast of mind helped to foster a form of apprehensive terror which tended towards persecution mania. The chances are, surely, that a less self-absorbed man would have mastered his fears more easily.

Warranted or not, those fears were powerful enough to make him leave the Paraclete. He writes with undeniable poignancy of the rather extravagant schemes that hatched in his tormented mind: 'Often, God knows, I fell into such despair that I thought of leaving Christendom; instead, I would live in a land of infidels and somehow purchase the right to lead a Christian life among Christ's enemies. I was sure that the pagans would give me a warm welcome since the accusation which had been levelled against me would make them doubt my Christian sentiments and see me as a likely convert to their idolatrous beliefs.'[48]

But at this point a surprising piece of news reached him: he had been elected abbot of a remote monastery in Brittany. It was at Saint-Gildas-de-Rhuys, in the diocese of Vannes, not far from Abelard's birthplace; in fact the monks' decision may have been prompted by the wish to install a local man who had risen to eminence. Be that as it may, Abelard appears to have leapt at the offer. He complained that the vexations which were being heaped on him had become too great a burden. Perhaps his school brought more problems than he cared to admit. And perhaps the idea of becoming an abbot appealed to his vanity: it would mean he was the canonical equal of Suger at Saint-Denis or Bernard at Clairvaux. His hopes of grandeur were soon dashed by the realities which he found waiting for him at Saint-Gildas: 'a barbarous clime, an unknown language, a wild, brutish populace, and – among the monks – forms of behaviour that simply could not be curbed.'[49]

Today Saint-Gildas is a pleasant summer resort. Holiday-makers flock to the beautiful sanctuary whose austere architecture and superb capitals probably still look the same as they did in Abelard's day. But when winter comes and the weather turns rough it is a lonely place and one can sympathize readily with the sense of isolation that is conveyed in the *Letter to a Friend*. It might indeed be 'farthest Thule' with its flat, almost treeless landscape, while the rocks thinly scattered along the shore seem to speak of the remotest past, and the slow, inexorable encroachment of the Atlantic. Brittany has retained its highly individual character, a character oddly out of key with the rest of France. In the twelfth century it must have seemed a wild, inaccessible region. Although it was a duchy (soon afterwards the title was held by the son of Henry II of England) the duke's authority over the local lords was largely theoretical. Yet the area contained many monasteries and many fine examples of romanesque architecture, even though granite is notoriously difficult to hew. So far, however, the reformist movement had made little headway there, its influence being confined to the neighbourhood of Nantes.

Abelard's arrival at Saint-Gildas became the subject of an anecdote which was still in circulation a century later.[50] He is said to have left his horses and baggage at the nearest town and gone to the abbey on foot, wearing a shabby cope; he received a rough and ready welcome and was told to bed down among the riff-raff who traditionally sought shelter in monasteries. Next day he returned in full pomp with servants and horses; he was greeted with fitting ceremony and ushered into the chapter-house, where his monks were assembled. His first act was to reprimand them and remind them of their Christian duties. It was only too obvious, he said, that they would have snubbed Christ himself had they seen him ragged and barefoot: their respect was not for the man but for the trappings. The scholar who has handed this story down to us, Stephen of Bourbon, lived about a hundred years after Abelard and it may be pure fantasy. However, it conveys the reforming zeal that burned within Abelard and was sufficiently in character to be widely accepted.

There was ample scope for such zeal at Saint-Gildas. 'The lord of those parts, whose authority knew no bounds, had long since laid his yoke upon the abbey by exploiting the unruliness that prevailed there. He had appropriated the entire estate and was subjecting the monks to even worse extortions than those inflicted on the Jews. The monks kept pestering me to supply their daily needs, for the community had no distributable possessions and only by drawing on his own inheritance could each member support himself, his concubine and his sons and daughters. Not content with tormenting me, they stole and carried off whatever they could so as to make life difficult for me and compel me either to stand down or to relax the rules of the order. Since all the rabble in the surrounding countryside were equally intractable, there was no one to whom I could turn. I felt completely cut off. Outside the abbey, the lord and his guards oppressed me without respite; inside the abbey, the brothers were forever setting traps for me.' Abelard certainly paints a hair-raising picture. Perhaps he is exaggerating. On the other hand his account may be strictly accurate. The conditions of which he complains had been all too common a century earlier. Before the Gregorian reforms many castellans had sub-jugated priests and religious and imposed their own temporal authority on churches, monasteries and other foundations. The end of the Carolingian era had been a time of grave crisis for the Church, and the situation had been further aggravated by the moral decadence of the papacy when, in the tenth century, it fell into the hands of Theophylact and his wife and daughters, that powerful Roman family which could make or break popes at will. The Cluniac Reform brought some improvement to the situation and in the eleventh century, as the religious revival gained strength, successive popes – stimulated by Hildebrand, the monk who was himself destined to become Pope Gregory VII – gradually freed the Church from the crushing mortgage laid on it by the secular powers; the evils of simony and lay-investiture were fought with increasing vigour. Yet the effects of these changes seem scarcely to have been felt in Brittany at the time of Abelard's appointment as abbot of Saint-Gildas. The monks still led dissolute lives; the local lord's whim was law; there was a desperate need for change, both spiritual and temporal.

As at Saint-Denis, Abelard – who this time had full authority to impose his wishes – would have liked to instil a pattern of life more in keeping with the monastic ideal. But the work of a reformer demands more than zeal: it calls for vigour and determination. At just about this time Suger, at the bidding of Bernard of Clairvaux, was introducing changes at his abbey which were very similar to those desired by Abelard. The latter, however, was not strong enough to institute a major reform at Saint-Gildas. 'No one can deny the mental and physical torments that beset me day and night when I thought of the refractoriness of the monks whom I had undertaken to govern. Any attempt to restore them to the monastic rule to which they had committed themselves would place my life in jeopardy; I had no illusions on that score. On the other hand I should incur eternal damnation unless I did all I could to bring about reform.' It was a dilemma that called for a man of action, and Abelard was better at talking than at doing. Certain passages in the *Letter to a Friend* show clearly how daunted and disoriented he felt in these alien surroundings, far removed from the atmosphere of civilized intercourse to which his years of teaching had accustomed him. He was quite lost among landscapes, seascapes, skyscapes that contrasted markedly with the bland countryside of Champagne or the Ile-de-France: '. . . on the shores of the Ocean, with its terrifying voices, banished to the uttermost ends of a region that denied me all possibility of further escape . . .' Escape had become his sole ambition, an ambition that did nothing to quieten his inherent instability. He may have come to terms with solitude on the banks of the Ardusson, but this was something different: complete isolation in a place that appalled him.

As it happened, an opportunity of escape was about to come his way.

Abelard had been at Saint-Gildas for some two or three years (although elected in 1125, he probably did not take up residence at the abbey until several months afterwards) when disquieting news reached him: Heloise and her companions had been expelled from Argenteuil, disbanded, and sent to a number of different abbeys.

What exactly had happened? Historians have recorded the event without ever adequately accounting for it. At the time of its foundation in the reign of Pepin the Short, Argenteuil priory was a daughter-house of the abbey of Saint-Denis. Under Charlemagne, it was declared autonomous and turned into a nunnery, with the emperor's daughter Theodrada as abbess, on the understanding that it should revert to Saint-Denis after her death. Abbot Hilduin, who has already been mentioned, secured confirmation of this promise of reversion from the emperor's son, Louis the Pious, whose chaplain he was. In spite of which, Argenteuil was handed on from abbess to abbess and had been a nunnery for some three hundred years when Suger took over the administration of Saint-Denis. He himself has described how, in adolescence, he used to pore over its charters and marvel at the irregularities and acts of negligence which his reading brought to light. On becoming abbot he brought great skill and experience, as well as boundless ambition, to the task of asserting the rights and privileges of which Saint-Denis had been cheated under his predecessors. In a work which has come down to us,[51] he sets forth the results of his efforts, noting with pride that a given area of soil which had previously yielded six *muids* of corn now yielded fifteen, while at Vaucresson – hitherto a wasteland infested with brigands – the ground had been cleared and cultivated on his instructions; today Vaucresson had farms, houses, a church and a population of sixty, consisting mainly of peasants who had moved into the area . . . And so forth. He tackled the problem of Argenteuil with characteristic energy. Special envoys were sent to Rome, asking Pope Honorius to examine the ancient charters and order a canonical inquiry.

All of which sounds straightforward enough until we con-

sider the contents of a charter drawn up in 1129 by the papal
legate, Matthew of Albano. 'Recently,' states the text, 'in the
presence of the illustrious lord and sovereign, Louis of France,
together with our brother bishops Reginald, archbishop of
Rheims, Stephen, bishop of Paris, Geoffrey, bishop of Chartres,
Gozelin, bishop of Soissons, and others in great number, we
discussed the question of reforming the monastic rule in
various French abbeys where zeal had waned; suddenly, from
the body of the hall, there was an outcry against the scandal and
infamy prevailing at a nunnery called Argenteuil, where a
small number of nuns were bringing disgrace upon their order
and had long since polluted the entire neighbourhood with
their lewd and shameful conduct.'

Naturally Suger was quick to voice his abbey's claims to the
priory, and it was decreed then and there that Argenteuil should
revert to Saint-Denis and that the nuns should be evicted and
replaced by monks. Later this decision was ratified in a papal
bull which emphasized that it was Abbot Suger's duty to
ensure that the evicted nuns were installed in convents of good
repute 'lest any of them should go astray and perish through her
misconduct'.

Thus the nuns were forced to leave Argenteuil because of
slanderous accusation; and what makes the accusation all the
more serious, from our point of view, is the fact that Heloise
was at that time prioress of the establishment; only the abbess
had more authority than she. So although she may not have
joined in the malpractices imputed to the convent she must at
least share responsibility for them. Admittedly, it seems something of a coincidence that this wholly unexpected charge
should have been made at the very time when Suger was
seeking to regain possession of the priory. On the other hand –
and this is certainly disturbing – there is no evidence that the
charge was ever disputed. Not even by Abelard. He who was
always so quick to detect and complain of wilful slander, and
who had not hesitated to speak out against the abuses he had
witnessed at Saint-Denis, does not say a word about these

139

accusations which had played so big a part in allowing Suger to get his hands on Argenteuil. Nor does Heloise; and their silence on so grave a subject can only give us pause. In the *Letter to a Friend*, Abelard merely states: 'It chanced that the abbot of Saint-Denis, having successfully sought permission to re-annex the abbey of Argenteuil, which had formerly been under [his abbey's] jurisdiction, and where my sister in Jesus Christ – rather than my wife – had taken the veil, violently evicted the religious community of which she was prioress.'

So we shall probably never know the full truth about these dark allegations. The most we can say is that Heloise's general behaviour, and the views and feelings expressed in her letters, place her completely above suspicion.

As for Abelard, he was fully alive to his responsibilities to her now that she had been uprooted. Ever since leaving the Paraclete he had worried about the oratory which he had built there. He felt it ought not to be left empty and neglected, but on the other hand the area was too poor to support a regular priest. Now a solution was providentially offered. Seeing Heloise and her companions 'scattered far and wide by exile, I realized that the Lord was giving me an opportunity to safeguard the upkeep of my oratory. So I went back there, invited Heloise and the members of her community to join me, and, when they arrived, made the oratory and its outbuildings over to them. With the approval of the local bishop, and indeed at his instigation, Pope Innocent II confirmed their right, and the right of their successors, to enjoy this privilege in perpetuity.'

There is a wonderful passage in Etienne Gilson's book, discussing this present from Abelard to Heloise. 'One would have no difficulty in citing two dozen more tragic moments in his painful career,' he writes, 'but I am not sure one can find any that is more deeply moving . . . All he now had in the world was the wretched plot of land which a benefactor had given him, together with this mean oratory and the small group of huts which his pupils had built for him. As soon as he heard that Heloise was homeless and adrift, he emerged from the depths of Brittany, hurried to her side and made these few last possessions over to her, completely and irrevocably. One hardly dares to hint at the wealth of feeling – of the noblest and this time the purest kind – that went into the gesture.'[52] His action revealed, in fact, 'the love of a priest for his church', the brotherly concern of a Benedictine abbot for his sister in Jesus Christ, and the warm feelings of a husband for his wife.

He had come to this decision without any thought of self, but suddenly a blissful prospect lay before him. Could it be that he, the eternal wanderer, the fugitive, had found his resting-place at last? Why not remain here at the Paraclete? Why not become abbot of this new cloister whose abbess was his wife in the sight of God? He was now a man of fifty or so. Soon he would have to reckon with old age and decline. His earlier ambitions had of necessity been renounced as abruptly as the pleasures of the flesh. Everywhere he had fallen foul of the hostility, persecution and misunderstanding of his fellow men:

> *Credit inhumanem mentem sapientibus esse*
> *qui nihil illorum corda dolere putat.*[53]

> They judge keen minds to be above distress
> Who think their hearts likewise immune to pain.

Worse still, his life was a failure – 'equally unprofitable to him and to others' – a view which he felt was borne out by his inability to exert the smallest influence on the monks at Saint-Gildas. Yet suppose he were to exercise the duties of priest, abbot and teacher here at the Paraclete, in and around the oratory which he had raised among the reeds? Living at the heart of a community which owed its survival entirely to him, he could forget the disasters of earlier years and bask in the warm, respectful regard for which he longed.

From the satisfaction with which Abelard outlines this scheme in the *Letter to a Friend*[54] it is obvious that he had long harboured such a dream. And good reasons abounded – above all his duty to provide for the material needs of the sisterhood, which had great difficulty in sustaining itself in the wilderness: '. . . all our neighbours criticized me sharply for not doing what I could and should to alleviate the poverty of the convent, when it would have been so easy for me to do so by preaching.' St Jerome, after all, had adopted the same solution when Paula and her companions joined him in Bethlehem. And what about the apostles and, indeed, Christ himself? Did they not have women with them, women who helped them with their preaching and shared in their apostolic work? The weaker sex, reasoned Abelard, could not be expected to cope without the help of the stronger. Moreover, public knowledge of his emasculation would surely render him immune from all suspicion; so why should he not – like Origen, also a eunuch – devote himself to the education of these women to whom he had given a home? 'Although unable to achieve anything worthwhile with the monks, I might perhaps do [the sisters] a little good.'

We do not know exactly what compelled Abelard to return to Saint-Gildas. He himself is content to allude vaguely to 'enemies' whose 'malevolent insinuations' made it necessary for him to renounce his dream and tear himself away from these fields by the banks of the Ardusson, now doubly dear to his heart.

'With their customary spite, my enemies shamefully mis-represented the actions to which I had been prompted by sheer charity. It was clear, they said, that I was still dominated by the lure of carnal pleasures, for I could not endure the absence of the woman I had loved.' There is a temptation, at this point, to resurrect Roscelin's letter accusing him of handing Heloise her 'reward for past debauchery'; but it is unlikely that Roscelin was still alive in 1131, and his letter was obviously written some ten years earlier, before Abelard was condemned for the first time.

Perhaps Abelard was taken to task by the bishop of Troyes, as head of the diocese containing the Paraclete, or by the bishop of Vannes, as head of the diocese containing Saint-Gildas. Or perhaps he came to realize, without prompting, that his visits might be a source of harm to the young community. Whatever the truth of the matter, he felt obliged to return, heavy-hearted, to Brittany. But the fruits of his industry and generosity were destined to outlive his stay by six and a half centuries. The abbey which he had founded at the Paraclete survived until the Revolution. Not until 1792, by which time the nuns had been evicted, was the convent sold by the state and gradually demolished by its unlikely succession of owners – first the parish priest's manservant, then a lawyer, and next a second-hand dealer from Paris. Admittedly, its decline began earlier, for in the seventeenth and eighteenth centuries it suffered the same decline as many other convents and monasteries; Marie de la Rochefoucauld de Chaumont was installed as abbess in 1599; thereafter the abbess was always a member of the family and the Rochefoucaulds came to regard the abbey as part of the family possessions. Yet, together with the letters, the Paraclete proved to be Abelard's most lasting and least controversial achievement. His philosophical writings stand condemned and, in spite of the influence which they once exercised, are seldom if ever read today; none of them has been translated. His poetical works, which have survived only in part, are unappreciated except by those few scholars who have made a special study of them. But for six hundred years after his death generations of nuns succeeded one another at the Paraclete, observing, as we shall see, the rule which he had prescribed and singing the hymns which he had composed for them.

Abelard, however, witnessed only the first-fruits of this success. He left the Paraclete with a renewed sense of failure, a sense magnified by his readiness to dramatize his own existence.

Saint-Gildas had not improved in his absence. On the contrary, the monks appeared to have lost all control of themselves, and he claims they even went so far as to try to do away with him: 'How many times did they not attempt to poison me in the same way as St Benedict . . .* To foil their attempts, I kept as close an eye as possible on the food and drink that were brought to me; so then they tried tipping poison into the chalice during the [Holy] Sacrifice [of the Mass]. On another occasion I went into Nantes to see the count, who was unwell. I spent the night at my brother's house. They had primed one of my attendants to poison me – presumably in the belief that I should be less on my guard against a plot of this kind; but thank God I did not touch any of the food which had been cooked for me. A monk whom I had brought with me from the abbey died instantaneously after eating some in all innocence. The lay brother fled, overcome by pangs of conscience and terrified at being caught red-handed.'

As if he had not sufficient misfortunes to bear, he fell from his horse and fractured his cervical vertebrae. This happened during one of his frequent journeyings from priory to priory – for he tells us that he spent as little time as possible at the abbey itself but kept on the move with a small band of brothers on whose loyalty he could rely. It took him a long while to recover from the accident. He did his best to expel the more dangerous monks from Saint-Gildas. He persuaded Pope Innocent II to dispatch Geoffrey of Lèves – bishop of Chartres and a lifelong friend of Abelard – as legate, in the hope that between them they would succeed in re-establishing law and order. But the monks 'could not be quieted; only a short time ago, after the expulsion of the monks whom I have singled out for mention, I went back to the abbey and risked associating

* This account of Abelard under attack from turbulent monks is oddly reminiscent of a similar episode in the life of St Benedict. The *Dialogues* of Gregory the Great tell how Benedict, who had been leading the life of a recluse at Subiaco, was invited to become abbot of a small community of monks at Vicovaro; but these monks were soon irked by the discipline which he sought to impose on them and so they tried to murder him. St Benedict, of course, was the father of Western monasticism and his Holy Rule had a profound effect on all who aimed to be true religious. And Abelard certainly had good reason to regard himself as a victim of persecution.

with the others, in the belief that I had less cause to mistrust them. They proved to be even worse. No longer content with poison, they turned on me with swords and knives. I had great difficulty in escaping them, and might not have done so but for the protection of a great noble living in those parts.'

Thus ends the narrative contained in the *Letter to a Friend*. Abelard concludes with a series of reflections inspired by the Scriptures and by St Jerome, 'as whose heir I regard myself in matters of slander and hatred. The Christian cannot hope to live without being persecuted: let us therefore show ourselves capable of enduring our ordeals with a confidence commensurate with their extraordinary injustice . . . God, in his sovereign goodness, lets nothing be fulfilled unless it coincides with the pattern decreed by Providence, and he personally ensures that whatever conflicts with that pattern is properly resolved.' He therefore urges the friend in question to follow his example and proclaim 'not only with your lips but in your heart: Thy will be done.'

IV

ABELARD

Parce continuis
deprecor lamentis
nec, qua vincularis,
legem amoris
nimium queraris.[1]

Cease, I beseech you,
Your constant moan,
Nor rail too much against the law
Of love which holds you bound.[1]

'THE letter that you wrote to a friend with the aim of consoling him has recently chanced into my hands, beloved... Surely anyone who reads or hears the account of such ordeals must be moved to tears. For my own part, I can only say that it is so expressively phrased and so accurate in detail that it has ripped open all my old wounds...'

The words, of course, are Heloise's. When she says that the *Letter to a Friend* had 'chanced into her hands' we have to remember that in those days manuscripts circulated much as the printed word was to circulate in after years. They were read aloud among groups of friends, and copies were made of them; the speed with which they gained currency is often startling. The contents of the *Letter* must fairly soon have been familiar to a great number of academics working in monasteries and schools. It has been suggested – with some degree of probability – that Abelard's real purpose in composing the document was to remind the world of his existence and call attention to his talents, and such allegations are not easy to dismiss. He was living in seclusion at the time – possibly with members of his family – and already paving the way for his return to Paris, where before long he would once again be teaching on the Montagne Sainte-Geneviève. Presumably he had by now relinquished his untenable position as abbot of Saint-Gildas.

Unwittingly, by dwelling so heavily on the events of his own life, he had struck a chord which was to reverberate long and loud. For this *Letter to a Friend* provoked a reply that nonplussed him completely – Heloise's first missive, which marked the beginning of their correspondence.

For the second time in our story we hear the voice of Heloise. On the first occasion it was raised in startling opposition to Abelard's offer of marriage. This time she spoke out in very different terms, a commingling of pain and indignation. It was the outcry of a wife determined to remain at her husband's side, if only to share his sufferings, and refusing to be excluded from his life and concerns. In short, she was at last giving voice to the anguish of the passionate lover who stubbornly declined to accept the enforced termination of a loving relationship, the memory of which was still, after all these years, the living substance of her daily life.

Abelard's letter had been a narrative. Heloise's was a cry of such force that even today it has the power to move the reader, despite the intervening centuries, the outmoded phraseology and the perils of translation. It was first and foremost a cry of pain prompted by the sufferings which he had endured: '. . . the manner in which your masters persecuted you, the vile outrages cravenly inflicted on your body . . . the loathsome jealousy and burning animosity with which you were hounded by Alberic of Rheims and Lotulf of Lombardy . . .'; also his humiliation at the Council of Soissons and the torments inflicted on him at Saint-Denis and later at the Paraclete; and, last but not least, the violent acts of aggression perpetrated by 'those evil monks whom you call your children'. The entire 'little flock' at the Paraclete had been distressed to hear of these events and now trembled daily at the thought that their benefactor and spiritual father might be slain at any moment.

But coupled with all this compassion was a sense of shock which she found almost equally hard to bear. Whether the unnamed friend to whom he had related his long series of misfortunes was real or fictitious, either he or the public at large had received a boon which should surely have been conferred on her, Heloise, in preference to any other person – a letter from Abelard! How deeply it had grieved her to be confronted by a missive intended for a third party! And she was intent on procuring a privilege which he had already extended to others: whatever might befall him, she meant to share his tribulations and his joys; she wanted to lighten his burden if it had become too great for him – unless, of course, by the grace of God, 'the storm should abate a little'.

She then proceeds to wheedle him with all the skill of a master logician. For her letter is not only a cry of pain: it is an appeal against sentence, adroit, superb, glowing.

Predictably she begins with a classical allusion: 'Seneca teaches us by his own example how pleasant it is to receive letters from an absent friend;' and she goes on to quote from the *Letters to Lucilius*.

Abelard, she reasoned, had responded to a friend in need, thereby fulfilling the duties of friendship. Surely he had much deeper reasons for satisfying the need which she herself was now expressing? In the first place, let him consider the other members of her community: 'Far more compelling are the obligations which you have contracted towards us, for we are not simply friends but the most loyal and devoted of friends, not simply comrades but daughters; yes, that is the right name for us – unless a holier and more loving term can be imagined.'

She develops this line of argument, showing remarkable restraint at first. She and her sisters in Jesus Christ lived in a foundation which Abelard had conjured out of the earth, at the heart of a 'wilderness which used to be the exclusive haunt of brigands and wild beasts, [which] had never known human habitation, never seen a house'. The small band of nuns eking out an existence there today owed everything to him. Instead of frittering away his time with worthless, fractious monks he ought to remember the 'vineyard' which he had planted with his own hands. 'You devote yourself to enemies; think what you owe to your daughters.'

And then the mask slips. The skilled manipulator of words and ideas stands revealed as the passionately committed wife. What, she asks, of his personal debt to her? At this point her tone becomes sublime. Reproaches and effusions jostle each other. Here we have the authentic language of love. '. . . I need not remind you of the obligation that binds you to me; we are joined together by the sacrament of holy matrimony, a bond made all the closer for you by the knowledge that I have always loved you, in the sight of heaven and earth, with a love which knows no bounds . . .' 'You, the sole cause of my sufferings, alone have power to bring me consolation. You only, from whom all my sadness springs, can restore me to happiness or at least afford me some relief.'[2]

Next she subtly counterbalances Abelard's wholly masculine account of their meeting and its consequences by telling the same story from a woman's point of view. There can be no denying that she tells it with far more depth and weight than he. For him their love had been a voyage of self-discovery, whereas for her it had been from the very first a transcendent experience in which self was quite forgotten; she had made him a total gift of her mind and body, withholding nothing. Her version of the facts is so much more lively and intense that I have not hesitated to use it, rather than Abelard's, as the basis of my story. No one could hope to convey better than she the extraordinary impact made on her life by the sudden advent of this teacher and philosopher whose fame was equal to a king's, whose gifts as poet and musician eclipsed those of all his contemporaries, and whose good looks and intelligence made him a creature beyond compare, as beguiling a man as any woman could imagine. 'You alone can judge the feelings which I have always had for you; you have certainly put them to the test.' And Heloise reiterates her old grievances with a new ferocity. The tone of her letters, so temperate and rational at first, now grows heated: 'Tell me, if you can, why after the two of us embraced the religious life – a decision which was yours alone – I had neither your presence to fortify me nor even a letter to console me in my loneliness. Tell me, I repeat, if you can, or else I shall tell you my own opinion, an opinion which is on everybody's lips. It was lust rather than true feeling that bound you to me, sensuality rather than love – which is why, as soon as your desires were extinguished, all the outward displays which they used to inspire vanished too.'

She could hardly have addressed a crueller reproach to Abelard in his capacity as man, husband and lover.* She relents at once. Her language softens. 'I beg you to consider my request. It is so small and simple a thing that I ask. If your presence must be denied me, at least let your soft words – a letter costs you so little – remind me of your sweet looks.'³ Here she displays all the natural cunning of a woman, and it is hard to believe that the lines which come next are the work of a nun, an abbess, who had pledged herself to a life of chastity: '[My heart] is quite lost without you. I implore you to let it be with you – as indeed it will be if only you treat it kindly, offering it love in return for love, crumbs in return for a banquet, words in return for deeds.'⁴

Yet even as she writes these words, Heloise seems to recall the barrier created between them by her veil and by their mutual dedication to the religious life; for at the end of her letter she reinvokes the name of the Almighty. But even here there is a distinct touch of feminine guile: 'In the name, there-

* A complete critical survey of the various errors that have stemmed from a misreading of the manuscripts is to be found in Gilson's book. Discussion of this topic would be out of place here, but let us not delude ourselves: there are still plenty of people for whom Heloise and Abelard were not really Heloise and Abelard, just as Joan of Arc was not really Joan of Arc, nor Christopher Columbus really Christopher Columbus. It is an attitude deliberately and skilfully fostered by much university teaching, which encourages pupils to rely on the logical deductions of a 'well-trained mind' rather than on the plain facts of historical evidence.

fore, of him to whom you have solemnly dedicated your days, in the name of the living God, give me back your presence in so far as you are able by sending me a few lines of consolation – if not for my sake, at least so that I may derive new strength from your words and serve God with greater fervour.'[5]

All this must have come as a violent shock to Abelard. For years he had steered a lone course, almost identical with the course which he had pursued before meeting Heloise. He had led the life of an isolated thinker, the life of a monk in the true, etymological sense of the word – for both at Saint-Denis and at Saint-Gildas he had been a solitary, incapable of adjusting to the communities around him. And now Heloise's letter prodded him to a full recognition of his duties as a partner in a deep human relationship. True, he had shown his concern for her in the most concrete and generous fashion by handing over the Paraclete. For a while he had even thought of living there himself and acting as father and priest, since he could henceforth fulfil no other role, to the woman who had once been his wife. And it had been no small sacrifice for him to renounce this project. But suddenly, without meaning to, he had sparked off a display of feeling whose intensity he was no longer able to share: a love superabundant, passionate, devoid of limitations. Her letter opened his eyes startlingly to a bottomless pit of suffering: all those years of pent-up emotion endured beneath the veil of a nun whose outward virtues had led to her appointment as prioress and later as abbess; all those confrontations at the Paraclete during which Heloise had avoided any reference to her sole obsession; and finally all those feelings which she had somehow kept to herself – for instance, the pain she had experienced when, after his mutilation, he insisted that she take her vows before he did, as if doubtful of her total commitment to him at that terrible moment when all her hopes as a wife were dashed . . . Nothing could have overwhelmed him more than the revelation of the total, irrevocable love which she had pledged to him. He was abruptly conscious of the gulf that divided them, a gulf whose existence he had not even suspected.

How much farther than he she had journeyed along the paths of human love! Her undeviating loyalty to him day after day, stemming from a heart still pristine and intact despite the wounds of the past and the deprivations of the present, showed up the selfishness of his preoccupation with *his* personal future, *his* loss of prestige, *his* wounds, *his* humiliations.

Heloise's letter, a cry of passion, was also an invitation to start afresh and re-establish their old relationship – though, of necessity, on a different plane. She was perfectly willing to sacrifice that element in her which must for ever remain unsatisfied. There had been a time when, in her loving desperation, she would rather have been known as his mistress, or even his concubine, than as his wife; yet now she demanded those very privileges that went with the title of wife. He could no longer manifest his love to her physically, but he ought at least to open his mind and heart to her. Why was he not prepared to look her in the eye? She was merely seeking her due as a deprived spouse, a claim she could press all the more in view of the total obedience she had displayed towards her husband.

And sure enough the relationship did revive, though not at all in the manner envisaged by Heloise. For Abelard, who had proved weak and shortsighted on so many occasions, now successfully faced up to a situation that had caught him unawares.

Heloise's letter had allied passion to shrewdness. Abelard's reply was more than a match for her; shrewder still, it endeavoured to redirect the intense feeling which she harboured for him towards the Way which had become his own. For if, as already suggested, Heloise had outdistanced him along the paths of human love, he could now legitimately claim to be ahead of her on the road to divine love.

He made no secret of his startled reaction to her message. Nothing in her previous behaviour had prepared him for such an outburst. And however suceptible he might be to flattery, however athirst for compassion, and however deeply attached to Heloise, he had certainly not bargained for declarations of this sort. On reading his reply, one is brought to a full realization of what type of man Peter Abelard had become and how deep-rooted was his acceptance of suffering and humiliation. For his tone is not merely that of a man to whom sexual pleasure is now denied, but also, to a far greater degree, that of a human being who has committed himself wholeheartedly to the task of serving God.

Moreover, there is no hint of reproach in his reply. Abelard – and herein lies his greatness – is not concerned with ordinary, conventional morality. He makes no show of offended virtue, for he realizes that the quality of love which Heloise evinces on the human level has sufficient intrinsic value to be, in time, re-channelled towards Another. He simply expresses surprise that such a conversion has not already taken place: 'If, since we forsook the world for God, I have not addressed a single word of comfort or exhortation to you, the cause must not be ascribed to my neglectfulness but rather to your own prudence, in which I have always had implicit trust. It never occurred to me that any such acts of assistance might be necessary to a woman on whom God has conferred all the gifts of grace, a woman who by her own word and example is capable of bringing light to troubled minds, of sustaining the faint-hearted, of breathing fire into the lukewarm.'[6] These few prefatory words are enough to give the correspondence an entirely different tone from that intended by Heloise. One might almost think that he had misread her letter, were not each word so carefully chosen and its effect so accurately weighed. Here we see the qualities that made Abelard so successful a teacher. And indeed his sentences are undeniably pedagogic in character, the words of a master addressing a gifted pupil and determined to bring out the best in her. This is no scolding, but a wholly positive exhortation. What need has Heloise for letters or guidance from him when she is capable of dealing so wisely and zealously with the community which looked to her for leadership? Abelard briskly reminds her that she is now an abbess and has already held the rank of prioress.

They may once have been lover and mistress, but all that belongs to the past. He writes solely in terms of their present stations in life and of the realities which now confront them. He can offer her nothing apart from purely spiritual words of admonition.

He was, however, keenly alive to the tension and distress which prompted her letter and had no intention of turning a a deaf ear to them: 'Yet if your humility impelled you to take a different view, and if – even in matters pertaining to heaven – you felt the need for our written counsel, write and tell us what subject you wish me to enlighten you about; I shall send as good an answer as Our Lord empowers me to give.'[7] Abelard has succeeded in clarifying the problem to his own satisfaction: Heloise's impulse to seek letters from him can only spring from a sense of humility; such letters can only treat of 'matters pertaining to heaven'; and the answers which he has somewhat reluctantly volunteered will deal only with topics appropriate to their religious vocations, topics concerning the life of the spirit. His comments leave no room for further misapprehension. Her first letter and his first reply are as distinct as works of music prefaced by entirely different key-signatures.

It might seem pointless for Abelard to go on with his reply after such a preamble; but in fact, although adhering to the same austere key, he develops the two themes which are especially close to Heloise's heart – their special relationship and the physical dangers to which he is at present exposed. If he is in peril, let her pray for him: God welcomes 'the prayers of women for the men whom they hold dear, and of wives for their husbands'. He then cites examples from the Bible, illustrating the power of prayer, a power capable of altering the course of events. One of these references is particularly significant. It concerns the Old Testament story of Jephthah's daughter and was later to inspire one of Abelard's finest poems, the *planctus* – a plaint, lamentation, or *planh*, as the form soon afterwards became known in the language of the troubadours. For Heloise and Abelard alike, this allusion to the sacrifice of a deeply loved and wholly innocent human being was all too clear in import. And he was, as I say, to enlarge on the subject in his poem – written in the first person and voicing the girl's own feelings – which so amply reveals the gifts that brought him fame in his own day.

Returning to the theme of the power of prayer, Abelard argues that God lends a special ear to a woman's prayers: 'You have only to skim through the Old and New Testaments and you will find that the greatest restorative miracles were worked largely or exclusively in the presence of women, and either upon them or for their benefit.' He reminds her of the widow living in Nain whose son was raised from the dead, and of Lazarus's two sisters.

And then, after these general observations, he addresses a personal appeal to Heloise, '. . . to you alone . . . to you whose holiness must surely carry considerable weight with God and upon whose succour I have first claim in my present ordeals and adversities.' The appeal is simple but bleak: the whole of Heloise's love is to be confined to, and summed up in, the special prayer which he asks of her and which is the sole form of exchange which is now possible between them. He reminds her that during his stay at the Paraclete they had adopted the habit of ending each office with a prayer whose antiphon and response were personal intercessions for himself, as the abbey's founder. He then gives the text of another prayer, one better suited to his present circumstances: 'Forsake me not, Lord, father and undisputed master of my life, lest I sink before my adversaries and my foe rejoice in my downfall . . . Preserve, Lord, thy servant who puts his trust in thee . . .' Finally he tells her what he wishes to be done in the event of his death: 'See to it, I entreat you, that my body, whether it has been buried or left to lie, be brought to your graveyard, so that the habitual sight of my headstone may prompt our daughters – or should I not say our brides in Christ Jesus? – to lavish their prayers for me more often upon the Lord.'[8] The call to transcend purely human love could not have been more complete: 'What I ask above all is that the overkeen solicitude which my physical perils arouse in you today be henceforth directed towards the salvation of my soul.'

And that, Abelard must surely have thought, marked the end of the correspondence. Displaying infinite tact and resourcefulness, he had dealt point by point with the issues of suffering and passion raised in her letter. He had turned this unrestrained outburst into a prayer, and he was convinced that he had sufficient control over Heloise's mind to persuade her to adhere faithfully to the pattern of behaviour he had laid down. Nor could he have indicated more plainly the precariousness of the life of the man she loved, or tried harder to reorient her concern for him towards an outlook more in keeping with earthly and heavenly realities.

But he had quite failed to realize that by so doing he had given more than sufficient grounds for a renewed sense of alarm, and that this very alarm would in turn provoke further emotional outpourings. The dialogue was to be such that one cannot read Heloise's letter without pondering the reply which it would undoubtedly prompt from Abelard, and vice versa; for, despite the entirely disparate keys of Letters I and II, Abelard suddenly had no choice but to meet Heloise on her own ground and take up her challenge at its face value.

Once again Heloise shows all her feminine guile by assailing him, right at the start, over a matter which is bound to disconcert her adversary. Comfortably in control of a situation which would have dismayed many another, she attacks him on a point of etiquette: 'I am astonished, O highest boon, that, deviating from the rules of epistolary style, and indeed from the natural order of things, you should have seen fit, when writing the heading and salutation of your letter, to put my name before yours – i.e. woman before man, wife before husband, servant before master, nun before monk and priest, deaconess* before abbot.'⁹

* In the early Church, deacons – who played a subsidiary role in acts of worship but were principally responsible for the care of the poor and the

Her stratagem is doubly effective. The series of antitheses is a reminder of all that binds them together in life, and the humble posture that she insists on adopting is yet another claim upon him. Come what may, they are husband and wife; come what may, there is a natural harmony between them which Abelard's aloof tone cannot dispel. Abelard, however, makes no allusion to the true motives of her complaint: 'As to the form of salutation, in which you say I have reversed the order, permit me to point out that I have merely fallen in with your own way of thinking. Is it not standard practice, as you say yourself, to place one's superiors' names first when writing to them? And you are my superior; you became my lady and mistress when you became my Master's bride.'[10] He replies at some length to this first, seemingly innocuous point, drawing on scriptural images of the Bride of Christ. 'It is true,' he writes, 'that the words are most often used to describe the contemplative spirit which is specifically termed the Bride of Christ. Yet the very habit which you wear is evidence that they refer even more expressly to you.'[11] And, adopting a metaphor which often occurs in the spiritual letters and discussions of the time, he exclaims: 'What a felicitous exchange of marriage ties: you, until recently the wife of the most wretched of men, are now privileged to share the couch of the King of Kings, and this signal honour has raised you not only above your first husband but above all the rest of that King's menservants.' He then makes abundant use of images derived from the Song of Solomon, images which throughout the twelfth century underlay all writings concerned with *caritas*, charity, divine love.

Heloise had also complained of something else which 'startled and disturbed' the members of her community: 'Your

---

material upkeep of parishes – included a number of women, especially widows. The term 'deaconess' has since been applied rather haphazardly to abbesses or nuns in general. Heloise seems to adopt it at this point mainly for literary effect, contrasting the humble church worker with the ordained priest who was empowered to say Mass.

letter, which should have afforded us some consolation, has merely added to our sorrows; the hand which was to brush away our tears has made them well up again. For which of us could refrain from weeping over the passage at the end of your letter in which you say: "Should the Lord deliver me into the hands of my enemies, and should those enemies triumph over me and kill me . . ."? Spare us such words, which merely add to the woes of women already so sorely troubled. Wait until we die before you rob us of the staff of life.' Abelard reacts sharply to this criticism: 'Why rebuke me for making you share my troubles, when it was you who badgered me into revealing them?' The whole of his letter is tinged with a certain harshness – on the surface, at least – which makes it a rational antidote to her own undisciplined feelings.

The theme elaborated by Heloise was: you speak to us of your death as if we could possibly outlive you! 'May God never so far forget his humble handmaids as to let them survive the loss of you! May he never bequeath us a life which would be harder to bear than death in any form! Even the thought of your dying is itself a kind of death to us.' To which Abelard replies: 'Should there ever come a time when you can no longer find a place for me in your happiness, I cannot think why you should want me to endure the prolongation of so wretched a life rather than death, which would be bliss . . . I cannot say what hardships lie in store for me beyond the con-fines of this world, but I know the hardships from which I shall be released . . . If you really love me, you will see no harm in this obsession of mine. Indeed, if you have any hope of God's being merciful towards me, you will long to see me set free from the tribulations of this life, and your longing can only be increased by the knowledge that they are intolerable.'

Here we are in the presence of an archetypal dialogue between man and woman, logic and feeling. Abelard stands firm, determined to confront the situation and stem a tide of emotion which merely vexes him. Heloise calls for 'an end to these words which pierce our hearts like lethal swords and bring us to a pitch of anguish more painful than death itself!'[12] He counters by demanding 'an end, for pity's sake, to these reproaches, an end to these wailings which certainly do not stem from a spirit of charity . . .'[13] She had pressed him for news; she must accept the possibility that the news might be bad; she should not expect to share his joys without sharing his trials as well; nor, on the other hand, should she wish to see him cling to a life doomed to unbearable suffering. His tone, at this juncture, is very much that of a stoic.

But the stoic is swiftly replaced by the theologian. Heloise had written in moving terms of the misfortunes that beset her existence: 'Were it not blasphemous, I could surely claim the right to exclaim: "Great God, how cruel you are to me in every way!" ' Perhaps from fear of venting too much anger on God, she almost immediately harks back to antiquity and substitutes fate for his holy name: 'What glory it has conferred on me by giving you to me! What blows it has dealt me through your person! How violently it has fluctuated from one extreme to the other! It has been equally unrestrained in bestowing good things and bad . . . The supreme ecstasies of sensual delight were succeeded by the burden of blackest despair.'[14]

They were sufficiently in tune with their own times never to deny the existence of God, not even at the height of their ordeals. It was open to them to resent him and blame him for their misfortunes – and this, indeed, was the attitude adopted by Heloise. God had treated them cruelly, worse still, in the eyes of this couple to whom logic was so important, he had acted illogically: 'All pretensions of fairness have been swept away at our expense. For while we were savouring the delights of an uneasy love affair – or, to use a cruder but more expressive phrase, while we were engaged in fornication – we were spared the wrath of heaven. Not until we legalized our illicit relationship, not until we cloaked our shameful excesses with the respectability of marriage, did the Lord lift his hand against us.' This was too much for Heloise. She could not understand why they should have been struck down at the very moment when they chose to give up fornication. 'The punishment inflicted on you would have been heavy enough retribution for men caught in the most heinous acts of adultery; what others might have merited for adultery, you incurred for marrying me.' Thus God had been unjust. Her belief in him remained unshaken, but she no longer had the same faith in his love. He had angered her by an act of spite which, in her opinion, was unwarranted by their past misconduct. For in the twelfth century the spirit of rebellion might lead to blasphemous or sacrilegious behaviour, but never to the denial of God as a living reality. His presence remained unchallenged even when a man or woman was taking him to task or heaping curses upon him. Human beings driven to extremes often reacted with hatred or impiety, but they never succumbed to the lure of atheism. They might well seek to dupe God or even tussle with him – but they knew, all the time, that he was there. Which, incidentally, is why suicide was so rare in those days. However low people were brought, they still had an ineradicable faith in God, and hence in life.

But to Abelard it was intolerable that Heloise should round on God: 'Finally I must refer to the way in which you everlastingly bewail the circumstances of our conversion. You hold it against God, when you ought to thank him for it.'[15] No one can deny that at this point Abelard touches the heights. He who had paid physically for their misdeeds, and who could legitimately claim that he had suffered more than she, suddenly turns the situation on its head by applying the term 'conversion' to the event which she insists on calling 'punishment'. The language of human logic has been replaced by the language of divine grace. This passage alone is ample evidence of the incredibly rich inner growth which had derived from his initial act of assent, from his deliberate acceptance of the blow which he had been dealt. And in this passage the man who seemed so harsh in condemning Heloise's somewhat self-indulgent laments is capable of appealing to the emotions in the most delicate and noble manner: 'Your first thought is to please me, you say. I don't know about pleasing me, but if you want to stop torturing me you must put all such feelings out of your head. By fostering them, you would forfeit the chance either to please me or to attain eternal bliss with me. Will you really let me make the journey alone – you who proclaim yourself willing to follow me into the fiery pit of hell? Exercise all your willpower to summon piety into your soul, if only to avoid being separated from me as I, in your own phrase, proceed on my way to God.'[16]

And with great gentleness, appealing once again to the better and deeper side of her nature, he continues: 'Think back to what you yourself have said and written about the circumstances of our conversion: that God, far from displaying feelings of hostility, showed conspicuous mercy towards me. At least be capable of bowing to a judgement which has brought such gladness to me, and which will bring equal gladness to you once, all sorrow appeased, you open the door to reason. Do not bewail the fact that you were the cause of so great a boon, when it is obvious that God created you for that special purpose.'

Besides, had God really been unjust? Abelard has no difficulty in showing that their 'punishment', if it can be regarded as such, is no more than their sins deserve. Remorselessly pursuing this line of argument, he pinpoints circumstances which in his view added to the seriousness of their misdeeds. He reminds her, for instance, of their sacrilegious behaviour at Argenteuil: 'We were unrestrained in our lewdness, despite the respect due to a place dedicated to the Blessed Virgin. Even if we were innocent of any other crime, that one surely merited the most terrible of punishments. Shall I now remind you of our early defilements, of the shameful licentiousness which preceded our marriage, or of the base treachery which I inflicted on your uncle by so brazenly seducing you at a time when I was his guest and table-companion? Was he not justified in his own act of betrayal? How can any other view be possible

when it was I, in the first place, who abused his trust so out-
rageously?' And as for Heloise herself: 'You do not need
telling that when you became pregnant and I smuggled you to
my own part of the country you donned the habit of a nun
and, by this irreverent charade, insulted a calling which you
have since adopted as your own. Say, after that, whether
justice – or divine grace, rather – was not right to drive you
against your will into the monastic state which you had un-
flinchingly ridiculed. It decreed that the habit which you had
profaned should be your means of atoning for the profanation,
that reality should redeem travesty and so make reparation for
the sacrilegious hoax.'[17]

Heloise had strenuously lamented the lot of women in
general: '[They] will always be the scourge of great men.'[18]
She had enacted the role of Eve, the temptress; it was her fault
that Paradise had been lost, that Abelard had been driven from
the Notre Dame schools, subjected to public humiliation, and
uprooted from his brilliant career. And her letter had gone on to
enumerate those passages in the Bible which depict woman as a
source of chaos and disaster: Eve and the serpent: the wives
who had lured Solomon along the road to idolatry; Job's wife,
who had incited the poor, afflicted man to blasphemy . . . She,
Heloise, was of the same lineage, the same breed. Reading this
letter, one senses the black thoughts that must have tormented
her, first at Argenteuil and now in the wilderness surrounding
the Paraclete.

In his reply, Abelard seizes upon these self-condemnatory
remarks and looks deeper into the meditations inspired by her
references to the Old and New Testaments. She speaks of
women as a 'bane'; but what relevance, he asks, have such
words to the realities of their own situation? He bluntly asserts
his own share of responsibility for their dissolute behaviour:
'You know what physical depravities we indulged in as a result
of my wild passion. Neither concern for decency nor respect
for God could keep me from rolling in the mire – not even on
the days of Our Lord's Passion or on the other solemn occasions

in the year.' The full significance of these words is lost until one
recalls the stringent customs prevailing at the time: throughout
Lent and Holy Week, on Ember days, and on the vigils of
feasts, all sexual relations were forbidden, even between
husband and wife; this, of course, was in addition to the usual
rules of fasting and abstinence. 'You were unconsenting, you
resisted with all your might, you remonstrated with me, and,
although your frailty as a woman should have protected you, I
used threats and actual violence to make you give in to me. My
longing for you was so intense that, for the sake of those foul
pleasures which I am now ashamed to mention, I was prepared
to forget everything – even God, even self. How could divine
mercy save me, except by denying me those pleasures for ever?
It was in a spirit of absolute justice and clemency, therefore,
that God consented to your uncle's unworthy act of treachery
. . . It was only fair that the organ which had sinned should
undergo attack and atone, through pain, for the crime of
self-indulgence . . . Surely the effect of this deprivation
has been to predispose me towards every worthwhile action,
precisely because it has released me from the oppressive yoke
of lust?'[19] Far from feeling crushed by the events which had
overtaken them, they ought to rejoice; for what the world
might think of as weakness and loss was in fact a cause for
rejoicing and an opportunity for fruitfulness of a different kind·
'What a deplorable loss, what a lamentable misfortune if,
surrendering to the impurities of carnal pleasure, you had
brought a few children into this world in travail instead of the
countless family which you are bringing forth in joy for the
joys of heaven! How tragic if you were only a woman, you
who today surpass us men and have turned Eve's curse into
Mary's blessing!'[20] It was, of course, common practice at the
time to link and contrast Eve's name with Mary's and to take
the view that the Gospels had raised woman from the lowest
depths to the greatest heights: after the Fall, for which she was
held responsible, came the Annunciation and all that stemmed
from it. These two extreme views of woman were present in

the mind of every theologian of the day and were more broadly reflected in every form of art – poetry, painting, sculpture . . . Her position had become far more privileged and exalted. One has only to think of the 'Most High Lady' of the troubadours and trouvères, or of the Virgin in majesty who was soon to sit enthroned above cathedral doors.

Abelard quickly showed himself a true pastor by ridding Heloise of the sense of guilt which still preyed so violently on her mind. For not content with harping on her wrongdoings ('Heaven grant that I may do adequate penance for this sin . . . [and] that what you suffered briefly through the flesh I, in turn, may rightly and properly suffer through lifelong contrition of soul'),[21] she came perilously close to despair, the worst sin that any Christian can commit, the sin of Judas Iscariot; she was haunted by the fear that her penitence might be unreal and unavailing. In this respect her letter can stand comparison with the most outspoken modern confessions: 'If I must indeed lay bare the weakness of my heart, I find no spirit of repentance within me that is likely to appease God. I cannot keep from condemning his pitiless cruelty with regard to the outrage inflicted on your person, and far from seeking to allay his anger by penance I merely offend him further by the rebellious mutterings which I pour out against his ordinances. Can one really claim to be doing penance, whatever the treatment inflicted on one's body, when one's mind still harbours the notion of sin and burns with the same old passions? It is easy to accuse oneself of sins and admit them in the confessional, it is even easy to subject one's body to external mortifications; the difficulty lies in tearing one's mind away from the ever-sweet lure of desire.'[22]

This, then, is the sickness that devours her. It is the theme of a particularly harrowing passage in the same letter: 'The sensual delights which you and I enjoyed together were so dear to me that I cannot help loving the memory of them and am quite unable to erase them from my mind. Whichever way I turn, they reappear and intrude upon my thoughts, bringing new desires in their wake. The fancies which they inspire obsess me even in my sleep. And at the most solemn moments of the Mass, when the mind should be so free from taint, the wanton images of those delights still exercise so firm a hold on this tawdry heart that I am more preoccupied with their lewdness than with prayer. I ought to groan at the sins which I have perpetrated, yet I sigh for those which I am no longer able to commit.' And she concludes: 'People extol my chastity, but only because they are blind to my hypocrisy.'[23] Abelard's sufferings were at an end, whereas her whole heart and body were still racked by the intolerable privation that had been inflicted on them.

Once again Abelard shows what an admirable spiritual director he is, with a highly developed aptitude for guiding the troubled spirit. He had turned her emotional outbursts aside with undeniable severity; but now, faced with these admissions of a tormented conscience, he is remarkably kind and understanding. He betrays no hint of reproachfulness or indignation. On the contrary: 'As for your rejection of other people's praises, I applaud your words for they show you to be even more worthy of the compliments addressed to you.'[24] Returning to the subject in hand, he dwells on the more positive aspects of the struggle in which she is engaged: 'By the simple expedient of letting my body be punished, [the Lord] instantly doused the burning lusts that used to consume me. He has saved me from the risk of ever stumbling again. In your case, by leaving your youthfulness to its own devices, by keeping your mind a prey to the everlasting temptations of the flesh, he has singled you out for the martyr's crown. You may block your ears and forbid me to say it, but you cannot escape the fact that the crown belongs to whoever is willing to fight without respite.'[25] He then proposes a mystical marriage in which merits and sufferings will be united: 'I am not sorry to see my own merits diminish when I feel so confident that yours are increasing, for we are but one in Christ; by the law of

165

marriage, we are one body.' Heloise has complained of being tortured by lascivious images; Abelard suggests that these be replaced by an entirely different image – that of a torture freely consented to for the greater good of husband and wife.

His conclusion is likewise in direct contrast to hers. She had ended her letter with a declaration unfaltering in its frankness: 'Until now, heaven knows, at all times and in all circumstances, it has been you rather than him whom I have feared offending; it is you, far more than him, whom I long to please.'[26] Abelard's closing words are as follows: 'God was already planning the event which was to bring you and me back to him; indeed, but for the fact that we had previously been united by the bonds of matrimony, the advice of your family and the enticements of the flesh would have kept you in the world after I withdrew from it. I leave you to judge the full measure of God's concern for us.'[27]

Their own private wishes had been of no account, since God had guided them against their inclination.

Abelard is not content with exhortations of a general nature. Applying a method in common use at the time, he urges Heloise to contemplate a particular image, a particular face, and draw on it as an example. He is fond of likening his own fate to that of Origen and he harks back to the comparison in this letter: Origen, too, had been a eunuch; he was said to have mutilated his own body in literal obedience to those words in which Our Lord speaks of 'eunuchs which have made themselves eunuchs for the kingdom of heaven's sake'.[28] He reminds Heloise that her name has divine echoes: 'By a kind of holy portent . . . God has specially marked you out for heaven by calling you Heloise, derived from his own name of Elohim.' He ends by entreating her earnestly to recite the prayer which he is eagerly engaged in drafting, even though she claims to be unworthy of addressing it to heaven on his behalf.

The prayer is so beautiful that it is worth quoting.

'O God, who at the very beginning of creation established

the great sacrament of marriage by drawing woman from the rib of man, you who honoured her and raised her so high by being born of a woman's womb and by working your first miracle at the wedding-feast at Cana, you have willed that I be cured of my incontinent weakness, spurn not the prayers of your handmaiden. I lay them humbly at the feet of your divine majesty in atonement of my sins and the sins of my beloved. Forgive, O kindly God – or, rather, God who is Loving-kindness itself – forgive the extreme gravity of our evil-doings, and may the boundlessness of your ineffable mercy match the multitude of sins which we have committed . . .

'You brought us together, Lord, and you parted us as and when it pleased you. Finish mercifully this day what you so mercifully began. May those whom you have separated for a moment in this world be united with you for all eternity in heaven, O our hope, our lot, our expectation, our consolation, Lord who are blessed for ever and ever. Amen.'

This letter from Abelard – Letter IV – marks the end of the series of exchanges dealing with their past, present and future relationship. And it is wholly in keeping with the spirit of the age that a correspondence that began with a barely restrained emotional outcry should conclude with a prayer. After all, many of the leading troubadours spent their last days in monasteries. Bernard de Ventadour retired to the abbey of Dalon, and so – after a stormy life – did Bertrand de Born. Peire d'Auvergne settled at Gramont and Folquet de Marseille at Le Thoronet, later becoming bishop of Toulouse.

And further testimony of the spirit of the age is to be found in the manner in which these letters were addressed. Even if the text of the correspondence had gone astray, we could still have fathomed its contents from the various superscriptions. For in those days there was a highly developed art of language. Words and phrases were selected for their innate expressiveness, and this entailed a training in the use of words which found reflection even in everyday life – as, for instance, in the widespread application of the cognomen, or nickname. Thus, Henry I of England became known as Beauclerk, and Henry II as Curtmantle or Plantagenet. The cognomen characterized a person in the spoken language as fully as a seal on a written document or a heraldic shield in the lists. Indeed, although it has now vanished without trace, the habit of conferring cognomens still persisted in French rural areas until not so long ago – and this feature of medieval life has survived in the form of the family surname.

This art of language was fostered in part by the pithiness and rich poeticism of the Latin then in use – a Latin, needless to say, far removed from Cicero's. Hence the concise phrasing at which Heloise is particularly adept, so brief and yet so eloquent that even a translator as superbly gifted as Octave Gréard was unable to render it without recourse to lengthy circumlocutions.

The superscription of the very first letter is a minor masterpiece in its own right. Each word captures and conveys the echo of an episode in their painful history: '*Domino suo, imo patri; conjugi suo, imo fratri; ancilla sua, imo filia; ipsius uxor, imo soror; Abelardo Heloissa*': 'To her master, or rather to her father; to her husband, or rather to her brother; his handmaid, or rather his daughter; his wife, or rather his sister; to Abelard, Heloise.' No one could summarize their respective situations in a more poignant yet incisive manner.

But Abelard's own superscription was no less pointed and significant: '*Heloisse dilectissime sorori sue in Christo, Abelardus frater ejus in ipso*': 'To Heloise, his most dear sister in Jesus Christ, Abelard, her brother in the same.' To her gloomy words of reminiscence, Abelard opposed a crisp statement of intent: the time for gazing into each other's eyes was past; instead, they must both look steadfastly in the same direction – the direction of Our Lord. Abelard was still prepared to treat himself and Heloise as a couple, but only in terms which matched their altered situation. And she was not yet ready to accept such terms. In her second letter she revised her salutation to: '*Unico suo post Christum, unica sua in Christo*', which, when rendered literally, means: 'To her only one after Christ, his only one in Christ.' But this is difficult to grasp unless we expand the meaning of every word: 'To him who is everything to her after Christ, she who is utterly his in Christ.' She had now gone so far as to relate their enduring partnership to Christ. Both Heloise and Abelard believed in God; they belonged to an age in which the patterns of everyday life were dictated by faith in Our Lord. Anyone who fails to grasp this basic fact is largely missing the point of these letters which seem so close to us and which, taken as a whole, are so profoundly human that their authors have become perfect prototypes of the Lover and his Mistress. But Heloise was none the less intent on pointing out that she must be everything to Abelard, just as he was every-thing to her. Abelard, as always, had an answer ready to hand: '*Sponse Christi servus ejusdem*': 'To the bride of Christ, Christ's manservant.'

The exchange opens our eyes dramatically to the state of conflict which was then considered the basic ingredient of the couple, the 'twosome'. At which point I cannot avoid alluding to a whole cluster of standard twelfth-century images come in to illustrate this theme. Two was considered an 'infamous' number – meaning, quite literally, a number of ill-repute. Two inevitably connoted a clash. It was on the second day, according to Genesis, that division and rift came into being. 'And God said, Let there be a firmament in the midst of the waters, and let it divide the waters from the waters. And God made the firmament, and divided the waters which were under the firmament from the waters which were above the firmament: and so it was.' On this second day God did not claim that what he had made was good. Abelard emphasizes this point – as indeed do all other contemporary commentaries on Genesis – in his *Account of the Six Days*, which he composed at Heloise's request: 'It will be noticed that . . . in respect of this day the Scriptures do not remark "And God saw that it was good", as they do in connection with all the other days.'* The cleaving of the upper and lower waters was a signal for all the divisions, confrontations and 'duels' of subsequent ages. And each new couple incorporates the original duel, temporarily resolved while husband and wife are 'two in one flesh' and transcended as soon as a child appears – for the child compels two pairs of eyes, previously absorbed in each other, to disengage and afterwards reassemble in rapt contemplation of one and the same external object, such contemplation being the basis of the couple's future harmony. For Heloise and Abelard – as the latter had realized without hesitation – such harmony could only be achieved in so far as their eyes were capable of looking beyond their own two persons. Otherwise there was a serious danger that their sad duet might die away altogether. Heloise was all for continuing it without departing from her initial terms of reference; but eventually she agreed to fall in with the plan put forward by the husband who was now her spiritual director. '*Domino specialiter,*' she wrote, '*tua singulariter*' – which might be freely construed as 'God's as a member of the human race, yours as an individual.' She remembered all the arguments which had gone back and forth between them; she recalled the various categories which her master had drummed into her; and, to please him, she became an abbess again; from now on, since that was what he wanted, she would address him exclusively in her capacity as abbess of the Paraclete.

'My pain and sorrow are still ready to break loose at a moment's notice; but I have, as you commanded, prohibited myself from expressing them, so that you cannot accuse me of disobeying you in any way. When writing to you, at least, I shall be capable of suppressing outbursts which, if we were to meet and talk, would be hard, indeed impossible, to avert. For

* I am indebted for this detail to the philosopher Jean Dahhan, who died at a tragically early age and whose *Commentaire sur la Genèse* has made an unforgettable impression on all who have been privileged to read it; the commentary is to be published in the near future. The biblical reference is, of course, to Genesis i 6-7.

we have less control over our hearts than over anything else; we are forced to take orders from them instead of imposing our will on them, and their onslaughts are so sudden that the feelings they bring may easily spill out in the form of words or actions . . . I shall therefore discipline my hand and not permit it to write those things which my tongue would have to blurt out. Would to God that my troubled heart were as biddable as my pen.'[29] There is no hint of dumb insolence or disobedience; instead, one is conscious of a heroic determination to transcend her own nature. She had deliberately elected to swallow feelings that refused to be obliterated; and because she mistrusted her own instincts she intended to be quite ruthless in her efforts at self-control.

Even so, she made one last request – and here she was conscious as being well within her rights. Abelard could scarcely turn it down. Moreover, she was encouraged by the success which she had already achieved in persuading him to write to her and show some awareness of her needs and sufferings. The exchanges prompted by her reaction to the *Letter to a Friend* may not have been exactly what she had in mind, but at least he had answered her and kept up the correspondence. He had broken the long silence for which she had upbraided him so fiercely. She had trapped him into re-evoking a past which was still so dear to her. And she felt quite confident that he would reply to this latest letter, for it questioned him earnestly about her present and future concerns. Furthermore she was now appealing to him on behalf of the community for which she was responsible: 'All of us, being servants and daughters of Jesus Christ, today beseech you that in your fatherly kindness you will grant us two things for which we feel an overriding need. First, will you please explain the origin of the sisterhood and the exact nature of our profession? Second, will you draw up a rule for us and put it in writing – a rule specifically designed for women and determining once and for all the role and habit best suited to our community. None of the Holy Fathers, so far as we know, has ever concerned himself with

171

these matters, which is why men and women living in cloisters are still subject to the same rule, and why the same monastic yoke is imposed on the weaker sex as on the stronger. Even to this day, men and women alike profess the order of St Benedict, although it is obvious that this rule was devised exclusively for men and can be observed by men only . . .'

It is a literary myth that Heloise fell silent after the celebrated 'lovers' exchange'. Apart from this present letter, so different in tone from its predecessors, there is evidence of a long and lively correspondence between herself and Abelard, who was now firmly cast in the role of spiritual director. After two letters establishing the rule which the convent was to observe came the hymns which he wrote, at her request. Then there were the problems which she laid before him and the sermons which she solicited for the community's edification. And later, as we shall see, came exchanges at an even deeper level, prompted by the storms which broke at the end of his life and which continued to rumble after his death. Thus, the whole of her existence was guided and illumined by Abelard. From now on they were united in a mutual determination. Heloise had won from him those tokens of solicitude which were hers by right; Abelard, in return, had secured the promise that all such tokens would be directed to one sole end: the greater service of God.

This long correspondence affords us a glimpse of Heloise's life at the Paraclete. What little remains of the old buildings gives an entirely misleading impression. The site is now occupied by a kind of fortress, complete with turrets, which was certainly not erected until after the twelfth century. The only part of the farmhouse that might date back to Heloise's time is a large room with a vaulted ceiling. What has *not* changed, on the other hand, is the scenery – the general atmosphere of this rather austere stretch of countryside, with its unexciting woods, meadows and river. But the splendid skyscapes are beautifully reflected in the ever-increasing number of ponds which materialize each autumn, and the sunsets are startlingly clear, a glorious suffusion of pink light.

It is easy enough to imagine the nuns singing in these 'picturesque' surroundings. Singing lent rhythm to their lives, beginning and ending each day, varying with the hours and seasons. The immense effort which Abelard put into the task of composing their hymns and anthems testifies to the importance which he attached to sung prayer, and it would be a betrayal to forget this aspect of his work: about a hundred and forty hymns written to punctuate each of the liturgical hours, crammed with Holy Writ and doctrinal riches, and containing verbal cadences of great poetic power – as, for instance, the famous O *quanta qualia*, set aside for Saturday vespers, or the special anthem for the first nocturn of Christmas. But his poetic achievement achieved its highest point in the six *plancti*, which invariably contain some echo of the experiences suffered by himself and Heloise. These six poems on biblical themes must have attained wide circulation, for – as has recently been pointed out – the melody of one of them (the Lament of the Companions of Jephthah's Daughter, referred to earlier) later provided the basis for a lay which became very popular in Old French: the Lay of the Maidens. Thus this melody composed by Abelard was still on everybody's lips more than a hundred years after his death.

It is in no way surprising that, according to the rule which he laid down for the Paraclete, the nun in charge of singing was also entrusted with the general education of the younger novices; this was entirely in keeping with the practices of an age which regarded singing as the starting-point of all instruction. 'She will teach the others to sing, read, write, and set down music; she will also take charge of the library, lending and recovering books, and will look after manuscripts and illuminations.' The rule which he promulgated was, as Heloise had asked, a sensible revision of the order of St Benedict, adapted to the spiritual needs and physical capabilities of women. Naturally, Heloise had expressed her own preferences: she was anxious that her nuns should not be expected to labour beyond their limited powers (St Benedict required his monks to till the land!) nor to pray at a length which would overtax them – to take but one example, she saw no reason why any psalm should be recited more than once a week. She had also suggested that dietary restrictions should be eased somewhat, so that the sisters might be allowed modest amounts of meat and wine. Her requests show a restraint which contrasts oddly with what we know of her passionate nature, but they also reveal her readiness to face up to the responsibilities which she had assumed by becoming abbess of the Paraclete. 'Would to God that our vows might so uplift us as to attain the level of the Gospel without rashly seeking to go beyond it; let us not aspire to be more than Christians.'

Abelard met her wishes with corresponding sense and fore-sight. There was no trace of undue asceticism in his rule. He decreed that the nuns who, whatever the season, had worn stockings, shoes or slippers, and plain cloth chemises under their black woollen robes, should be free to wear a sheepskin garment in winter and that they should have a cloak which would serve as a blanket at night; in the dormitories, each was to have a bed complete with mattress, bolster, pillow, sheets and a quilt. They would be expected to rise in time for matins, but the hours of waking and sleeping would be adequately apportioned. As for food, his instructions were full of good sense: 'Is there any great merit in abstaining from meat when our tables groan from the weight of other comestibles? We spend a great deal of money on all kinds of fish . . . as if the sin lay in the character rather than in the superfluity of foodstuffs. The aim, in this transient life, should be not to pursue high-quality food, but to make do with what is readily available.' Not that his rule contains a single feature which distinguishes it strongly from other monastic rules in force at the time. The most we can claim is that it occasionally mirrors certain personal characteristics – as, for instance, when he writes: 'In no circumstances must custom be allowed to prevail over reason, nor must anything be retained merely because it enjoys the sanction of custom . . . It is imperative that we regulate our conduct in the light of what seems sound rather than adhere strictly to usage.'

One is forced to admit that Abelard here shows none of the bold innovatory spirit of his compatriot, Robert of Arbrissel. When establishing the order of Fontevrault, Robert allowed for dual cloisters ruled by an abbess; monastery and convent would exist side by side, though naturally the monks and nuns would be strictly segregated. And a similar policy was pursued in other parts of Christendom, especially in Ireland and the other Celtic areas of Britain.

Abelard does indeed go so far as to envisage a monastery whose monks and lay brothers would be obliged to render service to the neighbouring convent, either by celebrating Mass and other offices or by helping with the manual work. But he adds: 'We desire that nunneries shall always be subordinate to monasteries in such a manner that the brothers shall look after the sisters, that one supreme abbot shall attend like a father to the needs of both establishments, and that there shall be but one fold and one shepherd in the Lord.' True, he afterwards palliates this suggestion: 'We desire . . . that the abbot shall preside over the nuns in a style that acknowledges his inferiority to the brides of Christ, whose servant he is, and that his joy shall lie not in commanding but in serving them.'

It was only to be expected that this prince of schoolmen would go out of his way to fill the nuns with a zeal for self-instruction. To this end, he reminded them how St Jerome had urged biblical studies upon the pious women who had gathered round Paula in Bethlehem. 'Bearing in mind the ardour which that eminent doctor of the church and those holy women devoted to the Scriptures, I urge and desire you to dedicate yourselves without delay – while you still can, since you have a mother thoroughly versed in those three languages [Greek, Latin and Hebrew] – to the task of studying them to perfection so that you will be able to elucidate any points that may prompt doubts because of discrepancies in translation. The very fact that the inscription on Our Lord's cross appeared in Hebrew, Greek and Latin seems to me a clear indication that a knowledge of these tongues should spread to the Church throughout the world, for the text of the Old and New Testaments is written in those languages. You are able to learn them without undue trouble or great expense . . . for, as I say, you have a mother with an adequate knowledge of these subjects.'[30]

In the early days, as Abelard himself testifies, living standards at the Paraclete had been extremely poor and precarious. The nuns found little shelter from the elements apart from the modest thatch-and-clay huts erected by the students and, of course, the chapel. This first chapel may well have stood on the same site as the one which today marks the spot where Abelard and, later, Heloise were buried. The cartulary* of the abbey has survived intact and testifies to the steady increase in the community's possessions. In 1134 Bishop Manasses of Melun devoted a small proportion of the tithes levied in his diocese to the task of 'relieving, at least in part, the penury of the poor handmaidens of Christ who offer him devoted service at the Paraclete'. By the year 1140 the institution was heavily in debt. Yet when, on 1 November 1147, Pope Eugenius III's legate came to Châlons to ratify the convent's independence, the list of property was imposing. As was usual at the time, this property consisted chiefly of a mass of small rights acquired more or less at random: the use of the woods at Courgivaux, Pouy, Marcilly and Charmoy, both for grazing and for building-timber; five sous from the toll-bridge at Baudement; two *setiers* (about eight quarts) of rye from the land of Walter of Courcemain; quit-rent amounting to twelve *deniers* from Thierry Goherel's meadow; a large barrel of oats and twenty hens donated by Margaret, viscountess of Marolles; and so on and so forth . . . But there were also more substantial gifts: a

* The name given to the book containing duplicates of the charters and title deeds of an estate. The original documents were preserved in the charter-room.

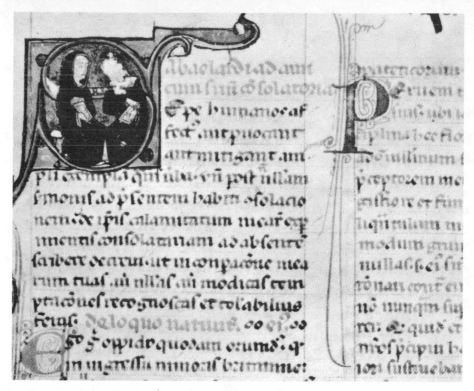

Abelard's Letter to a Friend became one of the most widely
copied texts in the Middle Ages. Above, a version in Latin; below,
a version in French

Mill on the Ardusson, where Heloise's convent of the Paraclete
once stood

The 12th c. well of the Paraclete

mill, a house, vineyards, meadows, arable lands – all of which added up to a sizeable estate.

And the Paraclete's protectors included persons of great power and substance. Most influential of all was the count of Champagne himself: Theobald had donated a barrel of wheat annually, together with the produce of the fishing-grounds near his mills at Pont-sur-Seine and about a hundred and twenty quarts of cereal from Le Moulin-de-l'Etang. Contributions had also been made by several lesser local knights, including Arpin of Méry-sur-Seine and two men named Felix and Aimé who are briefly and unenlighteningly described as *miles*. There had been offerings from many humble folk too: the wife of Payen the saddler, for instance, donated all that she owned: a house at Provins and the small income which she derived from land at Lisines. The nuns also appear to have been in great favour with the clergy: among the gifts which they received was one from Henry Sanglier, archbishop of Sens, who surrendered his tithes from Lisines and a portion of those from Cucharmoy; Atton, archbishop of Troyes, presented them with half the tithes from Saint-Aubin and also – an act of bounty indicative of the true flavour of those times – half the candles needed for the feast of the Purification (2 February). Several priests followed the example set by their superiors: as early as 1138 Father Gondry of Trainel parted with an estate which he had inherited from his father, and in later years Father Peter of Périgny-la-Rose presented the sisters with houses and vineyards.

Some of these gifts were made when novices entered the convent. For instance, a certain Galon and his wife Adelaide gave half of the mill at Crèvecoeur, together with the vineyards which they owned in the same district and a quit-rent of forty sous, derived either from Provins or from Lisines, when Adelaide's sister Hermeline took her vows at the Paraclete – which proves that the abbey started recruiting locally as early as 1133 (the date of Hermeline's dowry). Another tithe at Villegruis was contributed by a knight named Ralph Jaillac and his wife Elizabeth when one of their nieces took the veil.

All of which shows what an excellent administrator Heloise was – an astute abbess managing the foundation with the utmost zeal. And although her community had moved to this area in far from favourable circumstances (for these, remember, were nuns previously evicted from a convent which had a bad reputation), it soon began to enjoy widespread favour and esteem. The king himself – Louis VI – was quick to endow the abbey; his earliest gifts were conferred in 1135. Abelard cannot be accused of exaggerating when he records the rapid growth and development of the Paraclete in the following terms: 'The Lord willed that our dear sister who presided over the community should find favour in everyone's eyes. Bishops cherished her as a daughter, priests as a sister, and the laity as a mother; all were united in their admiration for her piety, wisdom and incomparably sweet and tolerant nature. The less she showed herself – the more she shut herself away in her oratory and gave herself over to pious meditation and prayer – the more ardently they solicited her presence and the revelations that were to be gained from conversing with her.'

This means that, like any other cloister at the time, the Paraclete received visitors. These were of three distinct kinds. First there were the paupers, pilgrims or tramps; it was the gatekeeper's task to receive them and minister to them, but the abbess or one of the other sisters was expected to wash their feet. Then there were the people who lived round about. And finally, from time to time, there were members of the clergy or representatives of the ecclesiastical authorities.

One day the Paraclete received a visitor whose presence caused a considerable stir. It was Bernard of Clairvaux. The nuns welcomed him 'not as a man but as an angel', and one can well imagine how they hung on his words. At one point, however, St Bernard himself received a considerable shock. He noticed that instead of saying 'Give us this day our daily bread' when they recited the Lord's Prayer, the nuns followed the Latin text of St Matthew's Gospel and said: 'Give us this day

178

our supersubstantial bread.' The visitor could hardly believe his ears. He asked Heloise for an explanation, and she presumably told him that this somewhat pedantic departure from common usage had been urged on them by Abelard. Bernard eventually let the matter drop.

But on the occasion of Abelard's own next visit, Heloise told him in confidence that the abbot of Clairvaux had seemed startled by this departure from the norm. Abelard wrote to Bernard without delay, and he certainly did not mince his words. The letter begins respectfully enough: 'You apparently assumed that this usage was of my devising; I must therefore seem, in your eyes, the author of a certain innovation. I felt I should write to you and outline my reasons for taking this step, especially as it would anger me more to offend your judgement than that of anyone else . . .' But his tone soon grows heated. Abelard justifies his decision to translate the word *super-substantialis* literally and argues that it is no crime to introduce an innovation. He refers Bernard to the words of St Gregory the Great and Pope Gregory VII. Both stressed the fact that Our Lord did not say 'I am the custom', but 'I am the truth.' And then, with sudden ferocity, he speaks out against some of Bernard's own innovations: 'You also, defying the practice of scholars and monks alike, an ancient practice still observed to this day, have introduced your flock to a new and revised form of divine service, yet you appear to feel no guilt on that score . . . Let me remind you of a few of your changes: you have spurned the usual hymns and introduced some which we have never heard before and which are quite unknown in all but a few churches . . . And astonishingly, even though you have named nearly all your oratories after the Mother of God, you celebrate none of her feasts, nor those of the other saints. You have all but excluded the hallowed custom of staging processions. Not content with continuing to sing the *Alleluia* up to Septuagesima, contrary to the standard practice of the Church, you even retain it during Lent . . .' He goes on to ask why he, too, should not be permitted to introduce innovations: 'For He who wished to be proclaimed by every tongue was bent on being served by various forms of worship . . . I do not seek to persuade anyone to follow me in this respect . . . For my own part, I shall invariably retain those words and their meaning to the full extent of my abilities.'

Bernard does not appear to have answered a missive which makes no reference to other points of disagreement between the two men. It must have been written some time after their first meeting on 20 January 1131 when, as abbots of Clairvaux and Saint-Gildas-de-Ruys, they jointly attended Pope Innocent III's consecration of the high altar at Morigny.

But, considered in the general context of Abelard's life and work, this letter – which tends to make too much of a rather trivial incident – can be seen as the opening shot in an unexpectedly serious polemical war, with Peter ranged on one side and Bernard on the other.

V

'THE MAN WHO BELONGS
AT YOUR SIDE'

O ros! o vanitas! cur sic extolleris?
Ignoras etiam utrum cras vixeris.
Hec carnis gloria que magni penditur
In sacris litteris flos feni dicitur
Ut breve folium quod vento rapitur.

O vanity like dew, why vaunt yourself?
Can you be sure tomorrow finds you here?
All flesh is grass, the Scriptures say; it withers
And vanishes, for all you hold it dear,
As leaves are wind-borne when they're brown and sere.

Poem attributed to Abelard

'HELOISE, my sister, once so dear to me in the world, today even dearer to me in Jesus Christ, logic has made me abhorrent in the eyes of the world.'[1]

This opening statement in Abelard's profession of faith – which, as we shall see, he composed in highly dramatic circumstances – shows how coolly and shrewdly he judged his own work and the reactions to which it gave rise.

For several years, he had been allowed to resume his teaching on the Montagne Sainte-Geneviève. No obstacle was put in his way. By 1136 at latest, and perhaps even as early as 1133, he was once again surrounded by a bevy of exuberant, captivated students. One of them, John of Salisbury, has bequeathed us an accurately dated account of these classes, adding that Abelard's departure seemed unduly sudden.

It may well have been during this period that Abelard wrote two tracts dealing with the question of morality: *Scito te ipsum* and the *Commentary on the Epistle to the Romans*. This is hardly the place for a detailed discussion of them, but the point does need to be made that there was no possibility of their gaining acceptance at the time of their composition. For Abelard argued that sin lay wholly in intention. This was tantamount to denying the importance of scandal, and his assertive stance was ill-designed to win approval and support in an age which took the view that no sin could be altogether private; individual and group were so closely interrelated that a community felt besmirched by the smallest transgression on the part of one of its members, and in some respects scandal was considered every bit as grave as sin itself. Abelard's emphasis on individualism in these matters had already been explored in depth in his treatises on morality, and so had the importance which he attached to penance.[2]

And it may also have been at about this time* that he began a work which he was never to finish – *Dialogus inter philosophum, judeum et christianum*, *Dialogue between a Philosopher, a Jew and a Christian*. The piece is exceptionally indicative of his mental attitudes. One night, he tells us, he had a vision in which three

* I cannot share the traditional view that the Dialogue was written at Cluny. The whole tone of the work is marked by that arrogant self-assurance which Abelard displayed in nearly all his writings and which did not desert him until he penned the *Apologia seu fidei confessio* and so put an end to all bickering. The phrase 'that admirable work of theology which envy could neither endure nor demolish, and which has been rendered even more glorious by persecution' may refer to the condemnation of his work by the Council of Soissons, but can scarcely be an allusion to the similar condemnation pronounced by the Council of Sens and immediately ratified by the Pope: it would totally belie his profession of faith, which is so different in tone.

I feel it is far more likely that the Dialogue was written in 1139 or 1140 – i.e. during or immediately after his series of meetings with Bernard of Clairvaux. The tone and character of the work are very much in keeping with this period when he and Bernard scored off each other at every opportunity. Bernard wrote his *Treatise*, exposing the various 'errors' perpetrated by Abelard, while the latter retained full confidence in his own powers of reasoning and in the continuing support of Rome; he was exclusively concerned with issuing public challenges against the abbot of Clairvaux.

men paid him a visit, each arriving from a different direction. The three men introduce themselves in the following terms: 'We are united in professing belief in one God, but divided by the faiths wherein we serve him and by the lives that we lead. One of us is a pagan, a member of that breed known as philosophers who are content with natural law. The other two have inherited the Scriptures; one is a Jew, the other a Christian. We have deliberated long and hard among ourselves about our various forms of faith. We arc looking to you to settle the issue . . .' Abelard lets the philosopher have his say first. It is he who takes the initiative in all matters pertaining to the mind – 'for that is philosophers' highest asset, that they seek the truth by way of argument and are guided in all things, not by men's opinions but by reason alone.' This particular philosopher, having decided to adopt the faith which seems most compatible with reason, has studied the Jewish and Christian religions in turn. All three men have prepared their lines of argument, and he is content to leave the final verdict to Abelard. In that shamelessly self-congratulatory manner which has never yet deserted him, the latter then proceeds to sing his own praises – though he makes the words issue from the lips of the philosopher: 'Such a verdict is certainly within your capability, for you are famed for your keenness of mind and for your knowledge of both Testaments, Old and New . . . Everyone knows the subtlety of your intelligence, and it is common knowledge that the treasure-house of your memory is richly stored with philosophical and religious knowledge of a range far transcending what is usually taught in the schools. You have unquestionably outshone all other teachers of any subject, whether sacred or profane . . . The proof lies in that admirable work of theology which envy could neither endure nor demolish, and which has been rendered even more glorious by persecution.'[3]

Clearly Peter Abelard thought that he was more competent than any other Christian thinker to rule on every question relating to faith, reason, or the no-man's-land between the two.

Yet this view was not held by some at least of his contemporaries . . .

'It bewilders me that I, the very least of men, should feel obliged to badger you, my lords and fathers. You have a duty to speak out, yet you remain silent on an issue which could not be graver and which relates to the common good of the faithful. How can I remain silent when I see the dangers which are being freely allowed to threaten the faith of our common hope, that faith which Jesus Christ sealed with his blood, which the apostles and martyrs defended with theirs, and which the tireless labours of the doctors of the Church have handed down, unblemished, to the wretched age in which we live. Yes, I am eaten up with sorrow, and the shock to my heart is so great that I have no choice but to alleviate it by raising my voice in defence of a cause for which, given the need and the opportunity, I should be happy to lay down my life.

'Do not delude yourselves into supposing that these are trivial matters. The issues at stake are no less than belief in the Blessed Trinity, the Person of the Intercessor, the Holy Spirit, the grace of God, and the sacramental means of our redemption. For Peter Abelard is once again propounding novelties in his teachings and writings. His books are spreading beyond the seas and the Alps, flitting from province to province, kingdom to kingdom. It is said that they even find favour with the Roman Curia . . . I must now tell you and the whole Church that by your silence you are courting disaster . . . Not knowing whom else to confide in, I have chosen you; it is you I turn to; it is you I call on to defend God and all the Church. This man fears you, he lives in awe of you. Whom will he fear if you shut your eyes to him? At this critical hour, when death has recently deprived the Church of nearly all her masters and doctors, this enemy within is pouncing on her defenceless body and seizing control of the magisterium. He is handling Holy Writ as he once handled dialectics . . .'

This letter was addressed simultaneously to Bernard of

Clairvaux and to Geoffrey of Lèves, Peter's lifelong friend and ally. And indeed the letter itself was not without a certain fellow-feeling for Abelard: 'I too have loved Peter Abelard and, as God is my witness, I should like to love him still. But in a matter such as this, I can make no allowance for friend or neighbour. It is too late to remedy the evil by private words of advice or admonition; the error is public and spreading like wildfire. It calls for solemn, public condemnation.'[4]

The author of these words was William, a Cistercian monk who had once been abbot of Saint-Thierry. It was probably in 1139, while writing his commentary on the *Song of Songs*, that he came into possession of two of Abelard's works, *An Introduction to Theology* and *Christian Theology*. By that time William was living in seclusion at the abbey of Signy, in the Ardennes. He had been driven to adopt this way of life by a process of inner development which urged him towards an ever more exacting rule of life, an ever greater shedding of inessentials. Born in Liège at roughly the same time as Abelard, he had first taken the cowl at the abbey of Saint-Nicaise in Rheims. In 1119 or 1120 he had been elected abbot of Saint-Thierry, on the outskirts of the same city, but some fifteen years later he had resigned the abbotship, donned a white habit in place of a black one, and committed himself wholeheartedly to the reformist movement which drew its vigour and inspiration from Bernard of Clairvaux.* In consequence, round about 1135, he had embraced the Cistercian order at the abbey

* The abbey of Cîteaux was founded in 1098 by Robert of Molesmes, with the aim of restoring the Benedictine rule to its pristine perfection; but these high ambitions proved hard to sustain and soon there were signs of a certain loss of vigour. One day in 1112 a group of about thirty young men appeared at the monastery gates. They were led by Bernard, son of the lord of Fontaine-les-Dijon. From that moment onwards, the Cistercians went from strength to strength. The first daughter-house was opened at La Ferté in 1113, and another at Pontigny the following year. In 1115 Clairvaux was founded, with Bernard himself as abbot. Before long the order, which reasserted the dignity of manual work and stressed the desirability of austere living conditions, had spread to all parts of western Christendom, giving rise to churches

of Signy. He may even have been tempted to adopt the still more austere and solitary life of the Carthusians, for he had spent some time in the charterhouse of Mont-Dieu.

William of Saint-Thierry was a gifted scholar. He had been through the schools – at Laon, probably. As a thinker, he played an important part in the development of twelfth-century philosophy. Like all his contemporaries, he had delved deep into the problem of love, which in those days was considered synonymous with the problem of the Blessed Trinity; and this was the subject of his principal works, *Of the Nature and Dignity of Love*, *Of the Contemplation of God*, and *The Mirror of Faith*.

Soon after dispatching his strongly worded letter, William sent his correspondents a detailed study of the errors which he had detected in Abelard's writings. He had read these pen in hand, jotting down every observation that struck him as unorthodox and summarizing his notes in thirteen propositions, each of which represented a departure from sound doctrine.

Such, then, was the origin of a conflict which was to be of far-reaching significance, not only for the disputants themselves, but for the general evolution of the Church and of intellectual thought. The ceaseless flow of comment which the duel has inspired over the centuries testifies to the enormously high stakes involved. The whole development of religious life in the twelfth century and beyond can be said to have hinged, in large measure, on the outcome of this clash.

In addressing his remarks to Geoffrey of Lèves, William of Saint-Thierry had solicited the aid of one of the most eminent bishops of his day – a bishop, after all, was by the very nature of his office the shepherd of the fold, the defender of doctrine. Bernard of Clairvaux was selected as the other recipient, partly because he was head of the Cistercian order, to which William

---

and cloisters constructed in a completely new style. In his thirty-eight years as abbot, Bernard founded sixty-eight monasteries – and by the time he died there were seven hundred monks at Clairvaux alone.

belonged, but chiefly because he was the perfect representative, indeed the living embodiment, of the reformist movement at work within the Church. Bernard was 'the watchdog of Christendom',[5] a man tireless in his opposition to all the errors and weaknesses of the age. He would have preferred to dwell undisturbed in the silence and solitude of his cell at Clairvaux, but the outside world would not leave him alone. He was first lured out to settle a quarrel between the archbishop of Sens, the bishop of Paris and no less a person than the king, Louis VI. Since then he had been summoned forth again and again, whenever men felt the need for higher arbitration. It was he who had to resolve matters when Pierleone, the ex-Cluniac monk, threatened the unity of the church by setting himself up as Pope Anacletus II; Bernard travelled to Etampes, where the bishops were assembled, and exerted his personal authority to such good effect that the waverers supported the claims of the lawful Pope, Innocent II, whose authority was thereby re-established.

By twentieth-century standards, his power and influence seem startling, for they did not derive from any particular rank or office within the Church. He was neither a bishop nor a cardinal. True, he was an abbot; but the powers attached to this post did not extend beyond the confines of Clairvaux. There was only one reason why his contemporaries looked to him when disputes needed to be settled or intricacies disentangled. He drew men to him by virtue of his personal magnetism; they were paying homage to his obvious, unadorned saintliness, reports of which had quickly spread far beyond his abbey. Such things do not happen in the modern world: one simply cannot imagine Pope Paul VI cabling a modern hermit to fly to Rome to dispense advice. Yet Bernard was universally regarded as the incarnation of the reforming process which was then considered the normal condition of the Church and men turned to him instinctively whenever they detected anything that they felt demanded reform. Which was why this would-be recluse had become an itinerant; why this man of delicate health, constantly on the verge of collapse, who likened himself to a 'plucked bird', had travelled the length and breadth of Europe, issuing reprimands not only to bishops and abbots, but to kings, to the Emperor, and even to the Pope himself.

So it was scarcely surprising that William of Saint-Thierry should write to Bernard of Clairvaux and tell him of the fear and concern which he had felt on reading Peter Abelard's works. A few years earlier the two men had exchanged a series of letters on the ever-topical question of how much luxury the Church might allow. The correspondence had inspired Bernard's celebrated *Apologia to William of Saint-Thierry*, in which he fiercely condemned all forms of wealth and ostentation: 'Tell me this, poor monks – if indeed you are poor – what place is there for gold in the house of God?'

William's attack on Abelard reached him some time in Lent 1139. 'Your strong feelings,' Bernard replied, 'strike me as warranted and desirable . . . Not that I have as yet read [your letter] with the close attention which [it] calls for; but what I have gathered from a swift perusal appeals to me, I must admit, and is, I feel, capable of overthrowing this impious doctrine. But as I seldom set great store by my own judgement, especially in such serious matters . . . I think it would be useful . . . if we met somewhere and talked all this over. I consider that we should wait until after Easter, however, so as to avoid disrupting the spirit of prayer demanded by this present season . . .'[6]

By the time the suggested meeting took place, he had made a much closer study of the detailed points raised by William (see Appendix I, p. 227). It was decided that Bernard should have a private interview with Abelard and try to persuade him to justify or correct the offending propositions. Most of these touched on the doctrine of the Trinity, which had been the recurring theme of Abelard's writings and which, as we have seen, was such an important element in the spiritual and intellectual climate of the age. So it would be impossible to overestimate the significance of the forthcoming duel. Neither protagonist was disposed to make light of the question at issue.

Each was determined to defend his views with the ardour reserved for the deepest commitments and beliefs.

Abelard's position must already be plain to the reader. He held that faith, in its essentials, could be approached by way of dialectic reasoning. He was fully prepared to admit that it was founded on revelation, but his temperament drove him to put his trust in the powers of intellect, at least in matters pertaining to what he calls the 'preliminaries of faith'.[7] Truth had been revealed; therefore it should be demonstrable.[8] And this attitude formed the basis of all his teaching.

Bernard, on the other hand, could not have been less rationalistic: 'The reason for loving God is God himself. The measure of that love lies in loving him beyond measure.' Those are the opening words of his treatise *On the Love of God*. For him, love came first – not logic. 'Of all the impulses, attachments and sentiments peculiar to the mind, love alone enables the creature to deal with his Creator, if not on equal terms, at least [with a sense of] offering him something akin to what one is offered . . . When God loves, he has only one wish – to be loved; he loves solely for the sake of being loved, in the knowledge that love will bring happiness to all who love him.'[9]

In Bernard's eyes nothing was of any account compared with this pre-eminence of love; it was on love that all faith was founded: 'No one can seek you unless he or she has already found you. This means that you wish to be found so that you may be sought, sought so that you may be found.'[10] The Word will remain unrevealed to anyone who approaches it without love: 'Love speaks through every line of the *Song of Songs*,' he writes. 'If one wishes to understand what is written therein . . . one must love. Otherwise there would be no point in reading it or listening to the song of love. A cold heart cannot understand words of fire . . .'[11]

It is easy to imagine how horrified such a man must have been by Abelard's methods. He maintained that, by its very nature, faith transcended reason and could not be subjected to the narrow, chilly processes of demonstration.

If one had to encapsulate their respective positions in a single phrase, one might say that Abelard was ever-ready to apply the word 'problem' to what in Bernard's judgement was a 'mystery' – and nothing was more likely to put the latter's back up than hearing the mystery of the Blessed Trinity discussed as if it were some abstract intellectual puzzle. One of his contemporaries, Otto of Freising, records that Bernard 'abhorred those masters who, relying on mere worldly wisdom, leaned too heavily on human reasoning; and if anyone informed him that they were deviating from Christian faith on this or that point, he immediately took note.'[12]

We have no exact record of what passed between Abelard and Bernard in the course of their meetings (for there was more than one), but they are unlikely to have achieved any true 'dialogue'. They were too far apart in their basic attitudes. We may reasonably infer, however, that Bernard was no match in debate for the most brilliant controversialist of the age. Abelard had been trained very early in the art of dialectic and had later imparted some of his own skill to several generations of students; so in this respect he could afford to look down on Bernard with a mixture of pity and contempt. Bernard was no intellectual: 'You will find more in our wilderness than in all your books,' he wrote in his famous letter to Henry Murdach. 'The trees and stones will teach you more than any master.'[13] Not that he despised scholarship; he was a scholar in his own right and was anxious – indeed at times insistent – that priests and religious should be 'learned'.[14] Even when he condemned the practice of acquiring knowledge for its own sake, or of treating it as an asset to be flaunted in front of others, he drew on his own knowledge of Persius and quoted the Roman satirist to good effect: 'Knowing this or that means nothing to you unless you are known to know it.' But he must have felt helpless against the supreme professional skill with which Abelard no doubt defended his theories.

One thing is obvious: these private talks merely served to

heighten the antipathy which already existed between the two men. Shocked as he was by Abelard's views, he took even greater exception to his arrogant manner and bearing: 'Of all the expressions in heaven and earth, there is only one that he condescends not to know – the expression "I know not".'[15] Not for the first time, Peter Abelard had made an enemy by his provocative attitude and his aggressive conceit.

But this particular enemy was to prove exceptionally tenacious. Bernard was now convinced that Abelard was preaching heresy: he might have a thorough knowledge of theology, but that knowledge had been warped by an immoderately humanistic approach: 'This man sweats hard to show that Plato was a Christian, thereby proving that he himself is no better than a pagan.'[16] It horrified Bernard that anyone should treat faith as if it were dependent on reason: 'Thus the human mind takes credit for everything and attributes nothing to faith. It aspires to what is loftier than itself and stares searchingly at what is greater, rushing headlong into the divine mysteries, profaning holy matters rather than explaining them; it does not penetrate to hidden knowledge but merely breaks the seals; and anything that seems unclear is held to be of no account and unworthy of belief.'[17] This evil must be stamped out at once – for the man was a teacher, idolized by his pupils and influencing them at the deepest level.

It was most likely in the weeks immediately after his talks with Abelard that Bernard set to work on his formal refutation – a treatise entitled *Against a Few of Abelard's General Errors*.[18] He may well have started preparing his mind for the task much earlier, at the time of his preliminary discussions with William of Saint-Thierry. Doubtless he had seen the necessity of establishing firmly and clearly that faith was transcendent and based on revelation: 'Our faith is rooted in the might and goodness of God, not in the devisings of our powers of reason.' And his keen irony at Abelard's expense betrays at least a hint of the exasperation which he had felt while under the lash of the schoolman's logic: 'Listen to our theologian: "What is the point of teaching* if the subject at issue cannot be expounded in intelligible terms?" Bedazzling his audience with [his personal grasp] of the most sublime and sacred elements hidden at the core of the Holy Faith, he establishes grades within the Blessed Trinity, degrees of divine glory, computations of eternity.'

Although the sequence of events at this point is none too clear, it seems likely that Abelard's first apology was written in reply to this treatise.† Unfortunately the work has not survived. Its contents are known only from the summary – *Disputatio anonymi abbatis* – which an unnamed abbot drew up for the benefit of a bishop. So far as one can tell, the Apology consisted of a point-by-point rebuttal of the charges levelled in Bernard's treatise. It was vehement in tone, labelling Bernard 'a devil disguised as an angel of light'.

The latent bitterness between the two men, already apparent in Abelard's letter of complaint following Bernard's visit to the nuns at the Paraclete, was suddenly brought into the open, creating a scandal in academic circles. Echoes of that scandal are to be found in the *Disputatio*, as when its anonymous author writes: 'The *Apologia* aggravates [the question of] Abelard's theology. He adds new errors to old, defending them with stubborn sophistry and sinking deeper into heresy.' The time for 'private talks' was over; the quarrel was now public.

Feelings must have run high among the students who still flocked to hear Abelard in the shade of Notre Dame or at the top of the Montagne Sainte-Geneviève. And, as always in those

* For a long time it was generally believed that the *Apologeticum* was composed after Abelard was condemned. Raymond Oursel has established, by means of textual criticism, that it was in fact written earlier. The hostile author of the *Disputatio anonymi abbatis* states that Abelard was still practising as a teacher – which would certainly not have been the case after his condemnation.

† In all, Abelard wrote three works in defence of his views. This was the first. The second – composed, in my opinion, immediately after the Council of Sens – was addressed to Heloise and later quoted in full by Berengar of Poitiers. The third, entitled *Apologia seu fidei confessio*, was unquestionably written at Cluny.

Seal of St Bernard of Clairvaux

The cathedral of Sens, west front

lobe: michaele. hildeburge sctimoniali. Amaltrico. Guille
Gertrude sctimoniali. & p omib; aliis frib; soroub; pare
nefactoub". Quoz nomina dt sctt.

...lus acctie secc Marie arg... silensdru... Anima donin al
...ore p o grex beolac adepto... anime omniu fidi
...ur miseras curba fidel sones... ctor in pace urra
...lor hunc morsu lublarii morr sf edacr... reqescant. Im
...lor aut genure uiuificare queunr... orcar sp'ob sp'n
...ad Ldimer eis cor hair q; dolores... Maslir abbnade la

On this roll, carried round from abbey to abbey, each community
inscribed the names of those who had died since the last visit. The
passage relating to the abbey of Argenteuil is believed to be in the
hand of Heloise

The crypt of the Paraclete, where the tombs of Heloise and
Abelard were discovered

days, rumours of the exchanges spread almost at once to regions far removed from the centre of the dispute; this is borne out by a letter from Canon Hugh Métel of Toul, a notorious wit and busybody who devoted much of his energy to the composition of unsolicited, floridly written epistles with which he hoped to capture the interest of some of his more notable contemporaries. Here was a splendid opportunity for him to meddle in other people's business; he was careful not to let it slip. He had already sent two letters to Heloise. Both were addressed to 'the abbess of immense renown, suckled by the Muses'. The desire for such an exchange appears to have been one-sided, however, and the correspondence went no further. But now, in the year 1140, Hugh Métel was prompt to add his voice to the chorus of abuse against Abelard, reviling him as the son of a Jewess and an Egyptian. These words could have only one meaning at the time – that Abelard was faithful to the letter of the Scriptures through his mother, was unfaithful to their spirit through his father, for Egypt was then regarded as the very embodiment of the pagan spirit. In contrast he saluted Bernard as a true Israelite on both sides of the family, in other words a man whose observance of the Scriptures was total and beyond question. Hugh Métel's letter is unimportant except as evidence of the widespread interest occasioned by the controversy.

The situation was further complicated when a number of highly suspect figures began to gather round Abelard, claiming to be friends or former pupils. Among them was Arnold of Brescia, a hotheaded advocate of religious reform. He was the kind of man who, failing to distinguish between zeal and violence, soon turns into a political agitator. He had whipped up a rebellion among the people of Brescia and urged them, successfully, to drive out their bishop. For this he had been banished from Italy in 1139, at the command of Pope Innocent II. He had then made his way to Paris and re-established contact with Abelard, to whom he owed his intellectual training.

Bernard realized that the matter must be settled; it could only be so at the court of Rome. He did his best to draw the Pope's attention to what he now called heresy, and dedicated the treatise summarizing his charges to him. But the document seems to have made little impression on Innocent, possibly because Abelard – or so he boasted – had powerful friends and protectors at the papal court. So Bernard began a series of letters, one of which was addressed to the Curia as a whole, and the rest to various individual cardinals. These included Guido of Castello, who later became Pope Celestine II. Bernard knew that Guido, who had studied under Abelard, was still on friendly terms with the philosopher; but this did not deter him. 'It would be an insult,' he wrote, 'to suggest that you love anyone so much that you even love his errors; for to love in such a manner is to show that one has not yet learned the right way to love . . .' The letter concludes: 'It is best for the Church of Christ, and indeed best for the man himself, that his voice be stilled.'[19] Another recipient was Stephen of Châlons, who had once been a monk at Clairvaux. Bernard took a sharper tone with him than with Guido: '[Abelard] glories in the thought of having infected the Roman court with this venom of novelty, of having planted his lips in Roman hands and his teachings in Roman hearts, and he seeks protection from the very men who ought to try him and convict him.'[20] He sent letters in the same vein to two former canons regular – Ivo of Saint-Victor and his friend Gerard Caccianemici (later Pope Lucius II): 'Master Peter Abelard, a monk without a monastery and a prelate without an office, adheres to no law and has no rule to restrain him . . . A Herod in the trappings of a John the Baptist . . . he was condemned at Soissons . . . but his new error is even worse than his old.'[21] He likened Abelard to that old enemy of the Church who had seized office as Anacletus II: 'After Peter the Lion (Pierleone) comes Peter the Dragon.'

All these letters were obviously the result of a single burst of activity; they are identical in style and imagery. They must have been dispatched at or around Easter 1140, with the object of putting paid to a controversy which had already dragged on too long for Bernard's liking. Three other letters show every sign of having been written at this same period, but were laid aside. One, addressed to the Pope in person, contains a similar allusion to the lion and the dragon and shrewdly harps on the friendship between Peter Abelard and Arnold of Brescia: 'Master Peter and Arnold, that pest of which you rid Italy, are actively in league against God and his Christ.'[22] The second of these letters was addressed to Chancellor Haimeric of Castres and the third to an abbot whose name is not specified.[23] None of the three was ever finished, for at this point a new development threw Bernard's plans into disarray.

On 2 June, the Octave Day of Whitsun, there was to be a solemn display of relics at Sens. Such ceremonies invariably brought a great mass of people together – nobles, commoners, and churchmen of every rank; this time even young Louis VII had promised to attend. Henry Sanglier, archbishop and metropolitan, would be surrounded by all his suffragans and by abbots and rural deans from every corner of the see. A distinguished gathering, by any standards, and the prospect sparked an idea in Abelard's mind. Why not turn this great assembly into a public forum? Those who attended would be treated to the most spectacular theological joust of the century: Peter Abelard would outline his theories and openly defy Bernard of Clairvaux to refute them. Well pleased with his inspiration, he wrote to the archbishop and begged leave to address the throng. Already he dreamed of a crushing victory that would more than make up for the base intrigues which had toppled him at Soissons twenty years earlier. He would demonstrate how pure his teachings were, how excellent his methods. He had taken his opponent's measure during their private talks together and was confident that he could demolish Bernard in debate. Four years of being idolized by a new generation of Paris students had made him as cocksure as ever. Before the whole world – or at least the world that mattered to him, the world of scholarship – and in the presence of the young king, who was himself a scholar, he would win recognition of his orthodoxy and expose Bernard's unsuccessful attempts to discredit him in Rome.

Henry Sanglier agreed, without apparently giving much thought to the possible consequences of this rather odd request. But he did at least inform Bernard of Clairvaux, who seems to have been somewhat disconcerted by a move which foiled his own bid to have the case tried before the Pope. Sens was not at all the setting which he would have chosen and he dreaded the prospect of a public confrontation with so skilled a wordsmith as Peter Abelard. He made these reservations plain in a letter to Innocent II: 'At [Abelard's] request, the archbishop of Sens has written to me and named a day on which we can meet so that Abelard may defend the propositions which I condemned in his writings. My initial reaction was to refuse. For one thing, he has been a debater from the cradle, just as Goliath was a warrior, and in comparison with him I am merely a child. For another, I felt it was unseemly that the cause of the faith, however unshakable its foundations, should be defended by the feeble arguments of one man. His writings spoke for themselves, I said, and were sufficient grounds for bringing a charge; this trial was none of my business; it was a matter for the bishops, who had a special duty to determine questions of doctrine. But Abelard pressed his demand more forcefully than ever, called his friends together, abused me in letters to his pupils and assured all and sundry that he would meet my objections on the appointed day. At first I paid very little heed to any of this, but in the end I yielded to the advice of my friends, who argued that if I failed to appear I should shock and offend the faithful and give my opponent even more cause to brag.'[24]

Yet, once he had mastered his instinctive reluctance, Bernard prepared for the fray with characteristic thoroughness. He stopped sending letters to Rome and wrote, instead, to members of the French hierarchy, bidding them come to Sens and prove themselves faithful followers of the Church and implacable foes of heresy: 'Wide publicity has been given to a piece of news which must surely have reached you: we have been summoned to Sens for the Octave of Whitsun and challenged to argue in defence of the faith, though by rights a servant of God should not wrangle but rather show patience to everyone. Were the cause his own, your servant might reasonably feel assured of your godly protection; but as this cause is yours – indeed more than yours – I boldly advise, earnestly entreat, that you show yourselves to be true friends in need . . . It is not surprising that we should write to you so suddenly and give you so little notice, for the adversary, with his usual guile and skill, has done his utmost to catch us unawares and leave us defenceless.'[25]

Abelard had leapt at the chance of appearing before a distinguished gathering. It was to be even more distinguished than he had foreseen. For, in response to Bernard's personal summons, eminent churchmen throughout the land prepared to set out for the old city where, some ten years earlier, Henry Sanglier had laid the foundations for a new building that would eventually replace his cathedral, now too small to meet the needs of the archdiocese. In Sens, as at Saint-Denis, a new art was beginning to emerge, an art that combined vigour and logic, the art of the ribbed vault and the flying buttress; in short, the Gothic style was taking shape.

Abelard does not seem to have been very alert to the architectural developments of his day; in the whole of his correspondence there is no indication, however fleeting, that they aroused the slightest intellectual curiosity in him. And yet he surely reached Sens before the main body of worshippers. And as he watched them advancing across the fields – all sorts and conditions of men, some on horseback, others on foot – he must have smiled with satisfaction at the thought that no other philosopher had ever dared dream of such an audience.

Of the suffragans who assisted Henry Sanglier on that Octave Day of Whitsun, the most eminent was Geoffrey of Lèves, bishop of Chartres, who had once been Abelard's pupil and who had remained a true friend to him in good times and bad;

at Soissons he had given him all the support he could. Possibly he had been as disturbed as Bernard by William of Saint-Thierry's letter, but we may reasonably suppose that he retained his confidence in his former mentor. At Geoffrey's side was Bishop Hugh of Auxerre, a close friend of Bernard of Clairvaux. The ceremony was attended by three other bishops from Henry Sanglier's archdiocese: Elias of Orleans, Atto of Troyes, and Manasses of Meaux. Samson of Les Prés, archbishop of Rheims, was accompanied by three of his own suffragans: Alvis of Arras, Geoffrey of Châlons, and Jocelyn of Soissons. Legend has it that, catching sight of Gilbert of La Porrée, the future bishop of Poitiers, Abelard mumbled some twelfth-century equivalent of 'People who live in glass houses shouldn't throw stones'; and, sure enough, Gilbert's writings were consigned to the flames seven years later. The young king was in the cathedral. His party may well have included Count Theobald of Champagne, with whom, at the instigation of Queen Eleanor, he was soon to clash; documents attest that it certainly included Count William of Nevers, a man of great piety who eventually retired to a Carthusian monastery. Yet it was Bernard of Clairvaux and Peter Abelard who were the centres of attention. The latter, we are told, was flanked by his supporters. Arnold of Brescia was presumably among them, and so – beyond all question – was a Roman deacon named Giacinto Buboni who years later became Pope Celestine III and who, in the days ahead, was to prove one of the philosopher's most ardent defenders.

Most of that Sunday, June 2, 1144, was given over to the display of relics and to various religious services. No doubt there were some of those huge processions which were then regarded as symbols of progress towards God during the Christian's life on earth.

But when evening came, Bernard of Clairvaux called a private meeting of prelates and asked them to consider the orthodoxy of the suspect propositions in Abelard's work. By the time the discussion closed, the list compiled by William of

Saint-Thierry had swelled from thirteen to nineteen. It was decided that Peter Abelard should be called to public account next day and obliged either to support his views or to repudiate them. The synod was no longer a forum but a court of law.

'The following day, a large throng gathered in the cathedral. The servant of God [Bernard] laid Master Peter's writings before the assembly and denounced the erroneous propositions contained in them. The philosopher was given the right either to deny that these propositions were to be found in his works, or to amend them in a spirit of humility, or to reply, if he could, not only to the refutations which had been advanced but to the testimony of the Fathers of the Church. But Peter refused to comply. Powerless to combat the wisdom and intelligence of his accuser, he appealed to the Holy See . . . Although urged . . . to answer without fear and in whatever way he chose . . . he stubbornly refused to speak.'[26]

There was general consternation at this dramatic turnabout: Peter Abelard had withdrawn from a duel which he himself had provoked. Admittedly, he had never expected to be cast in the role of defendant. As soon as he realized that the debate had turned into a trial, he refused to take part.

None of his contemporaries offers a satisfactory explanation. Geoffrey of Auxerre refers to the suggestion that Abelard came over faint: 'Afterwards, or so they claim, he told his friends that at that moment his memory deserted him completely. His brain had clouded, his thoughts had lost all direction.' The theory has been taken up in our own day and related to other circumstances in life which reveal his nervous sensibility. The medical explanations that have been advanced appear convincing. In the light of various items of information given by Geoffrey of Auxerre and Peter the Venerable, Dr Jeannin[27] has concluded that Abelard was suffering from Hodgkin's disease – a leukaemia-like condition causing chronic inflammation of the skin. The fainting fit can be seen as a classic symptom of the accompanying general weakness. None the less, one may reasonably suspect that there was more to this incident than physical weakness. Giacinto Buboni, or one of his other friends, may well have warned him of what had happened at the meeting the night before.

At all events, Abelard announced his intention of appealing to the Pope and promptly walked out of the cathedral, leaving the onlookers to draw their own conclusions. The prelates had no choice but to wind up the proceedings as best they could. They then went into secret session again. The nineteen propositions were raked over, reduced to fourteen, and forwarded to Rome for arbitration.

In his letter to the Pope, Henry Sanglier commented: 'Although this appeal is not strictly canonical (for no man is allowed to appeal against the judgement of a court which he has chosen of his own free will), respect for the Holy See has deterred us from passing sentence on Abelard. As for his false principles, which had been exposed several times in public, and which the abbot of Clairvaux – basing his arguments on rational proof and on passages from St Augustine and other Fathers – had demonstrated to be false, indeed heretical, we had already condemned them on the eve of this appeal.'

Henry's tone betrays not only the prelates' astonishment at Abelard's volte-face, but their embarrassment at having to refer to the Holy See a case which they had already tried.

Bernard of Clairvaux, however, was quick to adjust to the new situation. He began a fresh series of letters to Rome. First he sent Innocent II a full account of the affair, giving free rein to that fearsome verve which possessed him whenever he felt that the Church or Truth was in danger: 'It is Goliath himself advancing, arrogant, majestically girt for battle, preceded by his squire, Arnold of Brescia. The scales of their armour are so closely interlocked that even the air cannot penetrate. The bee of France has buzzed the bee of Italy. They have marched side by side against God and his Christ . . . He insults the doctors of the Church and heaps praises on the philosophers, preferring their inventions and novelties to the teachings of the Fathers, to faith. All men flee at the sight of him – yet he challenges me,

the puniest of all, to single combat . . . It is for you, the
Apostle's successor, to judge. You must consider whether he
who assails Peter's faith should find sanctuary beside Peter's
throne . . .'[28] And the last paragraph of this letter contains an
echo of the bickerings which must have marred the delibera-
tions: 'Giacinto showed us considerable ill-will, though not so
much as he would have wished – he did not have time. I felt,
however, that I should suffer him in silence, for . . . he spared
neither yourself nor your Curia.'[29]

The letters held over from his previous correspondence were
now sent off. The postscripts contained similar accounts of the
zeal with which Giacinto Buboni had defended Abelard.
Bernard was determined to have his say first, before Abelard
had a chance to undermine opinion in Rome. He composed
three new letters to individual cardinals, giving them notice of
the philosopher's appeal. It was imperative that the Vatican
ratify the assembly's verdict.

Meanwhile the throng dispersed. They all went back to their
homes or monasteries or dioceses, retailing what they had seen
and heard. Many of them felt cheated, for this was an age when
people relished a verbal duel, especially of the kind which had
so nearly taken place in Sens between two redoubtable
adversaries. Abelard was the most famed philosopher of his
time, Bernard the most influential preacher. Even today his
sermons, when read, convey something of the inspired vigour
which had the power to move whole congregations. Unfortunately we no longer have the text of the blazing exhortations which were to re-echo among the hills near Vézelay four
years later, but we know that they persuaded most of his
listeners to go on the Second Crusade.

Yet although the clash between Abelard and Bernard had
never fully materialized, it still left its mark upon the age. The
extent to which Abelard, the father of scholasticism, prefigured
the triumph of Gothic architecture has already been pointed
out by other authors. Cottiaux, for instance, writes: 'The many
and varied aspects of his thought are self-supporting, like those

ribbed vaults which he saw being built according to an entirely
new principle.' To understand Bernard, on the other hand, we
must meditate on Cistercian architecture and on the capacity for
renewal which it derives from its very plainness. The depth and
intensity of his reforms are mirrored in the buildings at Le
Thoronet and Sénanque, at Pontigny and Fontenay. His refusal
to make any concession to opulence, to embellishment, to any
of those things which charm the eye and lull the brain, had
revitalized romanesque art, awakening all its pristine energy.
The churches which he had inspired were not the fruit of
rational deliberation; they asserted their right to existence and
recognition in much the same manner as the transcendency of
faith. Their unadorned capitals and uncompromising arches
attest more powerfully than any words to the inner drive from
which they stemmed. Bernard of Clairvaux was the man who
had sacrificed everything, beginning with himself, to the
purity of that inner drive. His treatment of Abelard may seem
harsh, and some people have been shocked by the remorseless-
ness with which he carried on the fight against him; but his
severity in this matter is the same severity which had impelled
him to banish all superfluous decoration from his buildings, to
impose a truly austere rule on his monasteries, and to uphold
the integrity of the faith against all comers.

Yet undeniably many different views have been taken of
Bernard's attitude. This was so even in his own day. In the
schools, the issues raised at Sens gave rise to many heated
arguments. Students took sides and each defended his champion
with the utmost passion. The mood of the time can be gathered
from one of Abelard's own students, Berengar of Poitiers; he
had not attended the convocation, but this did not deter him
from painting a spirited picture of events or from launching a
violent attack on Bernard of Clairvaux. 'We were hoping,' he
writes, 'that in your words of judgement we should find the
clemency of heaven itself, the serenity of the air, the fertility of
the soil, the blessed abundance of the fruitcrops. Your head
seemed to touch the clouds and . . . your branches put even the

mountains in the shade . . . But now – woe! – you have shown your fangs . . . You chose Peter Abelard as your target. You spewed your venomous spite upon him . . . Before the bishops from far and wide . . . you declared him a heretic. You had bidden the ordinary members of the congregation pray to God for him, yet in your heart you were planning to excommunicate him. How could they pray properly when they did not even know what they were praying for?' And he goes on to describe a scene at which he had obviously not been present, the meeting of prelates held on the night of 2 June. We are asked to believe that after the bishops and abbots had finished dining, Bernard sent for Master Peter's works, and in the midst of a veritable orgy, read out a few cunningly selected passages and persuaded the gathering that Abelard must be condemned, without encountering a word of dissent. 'Anyone who had seen those pontiffs laughing, jesting, aiming kicks and hurling abuse might well have concluded that they owed their vows not to Christ but to Bacchus. All this while the bottles were circulating. The prelates swigged, appraised, drank their fill.' By the end, alleges Berengar, some were three-parts asleep, others were helplessly wagging their heads, and others kept saying thickly: 'Let us condemn, let us damn.' The entire letter was written in the same vein. Coming immediately after Abelard's condemnation, it can hardly have helped rally support to him. A few years later Berengar repudiated the composition, dismissing it as the work of a beardless youth. Nevertheless, it mirrors some of the indignation felt at the time. Above all, it preserves the text of an invaluable document which would otherwise have been lost to us: the apologia which Abelard addressed to Heloise.

For after leaving the cathedral Abelard decided that he must go straight to Rome and argue his own case there. But first he had a duty to fulfil, for he knew that Heloise must be desperately worried about him. She and her nuns were obviously aware of what went on at Sens. Their convent was barely a day's journey from the city. By 4 June at latest, therefore, she would know that Abelard had been condemned after refusing to answer the charges brought against him. No one, surely, can have followed all the stages of this controversy with as much alarm and concern as she. Was she now to be left in uncertainty? Must she apply the term 'heretic' to the man who had saved her community from disintegration and prescribed its rule, the man whose ideas had been the basis of all her own thinking? Abelard was well aware that she would have been willing, if necessary, to declare herself a heretic too. And for her he composed something which Bernard of Clairvaux had failed to elicit: a profession of faith as clear and unequivocal as the most demanding censor could have wished:

'Heloise, my sister, once so dear to me in the world, today even dearer to me in Jesus Christ, logic has made me abhorrent in the eyes of the world. Those corrupt corruptors whose wisdom is perdition say that, though a master of logic, I cannot fathom St Paul. Although acknowledging the penetrative power of my genius, they will not accept the purity of my Christian faith. In this respect, I feel that they exhibit the judgement of people misled by opinion rather than taught by experience.

'I have no wish to be a philosopher if it means rebelling against Paul. I have no wish to be Aristotle if it means severing myself from Christ, for it is in his name, and none other under heaven, that I must find my salvation. I adore Christ ruling at the right hand of the Father, I embrace him with the arms of faith when, divinely, he performs glorious works in a sinless human form conceived by the Holy Spirit. And, so that any concern or uncertainty may be banished from the heart that beats within your breast, I want to assure you personally that I have founded my conscience upon the rock whereon Christ built his Church. Here, in brief, is the inscription it bears.

'I believe in Father, Son and Holy Spirit, God by nature One, true God in whom Unity of Substance is unimpaired by Trinity of Persons. I believe that the Son is equal to the Father in all things, in eternity, in might, in will and in the exercise of power . . . I attest that the Holy Spirit is in every respect equal to, and consubstantial with, the Father and the Son; indeed I refer to him frequently in my books, calling him Lovingkindness . . . I further believe that the Son of God became the Son of Man in such a way that one Person consists and subsists in two natures. Having met all the demands of the human condition which he had assumed, even unto death itself, he rose again and ascended into heaven, whence he shall come to judge the quick and the dead. Finally I affirm that all sins are remitted in baptism, that we have need of Grace if we are to begin or complete good things, and that those who have erred are reformed by penance. As for the resurrection of the body, need I discuss it? In vain would I delude myself that I was a Christian if I did not believe that I shall one day rise again.

'Such is the faith to which I adhere and from which my hope derives its strength. Secure in this haven, I fear neither Scylla's bark nor Charybdis's vortex nor the fatal songs of the sirens. Let the storm break, it will not disturb me. Let the winds blow, they will not budge me. I am founded on firm rock.'

Any doubts in Heloise's mind must have been dispelled at once by this overwhelming profession of faith. And nothing could be more indicative of the new depth and closeness of her relationship with Abelard during the last phase of his life. After the Council of Soissons he had felt no need to open his heart to her, even though their love affair was then much closer in time; he had withdrawn from her completely and reasserted himself as the philopher, the intellectual, the solitary . . . But recently – by making him remember and give heed to her, by pressing him for hymns and sermons and letters of guidance – she had brought out the best in him, so that at last he was ready to forget logic and proclaim: 'I have no wish to be a philosopher if it means rebelling against Paul. I have no wish to be Aristotle if it means severing myself from Christ.' Surely these words, which put paid for ever to all ambiguity and misunderstanding, would not have been written had it not been for the presence of Heloise.

Vere Jerusalem est illa civitas
Cujus pax jugis est, summa jucunditas,
Ubi non prevenit rem desiderium
Nec desiderio minus est premium . . .

Nostrum est interim mentem erigere
Et totis patriam votis appetere
Et ad Jerusalem a Babylonia
Post longa regredi tandem exsilia.

Illic molestiis finitis omnibus
Securi cantica Sion cantabimus
Et juges gratias de donis gratie
Beata referet plebs tibi, Domine.

City of peace perpetual,
The ultimate in bliss,
Such is the true Jerusalem
Where highest pleasure is.
For there the heart's desire cannot
Outrun the boon required,
And the reward is never less
Than what the heart desired . . .

Meanwhile we lift up minds and hearts
And strive to reach anon
Jerusalem, our goal, from long
Exile in Babylon.

There all our sorrows have an end
As Zion's songs we sing,
Rendering grace for gifts of grace
For ever to our King.

> Abelard: *O quanta qualia*

The next day Peter Abelard set out for Rome. The hot June days were lengthening, and so were the stages of a journey that carried him ever farther from Sens. In Rome he would lay his writings before the Pope and secure recognition of their orthodoxy; better still, he would make the Curia realize the importance and usefulness of his methods, which provided a rational basis for the Church's teachings. He was determined to succeed. Bernard may have hoodwinked the French bishops, but in Rome he would be free to argue his case freely, and he knew that a number of cardinals were already in sympathy with him.

He rode along the valley of the Yonne and the Cure; he came to the Morvan mountains and their stormy foothills, where an occasional gap affords a distant view of the Saône plain; and finally he saw the seven towers of Cluny abbey rising in the golden evening from the Grosne valley. The abbey itself was surrounded by a vast complex of conventual buildings, mills, cottages, gardens, workshops, chapels, all bearing witness to the prosperity of this monastic town. Two centuries earlier, in the worst days of Carolingian decay, when the Normans were free to plunder wherever they chose and the south was left exposed to the 'Saracen terror', Cluny had imposed its law – the law of peace – on a world entirely dominated by force. By restoring monasteries, reclaiming arable lands and spreading the word each time a monk went on pilgrimage, Cluny had re-established pacific institutions. Above all, it had upheld the right of asylum. One of its abbots had set a striking example by personally opening its gates to the hunted killers of his own father and brother.

When Peter Abelard presented himself at the hospice he was

only one of a large crowd of pilgrims, travellers and other members of that assorted band of wanderers who liked to take to the road in summer. He announced his name, and immediately there was a good deal of hasty coming and going inside the monastery. Yet to imagine that he was about to be treated as an outcast would be to misconstrue entirely the nature of Cluny's hospitality. His identity made no difference, except that the monks felt it might be as well to inform the abbot, Peter the Venerable.

The abbot, often called away on official business, happened to be in residence. On hearing the visitor's name, he did not think in general terms of the celebrated philosopher or the theologian condemned by his peers; for him, this was the answer to two letters which he had sent twenty years earlier, soon after the Council of Soissons. The moment for which he had waited with 'burning patience'* had come at last. 'I shall welcome you as a son,' he had written. It was time to keep a promise which he had never retracted.

And he kept it, with infinite tact. His behaviour at this crucial juncture emerges plainly from the letters which he wrote and from the subsequent pattern of events, all of which centred on Cluny. Not a word about the past, not a line of reproach or mistrust. 'Master Peter . . . recently passed through Cluny on his way from France. We asked him where he was going. He replied that, exasperated by the antics of people who, to his horror, sought to depict him as a heretic, he had appealed to the Apostolic See and hoped to find refuge there. We applauded his intention and advised him to lose no time in reaching a place which is known to us all as a secure haven.'[30] Welcome, listen, encourage: that was his policy. It was with good reason that Peter the Venerable was regarded by his contemporaries as the embodiment of kindness. He must have known what had happened at Sens; he may even have been asked to attend. But at a glance he had gauged the physical and mental dilapidation

* The expression was minted by Pastor Roger Schutz, who has revived the work and spirit of Peter the Venerable at a point not far from Cluny.

of the old man who had come knocking at his door. The first need of anyone who has failed to get a hearing is sympathetic attention. The abbot of Cluny let him outline his plans and quietly encouraged him to go ahead. He added a word of counsel: Peter Abelard ought to take a few days' rest here at Cluny, while he himself would inform the Pope of the decision.

Abelard took this advice. And almost at once he sagged beneath the burden of fatigue, of all the tension of recent weeks, of a lifetime's violent emotions and strenuous ordeals; suddenly he came to an end of that astonishing energy which had kept him going till now, of that blind obduracy which had prevented him from appreciating the sheer length of a journey which was beyond his powers, the futility of an appeal to Rome which the Pope was sure to reject.

It was Peter the Venerable who had introduced the feast of the Transfiguration into the western liturgy. For centuries the Eastern Church had solemnly commemorated the event on August 6; the same date was adopted by Rome, and Peter composed a very beautiful proper for the occasion. And indeed one of the most extraordinary things about him was his power to 'transfigure', or at least transform, anyone with whom he came in contact. In the past he too had clashed violently with Bernard of Clairvaux. The Cluniacs and Cistercians were renowned for their squabbling. Yet in answer to Bernard's reformist promptings Peter revised the statutes of his order, introducing new regulations inspired by the Cistercian rule. When he found that the old rivalries persisted even after this measure, he reasoned that it might be better if the two sides got to know each other better. At his suggestion Cluniac priors spent part of each year in Cistercian abbeys, and vice versa.

But it was to be Abelard who provided the most striking example of this power to transform. For Peter, through his kindness, extracted what no one else had ever succeeded in obtaining: a complete renunciation, a total conversion. Afterwards Abelard showed no further sign of the hubris which had

209

marred too many of his deeds and actions. At Cluny, for the very first time, his combativeness melted like wax in the flame. And, having found the right setting at last after such a chaotic life, he ended his days as a self-effacing monk, indistinguishable from the rest, fervent in private prayer and always early at chapel.

In this extraordinary recovery from what had seemed a hopeless situation, the hand of Peter the Venerable is apparent at every stage. In his letter to the Pope he wrote: 'At this juncture the lord abbot of Cîteaux arrived and discussed with ourselves and [Abelard] the possibility of making peace between [Abelard] and the lord abbot of Clairvaux, who had occasioned [Abelard's] appeal. We likewise did our utmost to re-establish peace and urged [Abelard] to go and see [Bernard] in the company of the lord abbot of Cîteaux. We went on to advise that if he had written or spoken words offensive to Catholic ears he should agree, if so bidden by the lord abbot of Cîteaux or other wise and upright persons, to refrain from them henceforth in speech and then erase them from his writings. And so it transpired. He went, he came back, and on his return he told us that, thanks to the lord abbot of Cîteaux, he had renounced his previous protests and made his peace with the lord abbot of Clairvaux.'[31] The first major hurdle had been cleared: Abelard was no longer at odds with Bernard. From whom, in fact, had the initiative come? It would seem that the abbot of Cîteaux, Reginald of Bar-sur-Seine, arrived without being expressly summoned. Could Bernard himself have sent him, after hearing that Abelard was staying at Cluny? It is perfectly feasible. A few years later, in 1148, he asked John of Salisbury to arrange a private interview with Gilbert of La Porrée. He took this step soon after securing Gilbert's condemnation. Gilbert refused haughtily. Abelard, on the other hand, agreed. In both cases Bernard may have wanted a quiet man-to-man meeting which would dispel any personal bitterness caused by a measure which, in his view, had been necessary for the well-being of the Church.[32]

At all events, a reconciliation had been effected between the two. Furthermore, Abelard agreed to make a complete profession of faith concerning the articles condemned at Sens. This, the last of his apologiae, was addressed to 'all the sons of Holy Church' by 'Peter Abelard, one of their number, though the least among them'. Patiently, dealing point by point with the objections contained in the longest list – the one drawn up by William of Saint-Thierry and increased to nineteen by the hierarchy at Sens – he proclaimed his total adherence to the Church's teachings. When he felt obliged to correct errors of interpretation, he did so without a trace of rancour. 'May you, in your brotherly love,' he wrote, 'acknowledge me as a son of the Church who desires to receive in full all that she has received and to reject all that she has rejected, and who – although inferior to the rest in moral fibre – has never intended to depart from unity of faith.'[33]

News of his final condemnation may have reached him at this time, for his appeal was turned down in July 1140, only a few weeks after the Council of Sens. An examination of the letters setting forth the terms of the propositions extracted from Abelard's writings was sufficient to decide Innocent: 'Having taken the advice of our brother bishops and cardinals, we condemn the items garnered by your good offices and all the perverse doctrines of Peter [Abelard] together with the author himself, and we sentence him, as a heretic, to perpetual silence.'[34]

In a second letter, written the same day, the Pope ordered that 'Peter Abelard and Arnold of Brescia, fabricators of evil dogmas and assailers of the Catholic faith, be separately confined in whatever religious houses seem most suitable, and that their books be burnt wherever they may be found.' Abelard's works were ceremoniously burnt in St Peter's.

But Peter the Venerable had foreseen the verdict, and in his tactfully worded letter informing the Pope of Abelard's arrival at Cluny he had implanted the idea that punishment should be tempered with compassion: ' "Papal impartiality," we told

[Abelard], "has never been denied to anybody, not even to a stranger or a pilgrim; it will not pass you by." Indeed we promised him that he would find mercy too, should it be needed . . .' He went on to suggest how the situation might be solved: 'In accordance with our advice – but prompted rather, we feel, by some divine inspiration – he decided to renounce the noise and bustle of the schools and settle permanently [here at] Cluny. Such a decision seemed appropriate to his age, frailty and religious profession; and mindful of the fact that his scholarship, which is not entirely unknown to you, might benefit the community, we acceded to his wish. Subject to your kind approval, therefore, we have gladly and unreservedly given him permission to remain with us . . .

'So I – who, whatever else I may be, am at least yours – entreat you; this monastery of Cluny, which is utterly devoted to you, entreats you; Peter [Abelard] himself entreats you [. . .]: graciously ordain that he end his days, which may now be few, in your house at Cluny and that no authority drive or summon him from the home where this stray sparrow is so happy to have found a nest. Mindful of the honour with which you surround all men of goodwill, and of the love which you yourself have felt for him, graciously shield him with your apostolic protection.'35

The sentence imposed on Abelard took exactly the form which Peter the Venerable had planned. The 'heretic' found a gentle haven at Cluny. The 'stray sparrow', at long last reconciled to God and to his fellow men, entered a final phase which neither he nor anyone else, surely, can have foreseen. And subsequently Peter the Venerable had no difficulty in getting the canonical sanctions lifted so that Abelard was free to teach again. He knew that his guest had always felt lost without an audience, and it gladdened his heart that the monks should be taught by such a master.

Visitors to Cluny are usually shown a lime tree, several hundred years old, whose massive trunk stands at the far end of the avenue leading away from the flour store – one of the few parts of the great abbey to survive the early nineteenth century, when the estate agents who had acquired the site during the revolution tore the edifice down for the sake of the quick profit which they could make by selling the stone. According to tradition, Abelard used often to rest in the shade of this tree 'with his face turned towards the Paraclete'. Centuries later, Lamartine rested there too as he brooded on the work which he planned to devote to the scholar monk. And indeed, before it fell victim to the money-grubbing stupidity of a bourgeois civilization at its height, there were few places better suited to meditation. One would have difficulty in believing that Abelard, the ever-restless, the ever-tormented, spent many of his last days in these peaceful surroundings, were it not for the unimpeachable evidence of Peter the Venerable.

'Everyone at Cluny,' he writes, 'can bear witness to the edifying life, full of humility and piety, which he led here in our midst, and one cannot hope to depict it in the space of a few words. I do not think I have ever seen his equal for humbleness of bearing and attire . . . I invited him to take first place in our large flock, but his shabby clothes always seemed to suggest that he was the last and least member of the community. It often surprised, indeed astounded me, during processions, when he and the other brothers were walking ahead of me in order of precedence, that the bearer of so great and famous a name should humble and abase himself to this extent . . . Modest in dress, he made do with the simplest robe, aspiring to nothing beyond basic essentials. And it was the same with eating, drinking and all other bodily needs. Anything that was super-fluous, anything that was not utterly indispensable, he con-demned by word and example, whether for himself or for others. He was tireless in his reading, assiduous in prayer, and persistently silent except when forced to speak either by friendly questions from the brothers or by general discussions about holy matters. He used to approach the sacraments, offering the sacrifice of the immortal lamb to God as often as he could – indeed almost continually once, through my letter of mediation, he had been restored to favour with the Holy See. What else can I add? His thoughts, words and deeds were ceaselessly devoted to meditation, teaching and the elucidation of sacred, philosophical and scholarly things.'

Having wrought this change in Abelard, Peter continued to follow his progress as solicitously as ever. And yet how many other demands there were on his time! The years 1140–1 saw the fulfilment of one of his greatest projects: the translation of the Koran. This courteous interest in other faiths was typical of the man. He had already commissioned a translation of the Talmud and was the first Christian leader to acquaint himself properly with Islamic beliefs and impart them to his contemporaries. His exertions made it possible for all priests connected with the crusades to preach with a first-hand knowledge of the Koran. Not until our own day has there been a comparable concern with mutual understanding. He made every effort to ensure that the enterprise was brought to fruition in the best possible circumstances. He assembled what we would nowadays call a 'panel', consisting of two learned clerks – Robert of Ketene, from England, and Hermann the Dalmatian, from Carinthia – a Mozarab, Peter of Toledo, and a Saracen named Mohammed. The task of revising and co-ordinating the translation was entrusted to a first-rate Latin scholar, Peter of Poitiers. In his preface, Peter the Venerable hastened to assure the Moslems that he came bearing words, not weapons; that he dealt in reason, not force; that he was prompted by love, not hatred.

This outlook may have been an important link between him and Abelard. One of the latter's favourite themes was that even the pagans benefited from the effect of Christ's Redemption. He argued that the upright lives led by the great philosophers of Greece and Rome – Seneca, Epicurus, Pythagoras, Plato – were ample proof of this assertion. Moreover, it was generally believed in the twelfth century that the sibyls had foretold the Saviour's coming; Abelard reasoned that by so doing they had to some extent shared in the mystery of the Incarnation. He also spoke highly of the Brahmans. This may seem startling, but he and his contemporaries were at least vaguely familiar with the religious beliefs of the Far East. *Imago mundi* by Honorius of Autun, for instance, mentions the fact that some oriental sages 'hurl themselves into the flames for love of the world beyond'.

Peter's involvement in the enormous task of translating the Koran often took him away from Cluny. And so, of course, did his administrative duties. During his years as abbot he founded no fewer than three hundred and fourteen new monasteries, bringing the total number of daughter-houses to over two thousand. Yet he still found time to keep a close, discreet, personal watch on Abelard.

And Abelard himself was soon at work again. It was at Cluny, probably, that he made the final revisions to his *Dialectica*, a composition which the manuscripts indicate was several times laid aside and returned to; he dedicated it to his nephews. In addition, he wrote – or at least completed – his intellectual and spiritual testament: the long poem, composed in distichs, which he bequeathed to his son Astrolabe. Another work which would certainly appear to have been written at this time was his commentary on the six days of Creation, *Expositio in Hexaemeron*. He began it at the specific request of Heloise, and in the preface he addresses her in similar terms to those used at the beginning of his profession of faith: 'Heloise, my sister, once so dear to me in the world and now very dear to me in Christ.' The commentary covers the whole of the first chapter of Genesis, but it ends abruptly and inconclusively – as if this were the moment when his powers finally deserted him.

In his last months he was seriously troubled by illness – probably Hodgkin's disease, as noted already. Peter the Venerable decided that he should be moved to even quieter and more relaxed surroundings, a place with a smaller community and fewer visitors. The abbot chose Saint-Marcel-de-

Chalon, on the banks of the Saône, describing it as one of the most beautiful areas of Burgundy.

The priory stood on the site of a much earlier cloister, built as long ago as 584 in the Merovingian era; it was the first institution to be modelled on the ancient monastery of Saint-Maurice d'Augane, where the office known as *laus perennis*, or 'perpetual praise', was sung throughout the day and night by three alternating choirs. This practice, derived from the Eastern Church, must have died out amid the invasions and unrest which marked the end of the early Middle Ages.

Thus it was at Saint-Marcel-de-Chalon, in this house of 'perpetual praise', that Peter Abelard spent the final days of his life. 'There,' writes Peter the Venerable, 'resuming his studies in so far as his health would permit, he was forever bent over his books. Like St Gregory the Great, he could never let a moment go by without praying, reading, writing or dictating. It was in the exercise of these godly pursuits that the Visitor foretold by the Gospel found him.' He died on April 21, 1142. He was then about sixty-three years old.

Peter the Venerable might reasonably have considered his task at an end, but in his mind Abelard and Heloise were still one. She had already been informed of the death by a monk named Theobald; but on his first 'trouble-free day' (to quote his own expression) after returning to Cluny, Peter himself wrote to Heloise. He knew exactly, from Abelard's confidences, what manner of woman he was dealing with. He knew of the unrestrained love which had once burned within her and of the secret fear and remorse from which she still suffered – for this seemingly poised and perfect abbess was convinced that the sacrifice which she had made in taking the veil could mean nothing to God since she had not made it for his sake, but for the sake of the man whom she loved.

Peter could have confined himself to a formal letter of condolence; he could have taken the easy way out and, in the name of discretion, avoided all reference to the past; or again, for fear of the hidden complexities of the feminine mind, he could have appended his signature to a few vague exhortations. But his letter to Heloise obeyed none of the promptings of human wariness; it measured up to the exalted, uncompromising, self-forgetful love of this exceptional man and woman.

The early part of the letter is concerned entirely with Heloise herself. Peter reminds her of the great admiration which he had felt for her in his early years. His choice of language is true to the spirit of this century of courtly love: 'I wanted to show you the place I had reserved in my heart for the affection which I bear you in Christ Jesus. And this is no recent affection: it goes back almost as far as I can remember.' Next come pages extolling her high intelligence and the thirst for knowledge which she had displayed even as a young girl. 'Later,' he continues, 'when he who had singled you out at your mother's breast was pleased to call you to him by means of his grace, you chose a new and better path of study: a truly philosophical woman, you renounced logic in favour of the Gospel, physics in favour of the Apostle, Plato in favour of Christ, Academe in favour of the cloister.' He then praises her skill and determination in bringing the members of her community ever closer to God: 'I do not say this in order to flatter you, my very dear sister in Our Lord, but as a way of urging you to safeguard and bring to full fruition the admirable high endeavours in which you have long been engaged, so that by word and example you may fire . . . the hearts of the holy women who join you in serving the Lord . . . Like a lamp, you must both burn and illumine. You are a disciple of truth; yet at the same time, by virtue of the onerous role entrusted to you, you are mistress of humility.' He likens her to Penthesilea, queen of the Amazons, and to Deborah, prophetess and judge of Israel. Alluding tactfully to his knowledge of Hebrew, he recalls that the name Deborah means 'bee': 'You will amass a rich hoard of honey . . . Having gathered so many juices from a variety of flowers, you will instil them, by word and example and every

possible means, into the hearts of the women of your house –
and of other women, too.'

The words were a forceful reminder that Heloise had her
own life to lead and serious obligations to meet. Although
Abelard was dead, she must not succumb to the temptation to
dwell in the past; her life was far from over. She had committed all her energies to the service of her convent, and nothing
must be allowed to sap them. This was the reality she must
cling to. The rest was of no account.

Confident that he had by now reawakened Heloise's courage,
her sense of responsibility, and all her other positive virtues,
Peter added a personal note of regret: 'How it would delight
me to hold longer converse with you, for I am captivated by
your erudition and attracted, above all, by the many words of
praise which I have heard about your piety. Would to heaven
that our own abbey of Cluny had claimed you! Would to
heaven that you were among those handmaidens of Christ who
await their heavenly freedom in the captivity of that charming
house at Marcigny!' Marcigny was a convent especially dear to
Peter the Venerable's heart. His mother, Raingarde, had taken
the veil there, and so had two of his nieces.

Only after dealing with the situation now confronting
Heloise herself did he turn to Abelard: 'Divine Providence, the
dispenser of all things, may have denied us the advantages of
your presence, but at least we were accorded that of the man
who belongs at your side, the great man whom one need not
hesitate to call, respectfully, the servant and true philosopher of
Christ – Master Peter.'

'The man who belongs at your side . . .' It seems odd to find
such a phrase in a letter from an abbot to an abbess. One cannot
help thinking of the guarded terms which would be used in a
similar situation today. But sanctimoniousness was an invention of the seventeenth century. This sturdy simplicity, on the
other hand, belongs unmistakably to the same era as St
Bernard's uninhibited tone and language. Moreover, the words
had a specific root in reality: Heloise had asked Peter for

Abelard's body so that he might, as he had wished, be buried at the Paraclete. No one could have been quicker to grasp the full import of the request. At the end of his letter the abbot wrote: 'The man to whom you were united by the bonds of the flesh, and later by the stronger and more enduring bonds of divine love, the man with whom and at whose bidding you dedicated yourself to God's service – that man, I say, is today in God's bosom, being comforted in your stead, or rather as another you. And on the day of the Lord's coming, when the Archangel shall speak and the trumpet-blast proclaim the sovereign Judge as he descends from heaven, he shall mercifully restore him to you; he is keeping him for you.' According to Peter, God himself had become the guarantor and protector of the relationship which Abelard and Heloise had forged. Far from feeling that she was the target of reproof, she could rest assured that God was watching over her beloved on the far side of death.[36]

One task had still to be performed, however, and Peter the Venerable insisted on attending to it himself – the task of transferring Abelard's remains to a site doubly dear to him. The body was quietly removed from the cemetery at Saint-Marcel-de-Chalon and taken to the modest chapel which the philosopher and his pupils had built beside the banks of the Ardusson. This first meeting between Heloise and Peter the Venerable took place on 16 November, presumably in the year 1142. He said Mass, delivered an address to the assembled community, and established a 'spiritual coupling' between Cluny and the Paraclete, such a step being quite usual in the Middle Ages. Afterwards Heloise wrote to him and expressed her heartfelt thanks: 'It is a joy to us, excellent Father, that Your Lordship should have stooped to our low estate and we glory in the memory, for a visit from you is a source of joy even to the greatest. The others know how many blessings Your Lordship's presence brought them. As for me, I am incapable of expressing, or indeed conceiving, the boon and balm of your visit.' The rest of her letter contained three requests. She asked

Peter to have a series of thirty Masses said at Cluny Abbey after her death. She further asked him to draw up a general absolution of Peter Abelard and set his seal to it, so that she could hang the parchment from the tombstone; she was anxious that people should see, with their own eyes, that the brilliant teacher whose faith had for a while been called in question was now fully reconciled to God. Finally she asked him to ensure that their son, Peter Astrolabe, obtained 'some prebend from the bishop of Paris or any other diocese'.

This letter is her last surviving document. Although written many years before her death, it reads almost as if it were intended as her last will and testament. Significantly, she now cares nothing for herself and Abelard except in regard to their spiritual well-being. Her concern for Astrolabe is not without interest, either. We know nothing about him: his life was as obscure as the lives of his parents were notorious. Reference to the documents and cartularies of the time has proved exceptionally unhelpful. We find a certain Astrolabe presiding over the abbey of Hauterive, in the Swiss canton of Fribourg, between the years 1162 and 1165. Were Hauterive a Cluniac monastery, one's immediate impulse – especially in view of the uncommonness of the name – would be to suppose that this was indeed Peter the Venerable's spiritual son (Heloise herself hints at such a relationship by calling him '*your* Peter Astrolabe'). But in fact Hauterive was a Cistercian abbey and there seems little likelihood that the man whom we are seeking would have become a Cistercian. A more probable theory is that he became a canon at Nantes Cathedral; the cartulary of a church at Buzé, in Brittany, includes an Astrolabe in the list of canons holding office in 1150 and states that he was the nephew of another canon named Porchaire, who may have been Abelard's brother. The necrology found at the Paraclete records that '*Petrus Astrolabius magistri nostri Petri filius*' died on 29 or 30 October, but the year is not given, nor is there any indication of the dead man's calling.

The same necrology is almost equally terse about the death

of Heloise herself: 'Heloise, first abbess and mother of our religious order, renowned for her learning and piety, having given us hope by her life, blissfully rendered up her soul to the Lord.' The entry is dated 16 May, but here again the year is not specified. Cross-reference and deduction suggest that it was 1164; in which case she survived Abelard by twenty years and died, as he did, at the age of sixty-three.

EPILOGUE

So God created man in his own image, in the image of
God created he him; male and female he created them.

– Genesis i 27

When from the censer clouds of fragrance roll,
And swelling organs lift the rising soul,
One thought of thee puts all the pomp to flight,
Priests, tapers, temples, swim before my sight:
In seas of flame my plunging soul is drown'd,
While altars blaze, and angels tremble round . . .
Come, if thou dar'st, all charming as thou art!
Oppose thyself to heaven; dispute my heart;
Come, with one glance of those deluding eyes
Blot out each bright idea of the skies;
Take back that grace, those sorrows, and those tears
Take back my fruitless penitence and prayers;
Snatch me, just mounting, from the blest abode;
Assist the fiends, and tear me from my God!

EVEN Pope's most ardent defender would have to admit,
surely, that these lines from *Eloisa to Abelard* sound curiously
unconvincing when set beside the documents with which we
have been dealing. They are a travesty, rather than a translation, of Heloise's thoughts and feelings. And there is little need
to add that far worse travesties have been produced by far
worse poets, especially in the eighteenth century.

In our own day we like to talk about 'demythicizing' the
past. The best and simplest method of achieving this objective

is to go back to the earliest texts. One has only to read the records of Joan of Arc's two trials to strip off the countless layers of mawkish or chauvinistic gloss which have kept her true face hidden for so long; all the foolish nineteenth-century legends – that she was born out of wedlock, for instance – fall away in a flash. Similarly, no sooner does one turn to the original letters of Abelard and Heloise than their story stands revealed in all its intensity.

Its intensity and its symbolism. For of this there can be no doubt: the story would not have been handed down from generation to generation, and adapted to the style and outlook of each successive age, unless it were felt to be of timeless and universal import. The very names Heloise and Abelard, indissolubly linked, seem to speak of the person-to-person relationship within any human pairing – and perhaps it would not be too fanciful to suggest that they also seem to speak of the relationship between reason and faith in the individual psyche.

The Abelard who emerges from the *Letter to a Friend* must have been exceptionally hard to get on with. He seems to have been entirely lacking in empathy and to have shown no concern for others – except perhaps his pupils, but here he was swayed by vanity and the desire to strengthen his hold over them. It is extraordinary that he should have been thrown into contact with such an extreme 'temperamental opposite' as Peter the Venerable, and even more extraordinary that it was Peter who – quite literally, by publicly absolving him after death – had the last word.

By the time the two met, however, Abelard had undergone an inner change which opened his heart to Peter's loving-kindness and enabled him to feel its benefits to a degree which would have been wholly impossible at the time of Peter's earlier approach, soon after the Council of Soissons. But for the ordeals which he had suffered in the intervening years he would never have assented to the reconciliation with himself and others which Peter urged upon him.

By virtue of this assent he implicitly acknowledged that force within man to which, great as he was, he had always been blind. In his quest for truth he had depended entirely on reason, thereby violating the spirit of an age which held that reason was an effective tool only when allied to love.

Had he foreseen the consequences of his method, he would have been far from happy. For the renascence of Aristotelian thought, coupled with the influence of Arab philosophy, led to the total predomination of reason. By the seventeenth century, intellectualism was so rampant that even those voices which were still raised in defence of faith seemed to take on a note of desperation. 'I know not with all my heart,' declared Bossuet. Such words would have horrified Abelard and aligned him not only with Bernard of Clairvaux but with Richard of Saint-Victor and the other members of his school.

It was Richard, in fact, who formulated exactly the opposite view: 'I seek with all my heart.' For most of his life Abelard would probably have been content to say: 'I seek without respite', ceaseless questioning being the very essence of his method. But his last sufferings and final transformation brought him very close to the letter and spirit of Richard's pronouncement.

This inner change, which elevated him from narrow intellectual to fully alive human being, had begun with Heloise. It was she who had turned his physical craving into a loving impulse and made him respect the material world instead of despising it. And this is to take account only of the influence which she exerted during the brief phase when they were able to give physical expression to their love. Her influence in later years was even more telling.

For it is a remarkable fact that as soon as he took the cowl he slipped back into all his old ways. He seemed to forget her completely. Nothing mattered to him except his private worries and ambitions, his personal achievements and setbacks. Most of his energies appeared to be spent in riding the storms which he occasioned wherever he went. He had reverted to the

role of the single man, the lone wolf, the intellectual imprisoned by his own thought-processes. Only when Heloise
was in serious straits after her eviction from Argenteuil did he
show that he was still aware of her existence.

He then at once provided a new home for her community.
But a material gesture, however generous, is never enough in
itself, and one can well understand her angry insistence that he
should pay proper heed to her. With no care for what the
world, had it known, might have thought, she proceeded to
enact her feminine role to the full. She drew on Abelard's skills
as theologian and preacher; she made him the founder of an
order and a spiritual director. In short, she guided him into a
sphere which, left to himself, he would never have attained.
Again and again their now transfigured love impelled him to
reach beyond his apparent limits until he was ready for the final
transformation. She became incessantly involved in his labours;
when he composed his commentaries on the first chapter of
Genesis or the Epistle to the Romans, he was writing for her
benefit. What would Abelard have been without Heloise? The
first of the intellectuals? There was little room for the pure
intellectual in the twelfth century: people did not believe in the
'disinterested' approach; they cared nothing for 'art for art's
sake' or 'learning for the sake of learning'; they were concerned
only with what was likely to improve the human condition,
either in practical or – far more important – spiritual terms.

In our own day the stance of the 'pure intellectual' is regarded with similar lack of enthusiasm, and no one would think
it to Abelard's credit that he has come to be known as the
'father of scholasticism'. We remember him, and attribute
greatness to him, solely because of the love which he and
Heloise bore for each other, as rich and strange a love as the
world has ever seen.

ABELARD'S 'ERRORS'

The thirteen offending propositions singled out by William of Saint-Thierry (see page 186) are as follows:

1 Abelard defines faith as the appraisal (*aestimatio*) of the invisible.
2 In his view, it is wrong to differentiate between 'Father' and 'Holy Spirit'. The fullness of the Supreme Good is portioned out.
3 To the Father belongs fullness of power, and to the Son a certain measure of power; the Holy Spirit has none.
4 The Holy Spirit is not consubstantial with the Father in the same way as the Son is consubstantial with the Father.
5 The Holy Spirit is the *anima mundi*.
6 Free will is sufficient, without the help of grace, to ensure our ability, and our resolve, to do good.
7 It was not to deliver us from the power of the devil that Christ was made flesh and underwent his Passion.
8 Christ, God-made-Man, is not one of the three Persons in the Trinity.
9 In the Eucharist, the form of the original substance (*sic*) continues to exist in the consecrated vessel.
10 The devil uses physics (*sic*) to lead men into temptation.
11 We have not inherited original sin from Adam, but only punishment.
12 Without consent to sin and contempt of God, there is no sin.
13 Where concupiscence, delectation and ignorance exist, there is no sin but simply the handiwork of nature.

These thirteen items were the basis of the whole indictment.

HELOISE'S FIRST LETTER TO ABELARD

To her master, or rather to her father; to her husband, or rather to her brother; his handmaid, or rather his daughter; his wife, or rather his sister; to Abelard, Heloise.

The letter which you wrote to a friend with the aim of consoling him has recently chanced into my hands, beloved. I knew, by the very terms in which it was addressed, that it came from you, and I read it with an impatience and eagerness commensurate with my warm feelings for its author; his presence might be denied me, but at least his words would help to recapture his likeness. Alas, every line of that letter – which haunts me still – was full of gall and wormwood, for it rehearsed the distressing history of our conversion and of the cruel and unremitting hardships which you, whom I prize above all else, have had to suffer.

You have certainly kept the promise which you made to your friend at the very beginning: he now has good reason to know that his troubles are negligible in comparison with yours. After recalling the manner in which your masters persecuted you, and the vile outrages cravenly inflicted on your body, you go on to depict the loathsome jealousy and burning animosity with which you were hounded by Alberic of Rheims and Lotulf of Lombardy, both fellow-students of yours. You do not neglect to tell how your illustrious work of theology suffered as a result of their machinations, nor how you yourself were to all intents and purposes imprisoned. Next you turn to the schemings of your abbot and your false-hearted brethren, to the monstrous slanders of those two false apostles who were loosed against you by the same base rivals, and to the deliberate spreading of scandal in regard to your unusual decision to name your oratory The Paraclete. And you complete this lamentable picture by describing the intolerable vexations to which your life is still being subjected by that cruel oppressor and those evil monks whom you call your children.

Surely anyone who reads or hears the account of such ordeals must be moved to tears. For my own part, I can only say that it is so expressively phrased and so accurate in detail that it has ripped open all my old wounds; indeed, it has added to them by alerting me to the ever-mounting perils that confront you. From now on, your entire flock can only tremble for your life. Day after day we wait breathless and with troubled hearts, expecting to hear the worst news of all – that you are dead.

So we beseech you – in the name of him who still seems to enfold you with his protection in order that you may serve him; in the name of Christ, to whom, as to yourself, we are lowly handmaids – please write to us frequently and tell us of the storms that still assail you, so that we at least, who are all that remain to you, may share your tribulations and your joys. Sympathy usually brings relief to pain, and a burden shared is a burden eased. If the storm should abate a little, write to us as soon as you can, for it will be especially welcome news. But whatever the contents of your letters they cannot fail to be a blessing, if for no other reason than that they will prove that you are not forgetting us.

II. Seneca teaches us by his own example how pleasant it is to receive letters from an absent friend, when he writes to Lucilius: 'You write to me often, and I thank you, for in this way you are revealing yourself to me by the only available means. I never receive a letter from you without our instantly being together. If the portraits of our absent friends are a source of pleasure to us, calling them to mind and, in however false and empty a way, softening our regret that they are not with us, how much more pleasurable are letters – conveying, as they do, the distinctive stamp of the person whom we miss.'

This method of restoring your presence to us is still, thank heaven, open to you; neither jealousy nor anything else stands in its way. I pray that you yourself will not be responsible for any neglect or delay.

Your long letter to your friend was no doubt designed to comfort him in his misfortune, but it is of your own misfortunes that you tell. Although your purpose in recalling them so accurately was to bring him consolation, you have added in no small measure to our distress; in your desire to tend his wounds, you have inflicted new wounds on us and made the old ones gape afresh. You have gone out of your way to soothe hurts which others have caused; soothe, I beseech you, those which you yourself have occasioned. You have met the needs of a friend, a fellow scholar; you have satisfied the requirements of friendship and comradeship. Far more compelling are the obligations which you have contracted towards us, for we are not simply friends but the most loyal and devoted of friends, not simply comrades but daughters; yes, that is the right name for us – unless a holier and more loving term can be imagined.

III. Should you ever doubt how large a debt of gratitude you owe to us, we could furnish argument and proof in plenty. And even if we were all to remain silent, the facts speak loud and clear. You, after God, are sole founder of this haven, sole architect of this oratory, sole creator of this community. You did not build on a basis which others had established. Everything that exists here is your handiwork. This wilderness, which used to be the exclusive haunt of brigands and wild beasts, had never known human habitation, never seen a house. It was among the dens and lairs of those brigands and beasts, in a place where God's name is never even spoken, that you built a sacred tabernacle and dedicated a temple to the Holy Spirit. You took nothing from wealthy kings and princes, although you had only to ask and they would have given; you were anxious that nothing should be attributed to anyone but yourself. All the resources that you needed were supplied by the clerks and students who flocked to your lessons. Even those living on church benefices – men more used to receiving than to bestowing alms, men whose hands had, until then, taken rather than given – became lavish and importunate in their generosity.

This new plantation in the Lord's field is, therefore, yours and yours alone. Its host of young shoots call for continual watering if they are to thrive. It is intrinsically weak, by virtue of its feminine nature: it would be frail even if it were not new. So it requires more diligent tending, in keeping with the Apostle's words: 'I have planted, Apollos watered; but God gave the increase.' By his preachings, the Apostle had planted and established the Corinthians – to whom he was now writing – in the Faith; subsequently Apollos, his disciple, had watered them with his godly exhortations; and then, by divine grace, they received the power of growth.

You are vainly trying to cultivate a vineyard which was not of your own planting and whose sweetness has turned sour; your constant admonitions and homilies are of no avail. Remember your duty to your own vineyard, instead of devoting yourself to someone else's. You waste your time teaching and delivering sermons to rebels; you cast the pearls of your divine eloquence before swine; you lavish your energies on obdurate souls. You should be mindful, instead, of what you owe to biddable hearts. You devote yourself to enemies; think what you owe to your daughters. And, leaving my sisters out of account, consider the heavy debt which you have contracted towards me: perhaps your obligations to every one of these women will be honoured more energetically in respect of her who has given herself wholly and unreservedly to you.

You, with your great learning, know better than we, in our humble ignorance, how many earnest treatises the church fathers addressed to holy women as a means of enlightening, encouraging or even consoling them, and what pains they took over those compositions. It amazes me, therefore, that you have long since closed your eyes to the frail and rudimentary conditions of our religious life. There are times when my soul wavers and the burden of incurable sorrow becomes impossible to bear; yet nothing – neither reverence for God, nor love for us, nor the examples set by the church fathers – has ever induced you to come and fortify me with your words or even to console me from afar by sending me a letter. And yet I need not remind you of the obligation that binds you to me; we are joined together by the sacrament of holy matrimony, a bond made all the closer for you by the knowledge that I have always loved you, in the sight of heaven and earth, with a love that knows no bounds.

IV. You know, beloved – indeed, the whole world knows – all that I have lost in you; you know how lamentably you and I were together snatched from the world by the infamous act of betrayal which was inflicted on you; you know, too, that the manner in which I lost you was a far greater source of sorrow to me than the plain fact of losing you. The keener my sorrow, the more diligently it needs to be comforted. And you, the sole cause of my sufferings, alone have power to bring me consolation. You only, from whom all my sadness springs, can restore me to happiness or at least afford me some relief. This urgent duty is incumbent on you alone, for I have blindly carried out all your wishes. Powerless to resist you in any way, I did not shrink from abandoning myself when asked to do so. I went even further: my love, strange though this may seem, turned to delirium and sacrificed the sole object of its longings without any hope of recovering it. At your bidding I assumed a new habit, and a new heart to match, as a way of showing you that you were undisputed master of my heart as well as of my body. Never, as God is my witness, did I seek anything from you but yourself: it was you alone I loved, not your possessions. I had no thought for the circumstances of married life, or for the smallest dower, or for my own enjoyment, or for my personal wishes. It was your wishes, as you well know, that I was concerned to satisfy. The term 'wife' may seem at once holier and more substantial, but another was always dearer to my heart, that of your mistress, or even – allow me to say it – of your concubine, your whore. It seemed to me that the humbler I made myself in your eyes, the more I should be entitled to your love, and the less I should impede your glorious destiny.

You yourself, apropos of your own affairs, have not entirely forgotten these sentiments in the letter of consolation to your friend. You have condescended to recall some of the reasons why I sought to dissuade you from a fatal marriage, yet you say nothing of those which made me choose love rather than matrimony, freedom rather than a chain. As God is my witness, had Augustus, the master of the world, adjudged me worthy of marriage, and had his sovereignty of the universe been assured for ever, being known as your courtesan would have seemed sweeter and nobler to me than being known as his empress. For it is not wealth or power that makes a man great. Wealth and power stem from luck. Greatness stems from merit.

To marry a rich man in preference to a poor man, and to value the advantages of a husband's rank more highly than his innate virtues, is tantamount to selling oneself. Certainly, a woman who is prompted to marry by any such covetousness deserves to be paid rather than loved, for it is obvious that her attachment is not to the man but to his riches and that, given the opportunity, she would gladly have prostituted herself to an even wealthier man. Such was the plain conclusion reached by the wise Aspasia in her talks with Xenophon and his wife – the words being recorded by Socrates's disciple, Aeschines. This perspicacious woman, who had set herself the task of reconciling the couple, ended her remarks as follows: 'Once you come to realize that there is no finer man or more charming woman on the face of the earth, you will no longer aspire to anything save what will then seem the greatest boon of all –

you, to be the husband of the best of wives; you, the wife of
the best of husbands.' A godly observation, to be sure; ultra-
philosophical; or rather, this is not philosophy speaking but
wisdom itself. How blissful are error and deception between
husband and wife when perfect harmony keeps the marriage
bonds intact, less through chastity of body than of mind and
heart.

V. But that which is imparted to other women by means of
error was revealed to me by plainest truth. For what they alone
might think of their husbands the whole world thought of you
– indeed, not only thought but knew as clearly as I did; so that
my love for you was all the more sincere in that it was farther
removed from error. Was there anywhere a king, a philosopher, whose renown could stand comparison with yours?
What country, what city, what village did not long to see
you? You had only to show yourself in public, and who, pray,
did not rush out for a glimpse of you? Who did not stare
longingly after you when you chose to depart? What wife or
daughter did not burn for you in your absence and blaze up at
the sight of you? What queen, what princess did not envy both
my joys and my bed?

You, more than any other man, had two talents which are
instantly successful in capturing a woman's heart: talent as a
poet and talent as a singer; I do not know of any other philosopher who ever possessed them in the same degree. Armed with
those gifts, you found relaxation from your philosophical labours by composing all those poems and love-songs which were
performed far and wide because of the matchless grace of their
words and music, and your name was on everyone's lips. Their
mellifluousness was sufficient in itself to keep the greatest dunce
from forgetting them. It was this above all else which set
women's hearts yearning for you, and those verses, mostly
celebrating our love, soon spread my name through many
lands and sharpened the jealousy of countless women.

Indeed, what advantages of mind and body did not adorn your youth? Among all the women who used to envy my happiness, is there one today who, knowing that I am now denied such joys, would not feel for me in my distress? Where is the man or woman whose heart, even if it were the heart of an enemy, would not be softened by an appropriate sense of pity? Guilty as I may be, I am also – as you well know – very innocent. For the crime lies not in the deed but in the intention; justice is less concerned with weighing the deed itself than the thought behind the deed. You alone can judge the feelings which I have always had for you; you have certainly put them to the test. I place the entire matter in your scales, I entrust myself to your verdict.

VI. Tell me, if you can, why after the two of us embraced the religious life – a decision which was yours alone – I had neither your presence to fortify me nor even a letter to console me in my loneliness. Tell me, I repeat, if you can, or else I shall tell you my own opinion, an opinion which is on everybody's lips. It was lust rather than true feeling that bound you to me, sensuality rather than love – which is why, as soon as your desires were extinguished, all the outward displays which they used to inspire vanished too. This is not just my own supposition, beloved, but that of the world at large; it is not a private feeling but the general view, not personal opinion but common belief. Would to heaven that it were held by me alone and that your love might find champions whose arguments could allay my distress. Would to heaven that I could conceive of reasons which would excuse you and, at the same time, justify your handmaid.

I beg you to consider my request. It is so small and simple a thing that I ask. If your presence must be denied me, at least let your soft words – a letter costs you so little – remind me of your sweet looks. Can I expect generosity from you in material things when I find you mean with words? I had always imagined that I enjoyed strong claims to your consideration, having done everything for you – even to the point of lingering in a nunnery solely out of obedience to you. For I had no vocation: it was your will, and your will alone, that plunged me into the rigours of monastic life when I was still only a young girl. Unless you give me some credit for this, the sacrifice will have been entirely in vain; for I can look for no reward from God, having as yet done nothing for him.

When you entered God's service I followed you. Or rather I preceded you; for, as if obsessed with the memory of Lot's wife looking back, you insisted that I should don the habit and take my vows before you did; you bound me to God before binding yourself. This was the only occasion on which you have ever distrusted me, and I must confess that your action filled me with hurt and shame. Heaven knows, you had only to ask and I would have preceded or followed you into hellfire – for my heart was no longer with me but with you. And, today more than ever, unless it is with you it is nowhere. Or, to be more accurate, it cannot be anywhere without you. I implore you to make sure it is with you – as indeed it will be if only you treat it kindly, offering it love in return for love, crumbs in return for a banquet, words in return for deeds. Would to heaven, beloved, that you were less sure of my love; you would then be more anxious. But the safer I have made you feel, the more I have suffered your neglect.

I beg you to remember all I have done and to take account of what you owe me. While you and I were still enjoying the pleasures of the flesh, people may have wondered whether I was following the dictates of love or of desire. Now they are able to see what feelings drove me from the very beginning. My readiness to comply with your will has led me to forgo all pleasures; I have forfeited everything within me except the right to make myself wholly yours. How unjust, then, if you choose to accord less and less to someone who deserves more and more, if you refuse to give anything at all when faced with so small and simple a request.

In the name, therefore of him to whom you have solemnly dedicated your days, in the name of the living God, give me back your presence in so far as you are able by sending me a few lines of consolation – if not for my sake, at least so that I may derive new strength from your words and serve God with greater fervour. In the days when you still clamoured for earthly delights, you treated me to letter after letter and wrote so many poems and songs about me that the name of your Heloise was always on people's lips; it rang out in every street, in every home. How much better if you were now to awaken love of God within me, whom once you roused to love of pleasure. I beseech you again: ponder your debt and give thought to my request. And now – in brief conclusion to this long letter – farewell, my all.

NOTES
AND SOURCES

Chapter I: The Gifted Student

1   The *Moniage Guillaume*
2   A critical edition of the *Historia Calamitatum,* or *Letter to a Friend,* was published by J. Monfrin in 1962. The standard edition is contained in the *Patrologiae Cursus Completus, Series Latina* (abbreviated to *PL*), vol. 178. The correspondence between Abelard and Heloise is quite genuine, a point clearly established by Etienne Gilson in his *Héloïse et Abélard* (third edition, 1964; see especially Appendix 1, p. 169 *et seq.*). Enid McLeod arrived at the same conclusion in her book *Heloise* (London, 1938) which appeared at about the same time as the first edition of Gilson's. I propose to refer to the first Letter as the *Letter to a Friend* (abbreviated simply to *Letter*), giving chapter references, and to number the rest in keeping with their traditional order: *Letter I* (from Heloise), *Letter II* (from Abelard), etc.
3   *Dialectica,* ed. Cousin, V., *Ouvrages inédits d'Abélard,* Paris, 1836, p. 518 and introd. cxxii–cxxiii
4   Quoted in Raby, F. J. E., *A History of Secular Latin Poetry in the Middle Ages,* Oxford, 1957, vol. 1, p. 287
5   Otto von Freisingen, *Gesta Frederici,* I, 49, p. 55. Quoted in Lesne, E., *Histoire de la propriété ecclésiastique en France,* V, *Les écoles,* p. 105
6   *Letter to a Friend,* chapter 2. The subsequent quotations are from the same source.
7   Cf. extracts quoted in Raby, vol. 2, p. 25
8   Cf. Lesne, *op. cit.,* V, pp. 258–9
9   *Metalogicus,* I, 24
10 Pare, G., Brunet, A., Tremblay, P., *La Renaissance du XIIe siècle. Les écoles et l'enseignement.* Complete recasting of the work by G. Robert (1909). Published by the Institut d'Etudes médiévales d'Ottawa, Paris-Ottawa, 1938. Cf. p. 132

11 Lefevre, G., 'Les Variations de Guillaume de Champeaux et la question des universaux' Travaux et Mémoires de l'Université de Lille, vol. vi, no. 20, Lille, 1898

12 Cuissard, Documents inédits sur Abélard tirés des manuscrits de Fleury, Orleans, 1880; Carnandet, J., Notice sur le bréviaire d'Abélard conservé à la bibliothèque de Chaumont, Paris, 1885

13 The quotations from the Poem to Astrolabe are taken from the most complete edition: Haureau, M. B., Le poème adressé par Abélard à son fils Astrolabe, etc., Paris, 1895:
>   Major discendi tibi sit quam cura docendi
>   Disce diu, firmaque tibi, tardaque docere
>   Atque ad scribendum ne cito prosilias.

14 Letter, chapter 3

15 Letter, chapter 4

16 Letter, chapter 5

17 PL, clxxviii, cols. 371–2

18 Nigel Longchamp, Cf. Raby, II, p. 96

19 Fulke of Deuil, PL, clxxviii, 371–2

20 Raby, vol. 2, p. 40

21 Ibid., p. 273

22 Gautier of Châtillon. Raby, vol. 2, p. 193

23 Guy of Bazoches, ibid., p. 41

24 Gautier of Châtillon, ibid., p. 191

25 Letter, chapter 10

26 Letter I, chapter 5

27 Ibid.

28 Ibid.

29 These lines are taken from a mid-twelfth-century satirical poem, The Council of Rémiremont, relating how a group of nuns in a convent read Ovid and go on to argue about love. A rather unseemly work, it is generally assumed to have been written by a local clerk.

30 Altercatio Phyllidis et Floræ, composed in the first half of the twelfth century. Quoted in Raby, vol. 2, p. 293

31 See the Metemorphoses of Golias, which contains an account of a scene enacted before the god of Love, again concerning the respective merits of clerk and knight (Raby, vol. 2, p. 294)

Chapter II: Heloise

1 *Letter*, chapter 6
2 Letter from Peter the Venerable. The wording here and below is based on the translation by O. Gréard, Editions de la Bibliothèque de Cluny, 1959.
3 *Ibid.* The Latin text is contained in *Bibliotheca Cluniacensis*, L. I, 9. Translated extracts appear in Dom J. Leclercq's study of Peter the Venerable (1946).
4 Cf. Enid McLeod, *Heloise*, 1938
5 *Letter*, chapter 6
6 Cf. Raby, vol. 2, p. 239
7 *Letter*, chapter 5
8 *Letter*, chapter 6
9 *Letter I*, chapter 5
10 *Ibid.*
11 From the Haureau edition, previously referred to, p. 167
12 Author unknown. Published in Anglade, J., *Anthologie des troubadours*, p. 13
13 From a song by Christine de Pisan
14 *Letter*, chapter 6
15 *Letter*, chapter 7
16 See Gilson, E., *Héloïse et Abélard*, 3rd edn, 1964, p. 25 *et seq.*
17 Beauvoir, S. de, *La Force de l'âge*, p. 81
18 *Letter*, chapter 6
19 *Letter*, chapter 8
20 *Letter IV*, chapter 4
21 *Letter*, chapter 8
22 *PL*, 178, 174
23 *Planctus Jacob super filios suos.* Ed. Vecchi, p. 45
24 Bernard de Ventadour. Ed. Anglade, *Anthologie des troubadours*, p. 45
25 Baldry of Bourgeuil. Ed. Ph. Abrahams, *ibid.*, p. 199
26 Gilson, *op. cit.*, p. 111
27 From Lucan's *Pharsala* (VIII-v-94), in which Cornelia blames herself for her husband's death

Chapter III: The Wandering Philosopher

1 *Letter*, chapter 8
2 Cf. *Abbey of Saint-Denis* by S. McK. Crosby, Yale University Press, 1942; also *L'Abbaye royale de Saint-Denis* by Formige, Jules, 1960, a monograph incorporating Crosby's findings.
3 *Letter*, chapter 9
4 *Ibid.*
5 Ed. Haureau, p. 174
6 *Letter*, chapter 9
7 *Letter*, chapter 9
8 Ed. Haureau, p. 181
9 *Letter*, chapter 9
10 *Ibid.*
11 *Letter*, chapter 9
12 Ed. Haureau, p. 184
13 The subject is widely explored in the works of Father Henri de Lubac, especially the four volumes of *Exégèse médiévale*. A good deal may well remain to be said on this topic, which is serenely ignored by the exegetes and commentators of our own time.
14 *Letter*, chapter 10
15 For a long time, this treatise was presumed lost. The scholar Stöltzle traced it and published it, following the text of MS 229 in the library at Erlangen.
16 Cf. the edition of Richard of Saint-Victor's *De Trinitate* by Salet, G., 1959, No. 63 in the series 'Sources chrétiennes'. Cf. also Dumeige, Gervais, *Richard de Saint-Victor et l'idée chrétienne de l'amour, 1952*
17 By far the most comprehensive study of the theme of courtly love is *Les Origines et la formation de la tradition courtoise en Occident* by Reto Bezzola (5 vols., 1946–63). Cf. also the same author's *Le Sons de l'aventure et de l'amour au Moyen Age*, dealing especially with Chrétien de Troyes.
18 St Anselm, *De fide Trinitatis*. Cf. Vignaux, P., *La Philosophie au Moyen Age*, 1958, pp. 47 *et seq.*
19 *PL*, 178, 355–7
20 *Letter*, chapter 9
21 Cf. Victor Cousin's introduction to the 1836 edition of

Abelard's works, with particular attention to pp. cliv, clxiii and clxxiii

22 For the order of composition of Abelard's works, see L. Nicolau D'Olwer, '*Sur la date de la Dialectica d'Abélard*', in *Revue du Moyen Age Latin*, I, 4, Nov.–Dec. 1945, pp. 375–90 and Van den Eynde, '*Les Rédactions de la Theologia christiana de Pierre Abélard*', in *Antonianum*, 36, 1961, pp. 273–99

23 *PL*, 178, 357–72

24 Ed. Haureau, p. 184

25 *Letter*, chapter 10

26 *Ibid.*

27 Ed. Haureau, p. 160

28 Cf. Vecchi's excellent introduction to his edition, p. 16

29 *Letter*, chapter 11

30 Quoted in *Pierre le Vénérable* by Dom Leclercq, p. 6

31 See the *Dictionnaire de Théologie catholique* by Vacant-Mangenot, vol. 1, pp. 43–8

32 The works of E. Gilson are illuminating on this subject. See also Pierre Lasserre, '*Un conflit religieux au XIIe siècle. Abélard contre Saint Bernard*', 1930, *Cahiers de la Quinzaine*, Series 19, No. 13, and Ligeard, H., '*Le Rationalisme de Pierre Abélard*', published in *Recherches de Sciences Religieuses*, II, 1911, pp. 384–96

33 Otto of Freisingen, *Gesta Frederici imperatoris*, I, 47

34 Vignaux, *op. cit.*, pp. 47–8

35 See Stöltzle's edition, Freiburg, 1891

36 *Introductio ad theologiam*, *PL*, 178, 1056

37 *PL*, 178, 1314

38 *PL*, 178, 1349

39 Paré, Brunet, Tremblay, pp. 292 *et seq.*

40 *PL*, 178, 1353

41 *PL*, 178, 1051

42 *Letter*, chapter 11

43 *Letter*, chapter 12

44 *PL*, 178, 1855–6

45 Raby, vol. 2, pp. 177–8

46 *Letter*, chapter 13

47 *Letter*, chapter 11

48 *Ibid.*, chapter 13

49 *Letter*, chapter 14

50 Etienne de Bourbon, *Anecdotes*, no. 508. Ed. Lecoy de la Marche, p. 439

51 *Liber de rebus in administratione sua gestis*. Suger's allegations are studied and assessed in the relevant works by E. McLeod, pp. 73–83, and Ch. Charrier, pp. 154–74

52 Gilson, *Héloïse et Abélard*, p. 64

53 Ed. Haureau, p. 172

54 *Letter*, chapters 13 and 14

Chapter IV: Abelard

1 Poem attributed to Abelard. Cf. Raby, vol. 2, p. 313

2 *Letter I*, chapter 4

3 *Letter I*, chapter 6

4 *Ibid.*

5 *Ibid.*

6 *Letter II*, chapter 1

7 *Ibid.*

8 *Letter II*, chapter 4

9 *Letter III*, chapter 1

10 *Letter IV*, chapter 1

11 *Ibid.*

12 *Letter III*, chapter 2

13 *Letter IV*, chapter 2

14 *Letter III*, chapter 3

15 *Letter IV*, chapter 4

16 *Ibid.*

17 *Ibid.*

18 *Letter III*, chapter 4

19 *Letter IV*, chapter 4

20 *Letter III*, chapter 4

21 *Ibid.*

22 *Letter III*, chapter 5

23 *Letter IV*, chapter 4

24 *Letter IV*, chapter 3

25 *Letter IV*, chapter 4

26 *Letter III*, chapter 5

27 *Letter IV*, chapter 4

28 Matthew, xix, 12

29 *Letter V*, chapter 5
30 *PL*, 178, 332

Chapter V: 'The Man Who Belongs at Your Side'

1 Abelard's *Apologia*, *PL*, 178, 375
2 For a discussion of Abelard's moral attitudes, see especially *Peter Abailard* by J. G. Sikes (Cambridge, 1932), pp. 194 *et seq.* See also I. Vacant-Mangenot's *Dictionnaire de Théologie*.
3 See Fr. Damien van den Eynde, '*Chronologie des écrits d'Abélard à Héloïse*', published in *Antonianum*, No. 37, 1962, pp. 337–49, and R. Oursel, *La Dispute et la grâce*, p. 82. The text of the *Dialogue* is to be found in *PL*, 178, 1611–82.
4 Based on the translation by D. Dechanet, contained in his book *Guillaume de Saint-Thierry*, pp. 67–9
5 R. Oursel, *La dispute et la grâce*, p. 39
6 St Bernard, *Letter* 327
7 H. Ligeard, *Le Rationalisme de P. Abélard*, p. 396
8 Cf. P. Lasserre, '*Un conflit religieux au XIIe siècle. Abélard contre Saint Bernard*'. Paris, 1930. *Cahiers de la quinzaine*, series 19, No. 13, p. 91
9 Based on the translation contained in S. Lemaître, *Textes mystiques d'Orient et d'Occident*, vol. II, p. 147
10 *Ibid.*, p. 145
11 Lemaître, *op. cit.*, p. 147
12 Otto of Freisingen, *Gesta Frederici*, vol. I, p. 47
13 *Letter* 106
14 *Letter* 158
15 Cf. Lasserre, *op. cit.*, p. 91
16 *Ibid.*, p. 107
17 Letter 188
18 *PL*, 182, 1049
19 Letter 192. (The appeal to the Curia as a whole is No. 188)
20 Letter 331
21 Letter 193. (The letter to Gerard Caccianemici is No. 332)
22 Letter 330
23 Letters 336 and 338
24 Letter 189
25 Letter 187

26 Geoffrey of Auxerre, *Life of St Bernard*
27 Jeannin, '*La dernière maladie d'Abélard*', published in *Mélanges Saint-Bernard*, 1953
28 Letter 189
29 *Ibid.*
30 Letter from Peter the Venerable to Innocent II. *PL*, 189, 305–6
31 *Ibid.*
32 See Didier, '*Un scrupule identique de Saint Bernard pour Abélard et pour Gilbert de la Porrée*', published in *Mélanges Saint Bernard*, 1954, pp. 95–9
33 *PL*, 178, 105–8
34 Quoted by Vacandard in his *Vie de Saint Bernard, abbé de Clairvaux*, vol. II, p. 165
35 Gilson, *op. cit.*, pp. 136–7
36 Readers are recommended to read the beautiful passage in Gilson's *Héloïse et Abélard*, p. 141 *et seq*.

BIBLIOGRAPHY

Abelard and Heloise

Abelard: Works: vol. 178 of *Patrologie Latine de Migne (PL)*
Bourin, J.: *Très sage Héloïse*, Paris, 1966
Charrier, Ch.: *Héloise dans l'histoire et dans la légende*, Paris, 1933
Cousin, V.: *Ouvrages inédits d'Abélard*, Paris 1836
Gilson, Etienne: *Héloïse et Abélard*, Paris, 1938
Gréard, Octave: *Lettres complètes d'Abélard à Héloïse*, Paris, 1869
Jeandet, Y.: *Héloïse. L'amour et l'absolu*, Lausanne, 1966
MacLeod, Enid: *Heloise*, London, 1938
Monfrin, J.: *Abélard, Historia Calamitatum*, Paris 1962
Oursel, R.: *La dispute et la grâce*, Paris, 1959

The Schools and Philosophy

Chenu, Père M. D.: *La théologie au XIIe siècle*, Paris, 1957
Gilson, Etienne: *La philosophie au Moyen Age*, Paris, 1944; *L'esprit de la philosophie médiévale*, 2nd edn, Paris, 1944
Lasserre, Pierre: 'Un conflit religieux au IIe siècle – Abélard contre Saint Bernard' in *Cahiers de la Quinzaine*, 1930
Lesne, E.: *Histoire de la propriété ecclésiastique en France*; vol. V: *Les écoles de la fin du VIIIe siècle à la fin du XIIe siècle*, Lille, 1936–40
Lubac, H. de: *Exégèse médiévale. Les quatre sens de l'Ecriture*, 4 vols., Paris, 1960–4
Paré, G., Brunet, A. and Tremblay, P.: *La Renaissance du XIIe siècle. Les écoles et l'enseignement*, Paris-Ottawa, 1938
Vignaux, Paul: *Philosophie au Moyen Age*, Paris, 1958

The Church

Bihlmeyer, K.: *Histoire de l'Eglise*; vol. II: *L'Eglise de la Chrétienté, 692-1294* (by M. H. Vicaire), 1963
Calmette, J. and David, H.: *Saint Bernard*, Paris, 1953

Fliche, Augustin: *La réforme grégorienne et la reconquête chrétienne (1057–1123)*; *Histoire de l'Eglise*, vol. VIII

Foreville, Raymonde and Rousset de la Pina, Jean: *Du premier concile du Latran à l'avènement d'Innocent III (1123–93)*; *Histoire de l'Eglise*, vol. IX, Paris, 1953

Le Bras, Gabriel: *Institutions ecclésiastiques de la chrétienté médiévale*, 2 vols, 1962–4

Leclercq, Dom J.: *Pierre le Vénérable*, Saint Wandrille, 1946

Lot, Ferdinand and Fawtier, Robert: *Histoire des Institutions françaises au Moyen Age*; vol. III: *Les Institutions ecclésiastiques* (by J. F. Lemarignier, J. Gaudemet and G. Mollat), Paris, 1962

The Age

Aubert, Marcel: *Suger*, Paris, 1950; *L'architecture cistercienne en France*, Paris, 1947

Bezzola, R.: *Les origines et la formation de la littérature courtoise en Occident*, 5 vols., Paris, 1946–63

Bruyne, E. de: *Etudes d'ésthétique médiévale*, 3 vols., Bruges, 1946

Davenson, Henri: *Les troubadours*, Paris, 1960

Dobiache-Rojdesvensky, O.: *Les poésies des Goliards*, Paris, 1931

Duby, Georges and Mandrou, Robert: *Histoire de la civilisation française*, vol. I, Paris, 1958

Fawtier, Robert: *Les Capétiens et la France*, Paris, 1942

Focillon, Henri: *Art d'Occident*, Paris, 1947

Halphen, Louis: *Paris sous les premiers Capétiens (987–1223)*, Paris, 1909

Lavisse, Ernest: *Histoire de France*, vol. III, Part I (by Achille Luchaire), Paris, 1901

Luchaire, Achille: *Louis VI Le Gros*, Paris, 1890

Male, Emile: *L'art réligieux du XIIe siècle en France*, 6th cdn, Paris, 1953

Oursel, Raymond: *Les pèlerins au Moyen Age*, Paris, 1963

Petit-Dutaillis, Ch.: *La monarchie féodale en France et en Angleterre, Xe-XIIIe siècles*, Paris, 1950

Raby, F. J. E.: *A History of Secular Latin Poetry in the Middle Ages*, 2 vols., Oxford, 1957

Zumthor, Paul: *Histoire littéraire de la France médiévale*, Paris, 1954

INDEX

Abelard, Berengar (father), 13-14, 32

Abelard, Dagobert (brother), 11, 101, 144

Abelard, Lucia (mother), 32

Abelard, Peter

(1) LIFE (1079-1142), his arrival in Paris after renunciation of birthright (at Le Pallet in Brittany), 9-14; his early intellectual training under Roscelin and others, 15-17; in Paris, 18-19; his early contacts with William of Champeaux, 19-21, 23-6; at Melun and Corbeil, 25-27; at Le Pallet, 27; back in Paris, where again quarrels with William of Champeaux, and moves to Montagne Sainte-Geneviève, 27-32; again at Le Pallet, 32; returns once again to Paris and then goes to study at Laon, 32-6; teaches at Notre Dame (Paris), 36 *et seq.*; becomes acquainted with Heloise, 45 *et seq.*; lodges with her uncle (Fulbert) and becomes her lover, 52-3; progress of their love, 54 *et seq.*; its discovery by Fulbert and consequent flight with Heloise to Brittany, where their son is born, 59 *et seq.*; attempted reconciliation with Fulbert, 63-4; Heloise's refusal to marry, 65 *et seq.*; returns to Paris with Heloise and installs her at Argenteuil, 73-4; is castrated, 75 *et seq.*; forces Heloise to become a nun, and decides to become monk at Saint-Denis, 81 *et seq.*; situation at Saint-Denis, 85 *et seq.*; retires to priory of Maison-

celles-en-Brie, and continues teaching and writing there, 91 *et seq.*; his theological quarrel with Roscelin, 98 *et seq.*; arraigned before Council of Soissons, 104-10; confined to monastery of Saint-Médard, 110-11; declines invitation to Cluny, 111-13; continues his writings, 114 *et seq.*; returns to Saint-Denis, but again quarrels with authorities there, and retires to Champagne, 123-6; secures his freedom from Saint-Denis and establishes the Paraclete School, 127-34; becomes Abbot of Saint-Gildas-de-Rhuys in Brittany, 134-7; his reactions to Heloise's expulsion from Argenteuil, 138 *et seq.*; establishes her at the Paraclete, 141-3; his troubles at Saint-Gildas, 144-5; his correspondence with Heloise, 146-72; his arrangements for her life at the Paraclete, 173-9; his disagreements with St Bernard, 179-80; resumption of teaching at Sainte-Geneviève, 181; his theological views and quarrels with St Bernard and William of Saint-Thierry, 182-95; at Sens, where unsuccessfully confronts St Bernard, is condemned and decides to appeal to Pope, 195-203; last contacts with Heloise, 204-6; starts for Rome, but stops off at Cluny, 207-9; reconciled with St Bernard, 210; his condemnation upheld by Pope, 211-12; remains and works at Cluny, 212 *et seq.* and then at Priory of Saint-

B   Copy 1
He Heloise and Abelard
Pernoud
Heloise and Abelard

DATE DUE